A Great Day to Fight Fire

View from the south-facing slope of Mann Gulch, looking down
toward the mouth of Mann Gulch. Author's collection.

A Great Day to Fight Fire
Mann Gulch, 1949

Mark Matthews

UNIVERSITY OF OKLAHOMA PRESS : NORMAN

Also by Mark Matthews

Smoke Jumping on the Western Fire Line: Conscientious Objectors during World War II (Norman, 2006)

Library of Congress Cataloging-in-Publication Data

Matthews, Mark, 1951–
    A great day to fight fire : Mann Gulch, 1949 / Mark Matthews.
        p. cm.
    Includes bibliographical references and index.
    ISBN 978-0-8061-3857-2 (hardcover : alk. paper)   1. Forest
fires—Montana—Mann Gulch—Prevention and control—History.
2. Smokejumpers—United States—History.   3. United States.
Forest Service—Officials and employees—History.   I. Title.
    SD421.32.M9M38 2007
    363.37'9—dc22
    [B]
                                                                2006103030

The paper in this book meets the guidelines for permanence and durability of the Committee on Production Guidelines for Book Longevity of the Council on Library Resources, Inc. ∞

1 2 3 4 5 6 7 8 9 10

To Ellie and Hugh Saunders
An inspirational couple and eternal friends
of artists and activists everywhere

Contents

Illustrations

Photographs

Maps

Preface

In 1939, the U.S. Forest Service decided to train men to parachute into remote mountainous regions to put out small fires before they had a chance to blow up and spread. U.S. Forest Service worker Horace Godwin was the father of the smoke jumper program, while technicians Frank Derry, his brothers Chet and Buster, and Glenn Smith helped develop the early equipment and training techniques. The experiment started with a handful of guinea pigs from the Forest Service ranks, including Francis Lufkin and George Honey. The first fire jump occurred on July 12, 1940, when Rufus Robinson and Earl Cooley dropped to a fire on Martin Creek in the Nez Perce Forest in Idaho. The next year, the Forest Service expanded the project to include three eight-man squads. But in 1942, most of the pioneer jumpers enlisted in the military. As the agency was considering mothballing the project, a conscientious objector wrote to the Forest Chief asking if the agency would be interested in training men enrolled in Civilian Public Service to jump fires. The agency jumped at the chance and by 1945 had trained 250 "conchies." The Civilian Public

Service men performed so admirably that the Forest Service declared the experiment a success after the first year and expanded the project into a regular firefighting brigade. After V-E Day, some of the pioneer jumpers—such as Fred Brauer and Rufus Robinson—returned to their old jobs. Others, who had trained the conchies—like Cooley, Jim Waite, and Al Cramer—remained with the outfit. The assignment quickly became a popular summer job for college kids, especially those studying forestry. Over that first decade, the new firefighting brigade earned a reputation as hard workers and expert woodsmen. They also were very lucky. Smoke jumpers accrued their share of twisted backs and ankles, broken legs and bruised egos, but no smoke jumper had ever died fighting a wildfire. But as the fire season of 1949 heated up, their good luck was about to run out.

On August 5, 1949, a wall of flame roared up an isolated narrow gulch just off the Missouri River near Helena, Montana, killing thirteen wildland firefighters. Twelve of the dead were smoke jumpers, the elite of the elite when it came to fighting forest fires. The deaths stimulated the U.S. Forest Service to develop modern safety equipment and comprehensive training programs for its firefighters. Agency scientists also began to analyze fire behavior in the hope that they could teach firefighters how to avoid becoming caught in similar entrapments.

A handful of writers have written about Mann Gulch. Some, like Norman Maclean, concentrated on the fire's behavior and the controversy surrounding the deaths. Others—who often self-published—offered tantalizing bits of biographical information about some of the victims. In 1999, students from Helena High School contacted many relatives of the fallen men, requesting personal information about their lost brothers, sons, and cousins as part of a class project to commemorate the fiftieth anniversary of the tragedy. I was privileged to read those documents and handle the artifacts before they were sealed in a fifty-year time capsule and buried on the grounds of the Missoula Smoke Jumper Center at the Aerial Fire Depot. Working with these sources and from interviews with those who worked directly with the smoke jumpers in 1949, I have tried to reconstruct the events that led up to and occurred in Mann Gulch as well as bring to life the memory of those who died that day. I offer this "nonfiction novel" as a memorial to the young firefighters, hoping it will free their personalities from the emotionless confines of historical statistics and distant tragic events.

Acknowledgments

I would like to extend many thanks to Mrs. André Anderson for her help and encouragement for this project; to Fred Brauer, Skip Stratton, and Al Hammond for fact-checking the manuscript; to producer and cameraman Stevan Smith for the transcript of his video interview with Robert Sallee, which he filmed while producing *Firefighters from the Sky: The History of Smoke Jumping* for the Smoke Jumpers Association's sixtieth anniversary; to Judy Blunt and her fall 2005 nonfiction workshop at the University of Montana for their insightful criticism; and to the UM School of Journalism for its fine professional training.

I would especially like to thank Helena High School teacher Sandy Casey and X-CEL adviser Becky Stuker, who gave me access to the biographical material their students collected during a special class project for the fiftieth anniversary of the Mann Gulch fire. The students who contacted the relatives and friends of many of the jumpers included Stephanie Abraham, Nate Boyd, Dana Deininger, Greg Dorrington, Ashley Finnegan, Jenny Gambill, Mike Grevas, Allyson Hammill, Tanner Jackson,

Martin J. Kuhl, Kurt Michels, Mac Mullette, Heather Paulson, Val Platts, Kim Tallent, Karolina Topolski, Nate Warner, Crystal Warsinski, and Kit Watson.

Many thanks to Kate Babbitt for her impeccable copyediting and patience. And thanks once again to the folks of the Ninemile Ranger District of Lolo National Forest for the seasonal employment that keeps getting me through difficult financial times.

A Great Day to Fight Fire

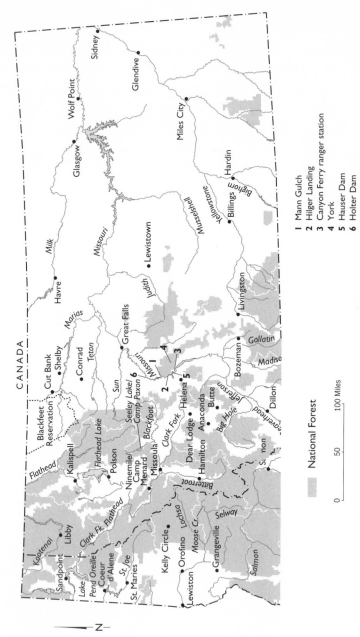

Northern Montana and Idaho, with national forests indicated by shading

National Forest

0   50   100 Miles

1 Mann Gulch
2 Hilger Landing
3 Canyon Ferry ranger station
4 York
5 Hauser Dam
6 Holter Dam

CHAPTER ONE

Julie Reba

Pierz, Minnesota
March 19, 1959

In her dream, Julie Reba stands so close to the string of men as they race up the steep slope that she could reach out and touch each on the shoulder as he passes. They all smile at her, even as they gasp for breath. Shirts soaked with sweat cling to muscular bodies, most of which have been toned in military boot camps and toughened by years of battle. But they never stop. In the deep gulch below, tongues of flame whirl hundreds of feet into the air. A scorching wind flattens the knee-high bunchgrass growing at Julie's feet, searing it to ash. A cloud of black smoke mushrooms into the tranquil summer sky. If Julie could feel the heat from the fire, as the men do, she would hold her hands to her cheeks to deflect the biting embers and ash. But she feels no pain.

As the last man in line approaches, Julie recognizes the soft brown eyes set in the big oblong face. Her husband, Stanley Reba, pumps his powerful legs like pistons, slightly dipping his broad shoulders as if he were a football player ready to burst through a defensive line. "Stanley," she says, "you're going the wrong way." But Stanley says nothing as he pushes past her, his feet kicking up loose pebbles.

Julie and Stan Reba's wedding portrait, 1948. Courtesy Mrs. André Anderson.

The air about Julie suddenly flashes red and orange. Her hair bursts into flames; the strands detach from her scalp and cascade to the ground. Still Julie feels no pain, even as her white chiffon dress transforms into red-embered tissue paper and then to ashes that swirl about her like a swarm of flies. She mutely watches as the pale smooth skin of her forearm shrivels, blackens, and breaks apart, curling up into tight scrolls. But Julie yearns to feel the pain. She realizes that until the flames consume her, she can never escape this nightmarish vi-

sion. Or the one occurring on the hillside above. Julie turns
in time to see the flames tackle her husband. When she trem-
bles, the spell breaks and she opens her eyes.

Julie Reba takes a package from her dresser—a mail-order
delivery from Sears, Roebuck and Co.—and carries it to her
bed. After slitting open the brown paper wrapping, she gropes
amid rumpled pieces of newspaper. When her fingers touch
cold steel, she lifts out a .38 caliber Smith & Wesson revolver
by the tip of its shiny blue barrel as if she were picking up a
dead mouse by the tail. Next, she locates the box of cartridges.
When Julie pushes the button on the side of the pistol's frame,
as Stanley had once demonstrated on his own pistol, the cylinder drops open. She appreciates how the bullet casings slide
snugly into each chamber. After clicking the cylinder shut, she
puts the loaded gun on the ruffled white chenille bedspread,
then kneels down and drags a small suitcase from under the
bed. The lid pops open as soon as she undoes the clasps, a pile
of letters and photos spilling onto the floor. A plaque dedicated to Stanley, presented to her by the U.S. Forest Service
ten years before, also tumbles out. Julie randomly picks up a
single sheet of stationery and sits on the floor with her back
against the side of the bed. Sometimes reading a letter from
Stanley eases the depression that has paralyzed her mind since
her husband died in the Mann Gulch fire.

"My dearest wife," she reads aloud.

CHAPTER TWO

Stanley Reba

Hale Airfield, Missoula, Montana
August 4, 1949

Stanley Reba set down his pen and flicked a drop of sweat from the tip of his nose. The sun had finally set over Missoula, Montana, but the temperature still cracked 80 degrees. What should he write to Julie this time? About the heat, for sure. More regrets about abandoning her for the summer? Of course. But if there was any place he'd rather be than by Julie's side, it was here, in the midriff of the Rocky Mountains, working as a smoke jumper. The only thing missing, of course, was a fire to fight and a chance to make some real money. But with the dry conditions in the forests, he would see action soon enough. Stan glanced down at the piece of stationery. So far he had written only the date: August 4, 1949.

Two days before, Stan had completed a three-day compacted refresher smoke jumper training course at Camp Menard, an old CCC camp about thirty miles west of Missoula. After the last training jump, Stanley and his best friend, Joe Sylvia, had ridden in the back of a pickup truck to join the standby crew in Missoula. He and the dozen other jumpers on standby alert had chosen to bivouac on the lawn of the Missoula

County Fairgrounds across the street from Hale Airfield rather than commute to and from the army barracks at Fort Missoula, about two miles to the southwest. Throughout the day Stanley had shaken out chutes in the parachute loft and repacked them on one of the long triangular-shaped tables expressly designed for that purpose. The loft, a long single-story structure, had once been a CCC barrack in Rimini, a small town a few miles west of the state capital, Helena. The army had taken over the CCC camp during the war to train sled dogs for rescue operations in Alaska, Canada, and Greenland. Near the end of the war a crew had dismantled the building and later reconstructed it at Hale Airfield.

The airfield was also home to the headquarters for Johnson Brothers Flying Service, which annually landed the contract to deliver the jumpers to the fires. Pilots like Bob and Dick Johnson, Slim Phillips, and Penn Stohr were the best at flying along mountain ridges and dipping into secluded valleys. They routinely landed the single-engine Travelaire and the Ford Trimotor on postage stamp–sized airstrips hidden in deep canyons throughout the Rocky Mountains in all types of weather conditions.

Stan looked down at his letter and wrote "My Dearest Wife."

Stan had missed a number of opportunities to jump two weeks earlier when lightning had peppered the 25 million acres of the Northern Rockies region, which included western Montana, northern Idaho, eastern Washington, and North Dakota. Sixty-four men had parachuted to fires in that first flurry of activity. A week later, thirty-four men had parachuted by twos and fours—in groups known as "sticks"—all across the Northwest, from the Gallatin Forest down near Wyoming to the Kaniksu up in Washington State. Even though the storms had ceased before Stanley's arrival, the scorching heat persisted, prompting the base foreman and project leader Fred

Brauer to recall three work details from around the region to stand by at Missoula and at Camp Menard.

Stanley was excited about the prospect of getting on a fire, but his excitement had nothing to do with the romance of being a smoke jumper. Stanley had jumped the previous summer, and he knew the script. After a two-minute float down to earth via parachute, the romance ended when the jumpers turned into ordinary groundpounders—their term for regular wildland firefighters. Once they reached a blaze, they typically dug fire line for up to eighteen hours a day, slept on the ground, went without bathing for days, survived on C-rations and K-rations, and then often hiked out twenty miles to the nearest road. That's what romance got them.

Stanley was more interested in the money. With one summer already under his belt, he was earning $1.43 an hour. While he was on a fire, he would be paid for twenty-four hours a day. Plus, the clerks didn't deduct meal expenses when he worked a fire. With any luck he might achieve every smoke jumper's goal—earning more than $1,000 over the summer. No matter how much he missed Julie, Stan recognized that smoke jumping was their best chance to quickly save up a nest egg. Last summer he hadn't fared too well. In between rain, rain, and more rain, he had made only two jumps. And then, when the season finally got going in late August, he had sprained an ankle on a landing and pulled radio duty in the dispatch office.

"I hope things will be different this year," he wrote to Julie. "If I have a good summer, maybe we can move out of the trailer into a nice apartment."

Their trailer in Minneapolis stood near the campus of the University of Minnesota, where the couple had first met. They seemed an unlikely pair. Stan, at six feet tall, was a swarthy big-boned guy, weighing 190 pounds, the upper limit for smoke jumpers. Both his parents had emigrated from Poland and settled in a Polish enclave in Brooklyn, where Stanley developed his distinctive accent. Before the war, Stan had entered Holy Cross College in Worcester, Massachusetts, and played the linebacker position on the football team. He had left school at the end of his freshman year to enlist in the Army Air Corps, where he served as a radio operator and gunner. Despite an occasional subconscious scowl that passed over his features, a trait inherited from his stern father, Stanley seemed a very gentle soul. He loved music—everything from classical string quartets to Hank Williams and Tex Ritter—and poetry. Alfred Lord Tennyson's "Crossing the Bar" was his favorite poem.

Maybe it was the music and poetry that had brought the two together. Julie—fair-skinned, light-haired, and slender—was cultured and refined. She played the piano and drew realistic portraits and landscapes. Her family home in Pierz, Minnesota, was full of light, music, and interesting conversation. The two had gotten hitched in the fall of 1948 at St. Olaf's Church in St. Paul and set up housekeeping in the trailer. Stanley, who majored in forestry, was planning to apply for a job as a forester in New York's Adirondack Mountains after graduation. Julie was taking business courses and hoped to start a family once Stanley found steady work.

When the spring semester ended, Stanley left for the East Coast to finish his training in the National Guard. Julie later rendezvoused with him in Atlantic City for a belated honeymoon and then took the train back to Pierz. After Stanley earned his commission as a first lieutenant, he hooked up with his best friend from the university, Joe Sylvia from Massachusetts, and they traveled together to the Nagel household in the small farming community about 100 miles northwest of the Twin Cities.

André Nagel, Julie's eleven-year-old sister, was excited to see Stanley again. The big lug always took time to play with her. When André had visited the couple last fall in Minneapolis, Stanley had taken her to the Como Park Zoo. Last winter, when word reached the newlyweds that André was ill, Stanley had not hesitated to make the two-and-a-half-hour drive through a blizzard to Pierz, despite a series of impending school examinations. André always wore the locket Stan had given her at Christmas, and at mealtimes she finished the skins of baked potatoes because Stanley had once told her that the skins were the most nutritious part.

André also took a quick shine to Joe Sylvia. She found Joe, who stood only an inch or two over five feet, to be friendly, well-mannered, and generous. André enjoyed the way Joe and Stanley kidded around. To her, they almost seemed like brothers, despite their dramatic physical differences.

The night before Stan departed for Montana, Julie beckoned him upstairs to show off a new locket that sat upon her bureau. Inside the square silver box, she had pasted bits of velvet backing. Over the cloth, she had glued fragments of black and white photographs of her and Stanley that she had torn from larger snapshots. In his photo, Stanley smiled broadly as he casually leaned against a railing on the boardwalk at Atlantic City. Behind him, the ocean waves glimmered with reflected sunshine. In her photograph, Julie wore a white sundress, with the sandy beach as the backdrop.

"When I close the locket, you and I will always be looking into each other's eyes," Julie told Stan that evening.

At 5:30 the next morning, the two smoke jumpers sat down with the Nagels at the large kitchen table for a breakfast of pancakes, bacon, eggs, homemade sausage, and pan-fried potatoes. Frank Nagel had hinted that he might be able to find work for both young men that summer selling cars at his Chevrolet dealership, but they didn't take the bait. Frank finally quit beating around the bush. "Isn't that smoke jumping rather dangerous?" he asked.

"Not really," Stanley shrugged. "I survived World War II, and that was certainly a lot more dangerous." Joe, a former marine, nodded in agreement. The father-in-law realized he couldn't argue with them.

As the Nagels washed dishes, Joe packed the duffel bags into the Chevy coupe that Julie's father had lent them for the summer. Frank had even provided two keys. After shutting the trunk, Joe turned to the dark-haired André and handed her his marine corps sharpshooter pin. The sixth-grader—who had already developed a crush on him—stood speechless.

In the living room Stanley kissed his wife good-bye and promised to send letters whenever he could.

So far, Stan hadn't missed a day of letter-writing.

As the light faded, he put the finishing touches on the epistle and slipped it into an envelope. A few moments later, an REO Speedwagon turned into the driveway of the county fairgrounds. The driver honked the horn, announcing the arrival of another detachment of smoke jumpers from Camp Menard.

CHAPTER THREE

Philip McVey

Camp Menard
August 4, 1949

Philip Rolla McVey, the agile shortstop for the smoke jumper softball team, wiped his sweaty forehead with the back of a well-stained baseball glove and looked over at the runner on first. The baseball diamond at Camp Menard lay between the dormitory and the office. A ball hit over the barracks counted as a homer. There was one out in the bottom of the fifth. Score: smoke jumpers nine, mule packers nine. Eight o'clock in the evening and the temperature still topped 85 degrees. The game would go on until dark, a couple of hours away.

McVey crouched as the pitcher wound up and delivered the underhand pitch. The batter cocked his head, flexed his biceps, leaned forward, and watched the grapefruit-sized ball bounce a foot before the plate. McVey stood upright and pushed back his billed cap. He wore a pair of blue jeans and a faded blue navy workshirt with the tails tied in a knot at his waist, sailor fashion.

Some of the mule packers now at bat had been around since 1930, shortly after the agency began building the Ninemile Remount Depot on a square-mile ranch just a mile down the road from Camp Menard. The Ninemile compound included half a dozen clapboarded Cape Cod–style cottages that functioned as administrative offices, a bunkhouse, and a cookhouse. Cottonwoods, cedars, ponderosa pines, and junipers shaded the manicured lawns. Lilac bushes bloomed beside the back porches of the cottages. In the center of the enclave stood a massive barn that was constructed with hand-hewn beams and sported a concrete floor. A small stud barn (modeled after the main barn), a tack house, and a blacksmith shop were located in front of a series of paddocks where the mules were kept before being loaded onto REO Speedwagons. All the buildings were painted white and topped with green-stained cedar shingles. The CCC camp had been built later, and many young out-of-work men had helped erect the paddocks, dig irrigation ditches, and hay the fields. The smoke jumpers had inherited the haying chores after the CCCs had disbanded at the beginning of World War II.

At first, the Forest Service had leased a small airstrip on Sixmile Road, a few miles from the depot, to accommodate the planes that transported the smoke jumpers. But when the farmer raised the rent on the lease, the agency built its own grass runway in one of the back pastures of the depot. Now, with the Hale Airfield parachute loft, the building where jumpers hung out, folding chutes, sharpening tools, and preparing food boxes, Region 1 fire supervisors routinely detailed men to Missoula to be near the planes. But during training jumps, the Johnson Brothers Flying Service planes still made the thirty-mile flight from Missoula to land and take off from the back pasture at the Remount Depot.

In its heyday, the Ninemile Depot supported scores of pack strings that supplied firefighters with food, tools, and other supplies. But as the smoke jumper program expanded—along with the growing network of forest roads—the mules saw less and less work. Nowadays, one of the major tasks of the packer was to retrieve the jumper's equipment after a fire. One mule could carry one jumper's 150 pounds of gear. Many times, only two jumpers would be dispatched to a fire. Consequently, packing wasn't much of a profession anymore. The mules were being auctioned off, and recruits from the depot for the evening baseball wars were growing scarcer.

CCC Camp Menard lay a mile north of the depot. During training, which usually occurred throughout April and May, the jumpers shared two of the low wooden barracks while the overhead team of trainers occupied the third. Army cots lined the interior of the barracks. When from fifty to one hundred men gathered there, clothes hung from hooks and pegs and foot lockers peeked out from under the beds. Family photos and pinups of movie starlets rotated on the wall as men came and went for the two-week sessions. In the dining hall, long wooden tables and benches crowded the front half of the building and the cook had the run of the kitchen in the rear. A wash house stood beside each barrack. In all, 150 men rotated in and out of Camp Menard every spring.

The training facilities surrounded the barracks. The most prominent structure in camp was the 40-foot-high tower from which the men dropped with a rope attached to their parachute harness. Most men professed that the jarring back-snap they experienced at the end of the rope was much more violent than what they experienced when a parachute popped open. Near the tower was a mockup of the rear section of a Ford Trimotor fuselage set on a platform about five feet off the ground. Over and over, the jumpers practiced squatting in the low narrow doorway and placing a foot out onto the metal step outside, then stepping out as soon as the spotter slapped them on the back of the leg or thumped them on the back. They finished the fall with a smooth parachute roll. The facilities also included an obstacle course featuring a 20-foot-

The parachute training jump tower at Camp Menard in 1949.
Courtesy Gerald Diettert.

high vertical rope net and a wooden wall of similar height for
climbing. Then there were the tank traps, a series of calf-high
wooden stakes pounded into the ground. A strap attached to
the stake slipped around the back of a man's calf while his boot
toes touched the bottom of the stakes. Then the men bent back-
ward until their heads almost touched the ground and brought
themselves upright using back and stomach muscles. They also
crawled through corrugated pipes, jumped ditches, and tip-
toed through old automobile tires.

After a dinner of steak, potatoes, vegetables, two desserts,
and plenty of fresh milk, the jumpers often congregated around
the red barrel used to burn trash outside the mess hall. Their

talk drifted from girls to fire adventures to baseball. Some were still sore that the Cleveland Indians had defeated the Boston Red Sox in the first-ever playoff game in American League history the previous fall. Others were surprised that the Indians had defeated the Boston Braves in the World Series despite batting only .199 as a team. The heroes that year had been player-manager of the Indians Lou Boudreau, the American League's Most Valuable Player. In the senior circuit, Stan Musial of the St. Louis Cardinals had won the honor. Pitcher Johnny Sain of the Braves had topped the major leagues with twenty-four wins, while Ted Williams of the Red Sox had won the American League batting crown, batting .369. Also of note, Cleveland's Satchel Paige had become the first black American to pitch in the American League and the first to pitch in a World Series. And Babe Ruth had died of throat cancer.

Phil McVey was one of many semi-pro baseball players among the smoke jumpers. In fact, Phil's big complaint about smoke jumping was that sometimes he couldn't follow the pennant races when he was dispatched to a fire.

McVey had heard the story of how conscientious objectors had scratched out the baseball diamond with pulaskis—double-headed ax-mattock fire tools. During training, pioneer smoke jumper Earl Cooley had bragged about how the big Mennonite farm boys could outwork anyone he'd ever seen on a fire line. But that comment hadn't sat too well with many of the war veterans. At first Phil couldn't understand how any man could have backed down from fighting against Hitler or Hirohito. He thought the conchies must have hidden behind their religion because they were yellow. But when Phil jumped his first fire, he quickly realized that cowards didn't volunteer for smoke jumping. Many other veterans also confessed to having a hard time sorting out their feelings about the conchies. As for the official Forest Service point of view, the administrators soon forgot the conchies had ever existed.

Earl Cooley, always the storyteller, did mention one tale about the conchies and the baseball diamond that always brought a laugh from the guys. When the conscientious objectors first started work on the diamond, the superintendent of the Remount Depot warned them not to cut down any trees. That meant they had to dodge a six-inch-diameter ponderosa pine after rounding third and heading for home. The tree had easily resolved any arguments about foul balls down the third base line but had made it hard on the runners. Finally, Cooley instructed the men to dig up the tree by the roots, thereby avoiding the literal order not to cut anything down. The next day, just as the game was breaking up, the depot superintendent had driven up to tell the boys that he had relented and they could remove the tree. "He never noticed we'd already taken care of it," Cooley chuckled, "and he could never figure out why all the guys were laughing."

McVey now called Babb, Montana, home, but he had been raised in a variety of towns along the Canadian border, where his father worked for the Immigration and Naturalization Service. Smoke jumping appealed to his innate sense of adventure and wanderlust. At age fourteen, Phil and a childhood buddy, Clarence Ames, had tied saddlebags and bedrolls onto their bicycles and pedaled from Northport, Washington, to the Grand Coulee Dam project to visit Clarence's brother. After a short stay at the construction camp, they had continued on to Spokane before heading back to Northport, a total of 400 miles.

When the war had broken out, Phil had been attending Browning High School on Montana's Blackfeet Indian Reservation, where the Great Plains unrolled from the Rocky Mountains. Before graduation he dropped out to join the navy. Counting his summers before the war, the curly-haired 22-year-old with the impish grin had already worked five years for the Forest Service. This summer would be his second year as a jumper, although, like Stanley Reba, he hadn't gotten much experience on actual fires during the cold wet summer of '48. Phil had spent most of that season at the Castle Creek Ranger Station, about thirteen miles southeast of Grangeville, Idaho, where he and a dozen other jumpers had cleared trails and roads and cleaned up slash from logging areas. Phil loved the camaraderie, good-natured teasing, and shenanigans in the backwoods camp. But he was eager to get back on a fire.

As the pitcher walked around the mound, Phil stretched down and touched his toes. By late afternoon, either during training or on work detail, Phil's body ached from head to toe. But by the end of dinner, he always found energy to play ball. Now, as the sun began to dip toward Stark Mountain at the upper end of the Ninemile Valley, he felt as if he could play all night long. At that moment, a crack echoed through the valley, but it wasn't the sound of a ball striking a bat. An echo of thunder bounced off the mountains, and the outfielders cheered.

"Hark," said the pitcher, a thespian tone to his voice. "The ka-ching of a cash register. See any lightning?"

"Nah, too far over the ridge," Phil said.

As a second crash echoed through the valley, the fielders whooped and tossed their gloves into the air. Before they settled down and refocused on the game, a pickup truck rolled up to the field. The superintendent from the Remount Depot leaned his head out the window.

"Get packed, boys," he shouted. "You're heading into Missoula tonight."

CHAPTER FOUR

Lightning

Colorado Mountain Lookout
August 4, 1949

In the early morning of August 4, 1949, a puff of cloud materialized in the azure sky over the Rocky Mountain Front. The lookout atop Colorado Mountain, ten miles southwest of Helena, mentally noted the innocuous wisp but didn't pay much attention. Some days the puffs remained suspended in place throughout the day, maybe stretching out a bit like strands of cotton candy, maybe multiplying like small white mushrooms. Other days they just rolled on through to disappear beyond the horizon. Most often they simply dissipated.

The old man in the lookout tugged down the brim of his oversized coffee-colored cowboy hat against the rising sun so that his eyebrows disappeared. Above his head hung an awning composed of wooden window shutters that wouldn't be dropped until he closed up the lookout for winter. He would soon have shade, once the sun rose higher than the mountaintop, which took some time. But at least the temperature was only 70 degrees Fahrenheit at 10,000 feet above sea level, not the 100 degrees the valley dwellers had complained about the day before. Vincent took a slow lap around the narrow catwalk that girdled the 12-by-12-foot cabin. Every few steps, he raised the heavy field glasses to the bridge of his nose and scanned the surrounding ridges for smokes. Nothing to report. Thank God.

Vincent wasn't a firebug like those crazy smoke jumpers who had come up last week to splice his severed phone line, a simple copper wire that was often broken by falling limbs. Throughout lunch all they talked about was fires, fires, and more fires. They brought no interesting news of what was going on in the world. No reports on how his favorite baseball team, the Washington Senators, was doing.

"Hey, Lookie, you think that cloud will turn into a thunderhead?" one young fellow had asked repeatedly. "Think we'll get some fires soon?"

How in blazes was he supposed to know? He wasn't a goddamn meteorologist (but with just one glance he knew the cloud didn't have a chance) and who the hell had told them they could call him "Lookie"? Maybe he should have told them his real name when they had introduced themselves, but he didn't like giving his name out to strangers right away. He was glad when the three young fellows had finally packed up their boisterous manners and headed down the trail back into the canyon. An hour of company a week fit the bill perfectly as far as he was concerned. Eventually he slipped back into his solitary routine. Today was window-washing day—all 210 panes. He poured a half-pan of water from a canteen, picked up his rag, and started on the outside. By 11:00 he was starting to sweat as warm damp air roiled up the sides of the mountain. Nature was about to play a little trick on him.

As the air climbed into the atmosphere, it cooled and condensed, forming another puff of white cloud, this time directly above the lookout. This cloud wanted to quickly expand upward, but the surrounding dry air kept knocking it down like a baker deflating a bowl of yeasty dough. Eventually the cloud grew into a full-fledged cumulus, but it was blocked from Vincent's view by the wide awnings.

Every fifteen minutes, Vincent put down the wipe cloth, picked up his binoculars, and made his rounds along the catwalk. While scanning northeast toward the Helena Valley, he hesitated and stared through the binoculars until his arms began to ache. He had spotted an ephemeral tendril of blue smoke rising above a ridge where he knew the Missouri River flowed at the edge of the Big Belt Mountains.

Different kinds of fire sent up different colors of smoke. This he knew. White smoke meant pine needles burning, yellow and tan was grass, black was usually a fresh ignition of pitchy pine, while hot burning wood sent up blue smoke. But after years of spotting fire, he had learned a trick or two. What appeared to be yellow smoke often turned out to be road dust, and what appeared to be white smoke could be spiraling ground fog or waterdogs. He also knew that the big tour boat that plied the waters of the Missouri River near the Gates of the Mountains often sent up a column of blue smoke. He'd bet a sixpack that the next time he looked in that direction, the slender thread of smoke would be gone. And when he finished his rounds two minutes later, the thread of smoke had disappeared. Vincent returned to his window panes.

Meanwhile, in the sky above, the expanding cumulous cloud continued to transform water vapor into rain droplets, that white solid material that makes clouds visible, but updrafts kept the rain and hail from falling. At a height where the air temperature registered above freezing, the rain particles got fatter and heavier until they fell within the cloud, but no farther, as dry air being drawn into the cloud evaporated them. The chilling of the air in this manner created a downdraft, which created friction against the updraft. These opposing winds began to charge the cloud like a battery. Not too much later, the cloud, with its immense cell activated, was ready to blow.

Finished with the outside panes, Vincent began tidying up the cabin. First he cleaned the alidade, a sighting mechanism that stood perched on a swivel in the exact center of the structure. Beneath it lay a map of the area, perfectly aligned so that Colorado Mountain was in the exact center and the compass points on the map exactly matched the surrounding terrain. After aligning a smoke through the alidade's crosshairs Vincent could look down at the map and see in which drainage or on what mountain slope the smoke might lay. Not that he needed to refer to the map very often. After twenty years on the job he could name just about every ridge, valley, and mountain from memory. If another lookout also got a read on the same smoke, the two plotted lines on a map would transect and give the dispatcher a good idea where the fire burned. With a third sighting the dispatcher could triangulate to almost the exact longitude and latitude, township, and range. Vincent checked his watch. Two o'clock. Time for lunch. He filled an aluminum pan with water and placed it on the two-burner propane stove.

Food sustained man, but lightning may have played an even more important role in the formation of life. Scientists theorize that lightning might have catalyzed the earth's primordial soup into forming the earliest organic compounds. But long after that event, it continued to play an important role. Since earth constantly leaked electricity into the atmosphere, the planet would lose almost all its electrical charge in less than an hour if lightning didn't restore the equilibrium. The feat required about 8 million cloud-to-ground strokes every day. Vincent was about to witness one of those jolts.

As the initial lightning stroke raced like a giant spark through the cloud parked above Vincent's head, it heated the surrounding air to 54,000 degrees Fahrenheit, causing the air to expand explosively. That process also stimulated a shock wave that simultaneously traveled outward in all directions as sound. From

within 300 feet or less, the sound of the thunder came as a CLAP
or a CRACK, followed immediately by a loud BANG.

Vincent flinched under the flash and boom and then skipped
out the door, leaned out over the railing, and looked up into
the ominous underbelly of the thunderhead. "Damn inconsid-
erate of you sneaking up on me like that," he said, ducking back
inside. He hopped up on a wooden chair that had thick glass
insulators stuck to its feet. Vincent wobbled the chair across the
floor as far away as he could from the metal alidade, the big box
telephone, and the cast-iron woodstove. A downdraft soon
rocked the lookout like a cradle, and the panes of glass seemed
ready to implode. The only thing keeping the structure from
toppling over was the inch-thick steel cables wrapped around it
and bolted to the mountain. A lighter wire ran from the lookout down into the mountain to carry off any lightning strokes.
Lightning hits sometimes electrocuted all living things with
twenty-five acres, including plants. The theory that lightning
didn't strike the same place twice did not apply to lookouts.

Pushed by prevailing winds, the battleship hulk anchored
above the lookout drifted east, moving far enough astern so
that Vincent could watch. The anvil-headed formation
stretched 60,000 feet into the atmosphere. Although Vincent
scoffed at the smoke jumper's obsession with fire, he was fascinated by lightning. "Now, let's see you fire your big guns in
some other direction," he said out loud.

As the cloud drifted, it tilted as strong interior winds prolonged
the life of the system by sustaining the updrafts and downdrafts.
That action would continue until the moisture in the cloud became too heavy for the updrafts to support it, then the rain and
hail would begin to fall—at least, that was the hope. Meanwhile,
the cloud reloaded. The liquids moved from one part of the cloud
to another, froze, and melted, exchanging positive and negative
ions during the process. As lighter ice crystals drifted into the

upper part of the cloud, hailstones fell toward the bottom, setting the stage for dueling opposite fields.

Vincent was watching one of more than 40,000 thunderstorms that formed that day throughout the world, one of 14 million that form each year. Most of them develop in the equatorial regions, where storms occur every one to three days. When they form over the ocean, the storms help distribute atmospheric heat toward the polar regions, maintaining a global heat balance. In the Northern Rockies they develop less often, about every twenty days, although Vincent swore that some summers they seemed to crop up daily for long stretches at a time.

But there was another important phenomenon occurring at the same time. The negatively charged bottom of the cloud created a positive charge on the ground directly below it. And as the cloud drifted away from the Rocky Mountain Front toward the Big Belts, it pulled the positive charge along in the ground like a dog on a leash. And whenever the ground charge dragged over a protruding object, like a tree or telephone pole, it intensified. After the initial stroke, the surrounding dry air, a poor electrical conductor, stifled the electrical potential of 10,000 volts per meter between the cloud and the ground. But as the cloud drifted closer to the Missouri River and entered the Gates of the Mountains, the insulating properties of the air broke down. As Vincent would have said, it was time for the cloud to fire its big guns.

Electrons from a localized electric field exceeding 3 million volts per meter rushed from the top to the bottom of the cloud and then out of the cloud toward the ground in a series of steps. Each discharge covered about 50 to 100 meters, then stopped for about 50 millionths of a second before continuing another 50 meters or so. This stepped leader appeared so faint that Vincent didn't even notice it.

As the tip of the leader approached the ground, the positive current in the earth started to move up into a ponderosa pine tree growing high on the ridge that separated Mann Gulch and Meriwether Canyon. When the positive and negative forces met, millions of electrons slammed into the ground. Instantaneously, a larger, more luminous return stroke, several centimeters in diameter, surged upward into the cloud along the path that had been forged by the leader. Vincent smiled as the long jagged flash ripped through the sky, unaware that what he was actually seeing was the bright return stroke from the ground up to the cloud. It happened so quickly—within 1/10,000 of a second—that his eyes could not resolve the motions. Instead, Vincent saw a continuous bright flash of light.

To be more precise, Vincent saw more than four lightning strokes at once, all flowing through the same ionized channel at intervals of about one-tenth of a millionth of a second. The second shot, called the dart leader, proceeded downward from the cloud, moving more quickly because of the lower electrical resistance of the path. As this leader approached the ground, a less energetic return stroke than the first one rebounded from the ground back up to the cloud. Two or three more followed, with the whole light show lasting less than a second.

Vincent checked his watch. Almost 4:00. He'd forgotten all about lunch.

Ten miles away, the trunk of a 70-foot ponderosa pine twisted and exploded with the intense heat. Its pine needles ignited and burned for about ten to fifteen seconds. From Vincent's position it looked like the ember at the tip of a puffed cigar. Vincent took an alidade reading of the stroke. He would check for smoke in that direction later that evening or the next morning, when the sun once again heated up the ground.

About one stroke out of twenty-five in the Northern Rockies packed enough punch to start a fire. There was little chance a fire would start that evening, with the storm cooling the ground temperatures, but some embers might survive the night as "sleepers." Lookouts didn't bother reporting lightning strokes. No use sending someone on a wild goose chase. But with lightning causing 10,000 forest fires a year across the United States, Vincent knew there'd be smoke popping up somewhere soon over the next couple of days.

The cloud continued to pepper the earth with lightning for half an hour until downdrafts cut off its supply of warm humid air. Vincent spotted intense rain showers trailing the cloud like a bride's veil. Although the rain seemed heavy from Vincent's vantage point, it remained spotty around the district and missed many areas. Eventually the rain ceased and the lower-level cloud particles evaporated, leaving only the cirrus anvil to reflect the rays of the setting sun.

Vincent sighed, popped open a can of Highlander beer, and sat down to enjoy the show. That was the second best part of his job—admiring sunsets.

CHAPTER FIVE

Jim Harrison

*Meriwether Campground on the Missouri River
August 5, 1949*

James Oliver Harrison awoke to a bird-chirping dawn in a small cabin 100 yards from the Missouri River in the Forest Service's Meriwether Canyon campground. At that point, the river resembled a lake because it was backed up behind Holter Dam about a dozen miles downstream. On July 19, 1805, explorer Captain Meriwether Lewis had noted that the area featured "the most remarkable cliffs that we have yet seen, rising perpendicularly to the height of twelve hundred feet." Almost 150 years later, adventurers navigated the tamed waters by motorboat, leaving their cars parked at the Hilger Landing Boat Club on Upper Holter Lake, about half a dozen miles upstream from the campground.

Jim slipped into a bathing suit, draped his Forest Service uniform over his arm, and followed a path through a thicket of brush to a small beach. At the shore he scanned the river for fishing boats before slipping out of his trunks and wading into the river, bar of soap in hand. The water was neither cold nor warm but right in between—plenty comfortable on a hot summer morning. No campers had caught him naked yet. And he hoped no one ever would. He didn't think his boss, Helena District Ranger Robert Jansson, would appreciate reports of his recreation guard running around *au naturale*. But Jim doubted that anyone would get upset if they did spot him. After all, the mouth of Meriwether Canyon was a doorway into a wild area devoid of roads and human development. The Forest Service didn't even allow livestock to graze there.

After toweling off, Jim slipped into his olive uniform shirt and khaki pants. He checked to see if the clip-on sunglasses and metal pen were still in his breast pocket. Outside the pocket hung the agency's tin badge. Then Jim took inventory of his pants pockets: one small linen-covered wooden box containing a standard pocket compass, two small pocket knives (he couldn't remember how the second one had gotten in there), a pocket watch, two Lincoln pennies, and a small metal tin with a sliding top containing a snakebite kit. Ranger Jansson had presented the kit when Jim last visited the Canyon Ferry Ranger Station, about twenty miles upstream.

Jim slipped on his wire-rimmed glasses before clipping the cord of his pocket watch to his belt, then sat down in the dry cheatgrass to pull on his high laced boots. He took a moment to gaze upon the calm sheen of the river's surface. He appreciated the canyon this way; he knew that in a few hours upcanyon winds and motorboats would roil the water's surface. Later in the morning, an excursion boat that could carry up to 100 passengers would leave Hilger Landing, chug through the famous cliffs of the Gates of the Mountains, and disembark its passengers at Meriwether Canyon for a picnic lunch and some hiking or fishing. Two hours later the boat would retrace the same route, unload new passengers, and retrieve those from the previous drop. In addition, members of the boat club often navigated their private crafts to the canyon for overnight excursions. The previous summer, more than 6,000 sightseers and campers had visited the campground and canyon.

As the recreation guard for the Canyon Ferry Ranger Station, Jim greeted visitors, cared for the facilities, and did his best to represent the Forest Service. His small cabin contained only a bed and an SPF radio. He cooked outside, either over the fire pit or on a propane stove. At certain times of day, Jim radioed the Canyon Ferry ranger station to let them know what, or what wasn't, going on.

A swirl in the water far across the bay caught Jim's attention. It could have been any number of critters, from fish to loons to river otters. Jim found spotting wildlife to be one of the job's best perks. Bald eagles and ospreys nested in small caves in the pockmarked limestone cliffs, and Rocky Mountain bighorn sheep lounged on narrow rock ledges. Mountain lions and black bears also frequented the area, as well as big game like elk and deer, both mulies and white-tailed. He'd probably spot more animals today when he hiked the trail up out of the canyon to look for smokes. Thunder had boomed the previous afternoon directly overhead, which meant a lightning stroke had hit nearby.

For the past two summers, Jim had trained as a smoke jumper, and in some ways he missed his old occupation, or at least one part of it—parachuting out of airplanes. This summer he got to fires the old-fashioned way—afoot, carrying a full canteen of water, a shovel in one hand, a pulaski in the other, and a heavy fire pack on his back. He had grown more sympathetic with the regular firefighters, or groundpounders, as the smoke jumpers referred to them. Jim had quickly realized that they worked just as hard, if not harder, than any smoke jumper.

Groundpounders also were often more knowledgeable about fire behavior. Maybe not the drunks they recruited at

James Harrison preparing for a jump in 1948, assisted by Merle Stratton. Courtesy Merle Stratton.

the taverns during an emergency, but the full-time guys, like his buddy Gary Nelson, knew a lot about fire behavior, especially the big conflagrations that smoke jumpers seldom got to work. The jumpers' main job was to put out the small ones before they got big. And during a wet summer, like the one in '48, many men hadn't even been called out. And few men thought of making a career out of jumping, especially when they forced you to retire your chute when you turned forty. Most hung around for a few years until they graduated from college, then they moved on. True, the foremen at the base, like Fred Brauer, Al Hammond, Earl Cooley, Chuck Pickard, and Wag Dodge, knew their stuff. But Jim realized that when compared to a rank-and-file jumper, many groundpounders knew a lot more about fighting fire, even if they couldn't dig fire line or saw down a snag as quickly as a jumper could. Unfortunately for groundpounders, they missed out on all the romance. Smoke jumpers got all the glory; groundpounders got to mop up.

Jim had given up smoke jumping at the insistence of his mother, Susan. "It's too dangerous," she complained to him. "I worry about you every time I hear a thunderstorm." Eventually his mother's words had sunk in. Jim was twenty years old, a college student. Smoke jumping was OK for a kid just out of high school, but not for a serious-minded young man. In 1945, he had been a member of the state champion high school football team. The Elks had awarded him a scholarship to attend Montana State University in Missoula, where he excelled in his chosen field of study—chemistry. Townsfolk expected great things from him. He couldn't let them down. So he had not applied for a smoke jumper position this summer. However, he had learned one statistic from Helena National Forest supervisor Arthur D. Moir Jr. that he did not pass on to his mother. Since 1910, thirty-five men had been burned to death east of the Continental Divide in fast grass fires, compared to just two in forest fires in Idaho and Montana. And no smoke jumper had ever died in a fire.

A smoke jumper pal had put Jim in touch with Bob Jansson, the Helena District ranger. Jim found Jansson a funny guy, describing him to friends as "a little wishy-washy." For some reason, Jansson had gotten it in his mind that Jim could type, and at first he wanted the new recruit to work in the office. Although Jim reassured him he had no typing skills, Jansson had given him a six-page report to type up anyway. That task took Jim almost four hours to complete. Jansson finally saw the light and offered Jim the recreation guard job he had originally applied for.

From the start, Jim's enthusiasm infected the other workers at the Canyon Ferry Ranger Station. During training, Jim would accompany the other workers to the Ferry Road Inn to drink beer and sing a few songs after hours. Although a tee-totaler, Jansson tolerated the "indiscretions." The men supposed the ranger felt that light carousing was part of the team-building process.

Jim found the country along the eastern front of the Rocky Mountains very different from that west of the Continental Divide. It was drier here, the trees were spaced farther apart, and the forest floors were thick with vegetation. Much of the high grass at the lower elevations was cheatgrass that was as volatile as gasoline once it cured early in the season. At higher elevations, the forests often opened up into meadows full of bunch grass and wildflowers.

Around the Gates of the Mountains, many canyons featured perpendicular walls. Other side gulches offered more gradual slopes but were still too steep for a man to run up. Many south-facing slopes were cooked throughout the summer by a relentless sun and did not support trees. Jim felt more at home farther back from the Missouri River at a higher elevation where the air was cooler, more rain fell, and the timber grew more thickly.

When Jim first arrived at the Canyon Ferry Ranger Station, the Bureau of Reclamation was putting the finishing touches on Hauser Dam. The project site reminded Jim of a small version of the Grand Coulee Dam site on the Columbia River; it was complete with its own village to house workers. In a few weeks, workers were scheduled to begin moving the buildings at the ranger station before the backing water inundated the site.

Jim's first assignment on the district had been to help cut a new hiking trail into the scenic Hanging Cliffs area along the river. But Jim never did get far enough along the trail to see the cliffs themselves. As the crew retired into the tent one night, a steady rain began to fall. In the morning, Jim opened the tent flaps to find eight inches of snow on the ground, with more falling. The crew hiked out that day in a blizzard.

Jim compared his assignment at Meriwether to that of a lookout, except that people visited him every day. He greeted strangers as if they were family and friends. And although it wasn't in his job description, Jim often helped people carry camping gear and sleeping bags from their boats to the campsites, welcoming the chance to get some exercise since there wasn't much strenuous work to do around the campground. That's another reason why he enjoyed hiking the steep trail to the ridge that stood between Meriwether Canyon and Mann Gulch to look for smokes. He had a pretty good feeling that he would find something cooking up there today. The evening before, he'd heard radio reports of a fire flaring up just a few miles to the east.

After his bath, Jim cooked up some bacon, scrambled eggs, and coffee. After breakfast he tidied up the cabin. Fifteen minutes later, he radioed Canyon Ferry. Just as he expected, the voice at the other end said: "Jim, I want you to hike up the top of Meriwether once things warm up and check for smokes. Radio back around 3:00 this afternoon. But first pick up the picnic grounds. I don't want you getting up there too early and missing any sleepers."

Jim smiled. His day was getting off to a great start.

Fred Brauer

Missoula, Montana
August 5, 1949

Fred Brauer rolled out of bed before dawn in the cozy bungalow he shared with his wife, Kathy, on Missoula's south side. The couple had been married two and a half years. "Fritz," as many of the old-timers called him, usually didn't get up this early. On a normal workday, he left the house around 7:30 to cover the ten-minute walk to Hale Airfield. Since most thunderstorms didn't develop until after noon and most smoldering embers didn't produce smoke until around the same time, there was no need for an earlier start. The rest of the jumpers punched in at 8:00. But after an evening of lightning, like the night before, Fred liked to open the dispatch office early to make sure no one had made overnight requests for jumpers. Last night, he hadn't gotten home until 10:00.

"The sky was sparking? Did you see it?" Fred asked Kathy as he struggled his feet into high-topped boots manufactured by the White Boot Company in Spokane. He wore work boots at the office only during high fire danger when there was a possibility he might be called out as a crew leader. "I just hope some planes get back so we can get everyone out where they're needed today," he added. "A bunch of sleepers should be popping up this afternoon."

Sleepers, Kathy knew, were embers that smoldered in the duff—a mixture of rotted wood, pine needles, and leaves that resembled peat moss—beneath trees that had been struck by lightning. Evening air often cooled the flames but seldom put out the heart of smoldering coals. They could cling to life for days or even weeks, until a hot sun and stiff wind fanned the heat into flame. Kathy placed the plate of pancakes and bacon before her husband. It could be days before he sat down to another home-cooked meal.

Fred, big-boned and broad-shouldered, had a face as rugged as a mountain cliff. His grandparents, who had raised thirteen children, had emigrated from Holland to Salt Lake City as part of a Mormon recruitment project, bringing along seven of their children. Fred's dad, John, and his Uncle George and Aunt Marie had later moved to Butte, Montana, where the two brothers worked in the copper mines. George had eventually died of miner's consumption.

Fred had been born at the Butcher Nursing Home in 1917. Three years later, John Brauer had filed a homestead claim on some acreage near Divide, Montana, about twenty-five miles southwest of Butte. For three years he improved the land, but a week before Christmas in 1924, a cat had knocked over a kerosene lamp and the ensuing fire burned the house to the ground. First it was back to the mines for John Brauer and then a move to Missoula to work for the Forest Service as a powder monkey in the construction of the Lewis and Clark Trail Road heading up and over Lolo Pass into Idaho. In Missoula, Fred attended the county high school, where he played football his first three years. But when his father became sick, Fred quit football during his senior year to work and help pay the bills. In 1938, Fred had entered Montana State University (now the University of Montana) and played guard on the 1941 football

Fred Brauer (rear) with President Eisenhower at the dedication ceremonies for the Missoula Smoke Jumper Center, September 22, 1954. Courtesy U.S. Forest Service.

team that lost to national champion UCLA by a single touchdown. The following September he joined the Army Air Corps and became a flight leader for the 439th air unit.

Fred trained as a fighter pilot but was eventually assigned to fly a C-47. Besides dropping parachute troops, he flew many supply missions across Europe and North Africa. On one assignment he had led a unit that dropped twenty-five gliders, each carrying a ton of supplies, to the beleaguered troops trapped in Bastogne, France. He eventually earned a Distinguished Flying Cross and seven battle stars. But his most satisfying detail had been hauling out wounded soldiers to safety, first from a metal landing strip erected on Utah Beach after the Invasion of Normandy and later from prisoner-of-war camps in Germany.

Fred had begun his smoke jumping career before the war, in the summer of 1941, during the unit's second experimental year. When Fred had returned to Missoula after VE-Day, the conscientious objectors were still smoke jumping. Fred had encouraged the administrators to let the conchies go, pointing out that the law stated that returning vets be given hiring preference for government jobs. Fred could forgive the conchies for evading the war based on their religious beliefs, but he had found it tougher to interact with the few able-bodied Forest Service employees who hadn't enlisted and later got deferments when the agency declared the smoke jumper program vital to national security. Fred still had a few problems with some of those "draft dodgers," as he called them. But one by one they had transferred out of the program. Now he was in charge of his boys, many of whom were veterans attending college on the GI Bill or kids fresh out of high school who had already worked the required two summers for the Forest Service.

Fred knew the jumpers to be a well-behaved, dedicated bunch of guys, self-motivated and responsible. Sure, in their free time they liked to fool around with the girls in town or maybe occasionally hit the Casa Loma, a bar located across from the airfield on South Avenue, but in the last five years, the sheriff had only called on him one time to spring a jumper from the brig. And Fred had put that guy on the first bus out of town. The project leader knew how to instill the fear of God in the boys without even raising his voice. Show up for work with a hangover and you miss your jump rotation, he warned them. The threat of erasing their name from the jump list proved enough to keep them in line.

Around the men Fred could be brutally brusque and brash. They always knew what he was thinking. As one jumper commented, "Fred's not always right, but he's never in doubt." He was also colorful. When he lectured the trainees about snakebites he warned them: "If you do get bit, you won't be able to get a hard-on for a while." But Fred also carefully watched out for the men. During the off-season he tried to fix them up on work details throughout the region, earning the nickname of "good deal Brauer." He also helped start a smoke jumper welfare fund from which the newcomers, who were often college kids without a dime to their name, could borrow money to buy a pair of new boots. Nowadays, as foreman for a 32-man crew, Fred jumped only the big fires.

After breakfast Fred scanned the headlines on the front page of the *Daily Missoulian*: "Greater Sugar Beet Acreage Is Sought"; "Truman Gives Up Request for Blank Check"; "Deathless Days' Campaign to Start Today"; "Forest Fire Reserves Called Out."

"Hey, we made the front page," he said. Then he read aloud:

> Fire conditions were so serious Thursday that the forest service's region No. 1 utilized all available smoke jumpers, about seventy, and all available airplanes in the fight to curb the ravages of flames. As a consequence it became necessary to send for reserve jumpers, who had been engaged in other duties about the region.

Yeah, yeah, yeah. Fred knew all that. He mumbled a few more incoherent lines as he quickly scanned the rest of the story to see if his name appeared. It didn't. Most of the quotes were

attributed to the other Freds: Fred Stilling, the head of operations, or Fred Fite, the dispatcher. Then Fred's mood sobered
when another headline on the front page caught his eye: "Fire
Fighter Fatally Hurt."

"Some kid got killed fighting a fire yesterday," he said.

Kathy looked up. "Not a jumper?" she whispered.

"No. Frank Moore was his name. Probably some teenager
they dragged off the streets to help out. Or maybe he worked
as a smoke chaser. Anyway, a snag fell and hit him on the head.
Up near Sawyer Creek. Isn't that up by Seeley Lake?"

Kathy ignored the question. "I'll never understand why the
Forest Service depends on those kids and drunks to help them
out," she said. "Why don't they just train more smoke jumpers?
Or at least keep some more trained smoke chasers on hand?"

"Amen," Fred said. "But not everyone is as sharp as you."
He pushed his chair away from the table. "Hopefully, I should
be home tonight."

Fred decided to drive to work. Instead of pulling into the
airfield lot, he parked on South Avenue. His clerk, Jack Nash,
who had beat him into the office, waved a handful of papers
in the air. Nash had jumped with Fred for a few seasons after
the war but had had to give it up when he turned forty. Fred
had hired him to do the paperwork. Nash kept track of where
the men jumped and made transportation arrangements for
them to get back to the base. When the base was shorthanded,
Nash often accompanied flights to kick out the cargo.

"Any of the project crews report in last night?" Fred asked.

"Yeah, and a few more should be in this afternoon," Jack
said.

By 7:00, the two men had compiled the new jump rotation
and the day's destinations for the pilots. One of the Ford
Trimotors, or Tin Gooses, as the jumpers affectionately called
the lumbering slow-flying crafts, would deliver jumpers to
Kootenai National Forest. The other Ford would pick up

jumpers and equipment from a fire in Gallatin National Forest. They also scheduled the lone Travelaire to deliver jumpers to a fire in the Kaniksu National Forest. However, one of Johnson's two big Douglas C-47s sat in the hanger with one of its engines dismantled, leaving only the other C-47, also known as a DC-3, available for standby duty.

A few years after the war, Bob Johnson of Johnson Brothers Flying Service had traded in a couple of Ford Trimotors for the larger Dougs at the urging of Forest Service brass, who wanted to move more men in fewer trips to save money. When the first big cargo plane had landed on the base strip, Johnson had commented that it "pretty near took up the whole field."

For years Johnson had experimented with the Trimotors and Travelaires, carefully figuring out the distances the craft required to land at and take off from small wilderness airstrips like Big Prairie. With the big silver Dougs he had had to do his homework again, figuring out just how slowly the behemoths could fly and still be safe to maneuver. His tests on actual fire flights showed that the Dougs could do seventy-five miles per hour in good air and eighty miles per hour in fairly rough air. Some of the pioneer jumpers were at first reluctant to jump out of the big bird, since the Fords and Travelaires could fly as slow as sixty. But the added speed hadn't proved to be a problem. The Doug had a curved open doorway because of the bulge of the plane's side, and when he worked as the spotter, Fred liked to stick his head up into that roaring slipstream for a blast of fresh air.

The Dougs could carry twenty-one men and their equipment or sixteen jumpers suited with fire packs. The long-distance cruising planes also sometimes aided other districts. In 1947, Johnson Brothers Flying Service flew a C-47 loaded with marine pumps, hose, and radios from Spokane, Washington, to Concord, New Hampshire, to help fight fires that had burned over much of the state of Maine, including Millionaires' Row, located in what was to become Acadia National Park. For the East, the Maine fires had been the equivalent of the 1910 fires in northern Idaho and western Montana.

Fred was a little worried that only one plane remained at the base, but he had no recourse. No use keeping anyone around for an emergency. They were all emergencies now. "I think I'll head over to the fairgrounds to rustle up some bodies," Fred said. He walked out of the office and started across the floor of the parachute loft. When he was halfway to the exit, the door swung open and a group of men shuffled in. The one in the lead cast an expectant look Fred's way.

"Get your gear together, Stan Reba," Fred said. "You'll be breathing smoke today for sure."

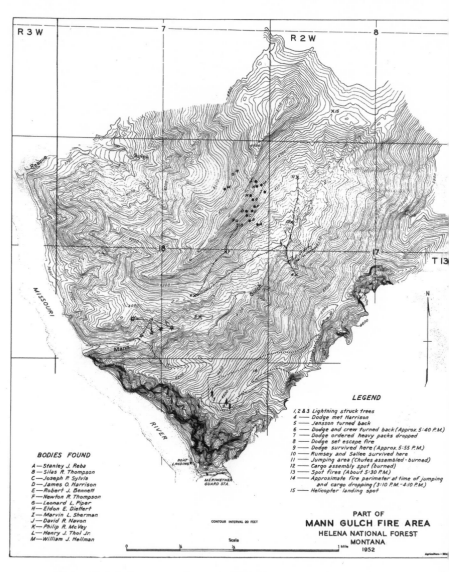

LEGEND

1, 2 & 3 Lightning struck trees
4 —— Dodge met Harrison
5 —— Jansson turned back
6 —— Dodge and crew turned back (Approx. 5:40 P.M.)
7 —— Dodge ordered heavy packs dropped
8 —— Dodge set escape fire
9 —— Dodge survived here (Approx. 5:55 P.M.)
10 —— Rumsey and Sallee survived here
11 —— Jumping area (Chutes assembled - burned)
12 —— Cargo assembly spot (burned)
13 —— Spot fires (About 5:30 P.M.)
14 —— Approximate fire perimeter at time of jumping
          and cargo dropping (3:10 P.M.- 4:10 P.M.)
15 —— Helicopter landing spot

BODIES FOUND

A — Stanley J. Reba
B — Silas R. Thompson
C — Joseph P. Sylvia
D — James O. Harrison
E — Robert J. Bennett
F — Newton R. Thompson
G — Leonard L. Piper
H — Eldon E. Dieffert
I — Marvin L. Sherman
J — David R. Navon
K — Philip R. McVey
L — Henry J. Thol Jr.
M — William J. Hellman

CONTOUR INTERVAL 20 FEET

Scale

PART OF
MANN GULCH FIRE AREA
HELENA NATIONAL FOREST
MONTANA
1952

Mann Gulch fire area. Courtesy U.S. Forest Service.

CHAPTER SEVEN

Fire

Mann Gulch
August 4–5, 1949

On the evening of August 4, 1949, as lightning plugged into the crown of the ponderosa pine tree on the ridge top south of Mann Gulch, the 3 million volts of electricity radiated through the ground surrounding the tree, electrocuting all the plants within a few hundred feet. The few grasses and other plants that escaped the ensuing fire would eventually succumb to insects or disease by the end of the summer.

In the tree itself, intense heat ripped through the pine's cellulose fiber, instantaneously evaporating the sap from tip to root. The trunk jerked slightly, like a person having a heart attack. A scar spiraled down through the bark, slashing open like a knife wound as the wood fiber twisted. Splinters of burning wood and bark exploded from the trunk; the needles on the branches ignited with a great whooshing sound as the crown of the 80-foot tree flamed like a match head. And in the moments it takes for a match to burn down to a smoker's fingertips, the great puffball of orange dissipated as curling cinders of disintegrating needles floated down in a red snowfall.

The clumps of fescue grass growing beneath the tree were well cured, the moisture in their stems having retreated to the root systems by the end of July. Thickly growing stalks of cheat-grass felt even crisper to the touch. A native of the Russian steppes, the knee-high grass earned its name by cheating other plants of water and nutrients with its deep fibrous root system. Plus it cheated ranchers out of money by displacing nutritious grass livestock liked to eat. Since late June, the cheatgrass had waited, eager to burn. A discarded cigarette or hot tailpipe would have ignited it. Cheatgrass spread by following fire's sooty path, its seeds germinating before native plants had a chance to reclaim their territory.

All the grass species in Mann Gulch had grown thicker over the last few seasons, thanks to a prohibition on livestock graz-ing because of the proposal to preserve the Gates of the Mountains as a wild area. Most grasses stood two to three feet high. Interspersed among the grasses sat the yellowed stalks and leaves of elephant ear balsam root and other spring and early summer wildflowers.

As the eastward-drifting thunderhead and its turbulent air currents slowly dissipated, the ground winds calmed down. A thumbnail-sized ember gently settled beside a blade of grass. Its heat caused the plant tissues to chemically break down, re-leasing the sun's energy the stalk had stored through photo-synthesis. As soon as combustible gases escaped from the decomposing tissue, they ignited into a flame that further de-composed the blade of grass, which sustained the flame. With enough heat, fuel, and oxygen in the immediate surrounding area, the tiny fire expanded exponentially.

Heat radiated from two sources: the smoke and the flame. The more intense heat from the flame zoomed in straight rays with the speed of light into the surrounding atmosphere and penetrated another blade of grass, a dried leaf, and a cluster of pine needles. As these materials decomposed, they released more gases until enough accumulated for the tiny flame to leap across to ignite them. In an area of twenty square feet, hundreds of other tiny individual embers started hundreds of other fires that flickered like candle flames. These hundred flames soon spread out and melded into one another so that in a matter of minutes fire had consumed most of the litter and vegetation within a few yards of the expired tree, with flames sometimes flickering up to two feet high.

Like an ever-extending fairy ring of puffballs on the prairie, the flames expanded outward until a black spot of ash appeared where the flames had consumed all the available fuel. The black circle followed the extending ring of fire. In some places, flames stuck to larger fuels like broken branches and pine cones, erratically burning in the black zone like untended campfires. Eventually the flames devouring these objects withdrew into red-hot coals, burning the carbon contained in the wood as a solid instead of as a gas. A fire burning in charcoal in this manner could sit unnoticed for days until a breeze blew the flame back to life. But because wood is a poor conductor of heat, the fire would eventually die out without the whiff of wind-driven oxygen. Once the charcoal cooled, the branch would take years to decompose, with the charred wood remaining a potential fuel source for re-burns.

Eventually the circle of fire reached a mature ponderosa tree and licked the bottom of the tree trunk. The species had developed a bark formed of layers of flexible wafer-thin strips that could get as thick as three inches in a 100-year-old tree. Deep crevices about a quarter-inch wide divided the bark into irregular pieces so that the surface of the trunk resembled a jigsaw puzzle. When the flames kissed the foot of the tree, the outer wafer of bark sprang away from the trunk, carrying any ignition three to four feet away. When the flame persisted, the next layer took up the line of defense.

But fire had few problems moving up the smooth trunks of Douglas firs that grew in the shade of the pines. When flames ignited the whip trunks of a few shoulder-high firs, the trees flashed like Roman candles with a startling poof. But for the most part, the trees and higher brush on the slope remained unscathed that evening. As the breeze died down, the air cooled and the fire lay down. But the heat from embers that had burned deep enough into the layer of pine needles and duff continued to decompose the fuels without producing flames. The fire only slept.

Before the turn of the century, fire had frequently visited these low-elevation forests, sometimes as often as every fifteen years or less. Nature used fire to clear the ground of dead grass, broken branches, brush, and crowded seedlings. In the old days, if ignition did not arrive from the clouds, man purposely set it by hand. Montana's Indians, like those in the East, used fire to keep the undergrowth down to aid hunting. The fires also regenerated the grasses and berry bushes. Because the frequent fires kept the fuel level light, the flames hugged the ground and seldom climbed into the crowns of the trees. When wind did push fire to an extreme level and spread it through a forest, killing berry bushes and other vegetable food sources, the nomadic people packed up their teepees and moved to another location.

At first, European immigrants embraced the Indian practice of light burning. Unless flames threatened lives, buildings, agricultural land, or other developed private property, early settlers let wilderness fires burn. Rural Americans regarded the occasional wildfire in the same way as they did floods and tornadoes. They also believed that wildfires would disappear as the march of civilization transformed the wilderness into farms, pastures, towns, and industrial forests. Those attitudes changed after the summer of 1910.

Snow fell abundantly in the Northern Rockies that winter, but the spring brought scant rain. The summer that followed was even drier. The drought got so bad that the Northern

Pacific Railway laid off about 4,000 men because crop failures along the line undermined the shipping business. By August, hundreds of wildfires ignited by lightning, abandoned hobo cook fires, and sparks from steam locomotives were smoldering in northern Idaho and western Montana. The fledgling Forest Service, formed only five years earlier, rounded up 3,000 men from saloons, logging and mining camps, and towns like Butte and Spokane to suppress the blazes. The army chipped in with thirty-three companies. The firefighters corralled some blazes even as new ones kept popping up. By mid-August the agency reported that it was controlling 3,000 small fires and 90 large ones. Then all hell broke loose.

On August 20, shallow cold fronts rushing across the Palouse Prairie in central Washington and the deserts of eastern Oregon pushed strong winds across the Northern Rockies, from north of the Canadian border to the Salmon River in Idaho. Canyons and valleys acted like wind funnels, and small fires became roaring conflagrations. Fire lines that had held for days melted away. Smoke turned the sky a ghastly yellow, then black. Hundred-foot-tall white pine trees toppled like matchsticks in whirlwinds created by the heat. Within a 36-hour period, individual fires swept up to fifty miles through mountainous terrain, jumped rivers and streams and then melded with other fires. Special trains ferried thousands of refugees to the safety of Missoula and Spokane.

But not all survived. Seventy-eight firefighters died that day, and a dozen towns burned, including the mining center of Wallace, Idaho. In all, the 1910 fires charred about 2.6 million acres, most of which burned during that day and a half.

Before the Great Burn, as it was called, a political debate had simmered among foresters and land managers over whether to use fire as the Indians did or to totally suppress it in the nation's forests. Gifford Pinchot, the first Forest Service chief, championed fire suppression. He pushed to build roads, trails, telephone lines, and lookout towers and hire more fire patrols, basing his model on the industrial forests of Europe. Other Americans embraced a modified version of "Indian" burning by taking some precautions to control the damage light fires did to merchantable timber by protecting the bases of mature trees. In August 1910, before the Great Burn, Interior Secretary Richard Ballinger publicly came out in favor of a policy of light burning. But after the conflagrations in the Northern Rockies a few weeks later, the tide turned in favor of fire suppression. In 1911, Congress passed the Weeks Act, which provided for federal-state cooperative fire control programs. Eventually foresters outlawed light burning on public lands. The agency poured more and more money into fire suppression. In 1935, fire suppression advocates secured complete victory when Forest Service chief Ferdinand Augustus Silcox established the "10 AM Policy." From then on, Silcox wanted firefighters to control every wildfire by 10:00 on the morning following the report of the fire.

Americans soon anthropomorphized fire, referring to it as "good" or "evil." Fighting wildfire took on military trappings as men "battled" blazes and fires "destroyed." Even the chain of command in the firefighting brigades mirrored the military, with an incident commander, squad bosses, and groundpounders. But there was one major flaw in the agency's arguments for total fire suppression: its science was not perfect.

The fires that swept through the Northern Rockies in 1910 burned mostly through mid-elevation white pine forests. Before that species was almost wiped out by blister rust in the 1960s, white pine grew in dense forests on cool moist slopes. Since scant ground vegetation grew in the shadows of the 200- to 300-year-old forests, fire seldom visited that ecosystem. But as the white pines overmatured, they came to depend on wildfire for regeneration. When the weather conditions were perfect (as they were in 1910 with prolonged drought and high winds) and an ignition source was available, the rare crown fire would mow down a stand of white pine. The next year, its seedlings would shoot up like weeds.

This infrequent stand-replacement fire regime also worked well for other "fire-dependent" species such as lodgepole pine, aspen, whitebark pine, and Pacific silver fir in the West and loblolly pine in the East. In marked contrast, the ponderosa pine, which grows at lower elevations, is a "fire-resistant" species. It tolerates fire and needs it to periodically knock down ladder fuels in order to prevent crown fires. It would take the Forest Service about sixty-five years to admit that it had made a mistake by removing fire from the forest ecosystems.

On the morning of August 5, 1949, when the sun's rays hit the ridge top, a tendril of pale smoke twisted into the sky. The lookout on Colorado Mountain crawled out of his sleeping bag and put a pot of coffee onto the stove. After splashing water onto his face, he broke a couple of eggs into a frying pan. About fifteen minutes later, when he had finished eating, he picked up his binoculars and stepped out the door onto the catwalk to scan the horizon. By that time, warm air rising up from Mann Gulch had blown away the ethereal string of smoke. When the lookout radioed into the ranger station in Helena at 9:00, he reported no new smokes.

Throughout the morning, the relentless sun warmed the hillside. By midmorning, the embers had spawned flames. Still hugging close to the ground, the red line casually drifted away from the river up toward the ridge. Sometimes it torched a small tree, but for the most part it crept along, the light smoke hugging the ground like fog. In Helena, twenty miles away, thermometers recorded temperatures in the low 90s. But with no smoke column, the fire was still undetected by the lookout as high noon approached. Just before noon, a plane flew directly overhead searching for smoke. The spotter saw nothing in Mann Gulch and continued on. But soon after the plane departed, an updraft of hot air pushed the flames upslope to the top of the ridge and the fire announced its existence with a plume of white smoke.

Under the smoke, the flames burned through an area of thick-growing shoulder-high trees before climbing the trunk of a mature Douglas fir and fizzling its crown. But the wind was not strong enough to propel the radiant heat into the crowns of the surrounding trees and the flames eventually fell back to the ground. For a couple of hours the fire steadfastly moved in an easterly direction, expanding from two acres to fifteen acres. Then, with new shifts in the wind, it surged across the top of the ridge. The heat from the burning juniper bushes caused some ponderosa pine reproduction to crown. The flames raced across about sixty acres before the firefront petered out in a small saddle where rocky soil could not support much plant life. The fire then lay down for a nap, stymied again.

But it was a good day for fire; the temperature was high and the humidity was low. The fuel moisture readings stood at 5.9 percent (5 percent or less is considered critical). In Helena, officials set the fire danger at seventy-four, approaching the explosive stage on a scale of zero to one hundred. These statistics would not be reported until after 5:00 in the evening. But as Helena Forest supervisor Arthur Moir once said, most veteran firefighters "had a feel for that sort of thing."

CHAPTER EIGHT

Bill Hellman

Hale Airfield, Missoula, Montana
August 5, 1949

Dressed in khaki-colored pants and wearing a bill cap of the same color, Bill Hellman sat on the edge of the loading dock of the L-shaped buildings at Hale Airfield that housed the fire cache and parachute loft. He stretched out his legs and took a puff from a cigarette. Through the open doors he watched his mates assemble fire kits and stuff parachutes. On the roof above, a squad of men was tearing off shingles and laying down new green tarpaper. A squad leader's days off split on the weekend, so Friday was Bill's to do whatever he wished, but he happened to be second in line for squad leader on the jump rotation list. With a two-month-old baby boy at home, he didn't want to miss an opportunity to earn some overtime pay. He just wished they had a pot of coffee brewing in the loft, which they never did. Instead, he'd head over to the six-stool lunch counter in the headquarters of Johnson Brothers Flying Service in a little while, where they also had a pop machine.

Until recently Bill had felt as if his adolescence and early manhood had been like a perpetual smoke jumper camp—serious training to prepare for something bigger. All the exercising, all the studying, all the skills practice were about to pay off. Bigger and better things waited. The feelings of confidence and optimism had started to crescendo a little more than a month ago. On June 26, Bill had crowded into a Ford Trimotor with veteran jumpers Skip Stratton, Bill Dratz, and Ed Eggen to fly to Washington, D.C., to help the Forest Service celebrate the success of the smoke jumper program. Al Cramer had come along as the spotter, while Jim Wait had served as the chute technician. Bob Johnson had sat in the pilot seat; Bud, Johnson's mechanic, in the copilot seat.

Because the Ford had no navigation lights, Bob Johnson had flown only during the day. Topping out at ninety miles per hour, the Trimotor took three exhausting days to reach the District of Columbia. Johnson had made one adjustment to the Tin Goose's equipment for the flight by installing a radio, a device that wasn't necessary for landing at isolated mountain airstrips. But Johnson had recognized that a transmitter and receiver might come in handy when approaching commercial airports like Washington National.

The boys knew Bob Johnson as a daring mountain flyer, but they hadn't expected him to practice his barnstorming ways as he flew over more civilized country. At one point over the Midwest, Bud, who had acted as navigator, couldn't match a town on the horizon with the dots on the map. Bob brought the plane down to about twenty feet above a set of train rails. As the plane zipped past the depot, he yelled out, "Did anyone make out the name on the depot sign?"

Even though Bob Johnson bought a new Cadillac every year and spent winters in Hawaii, he often complained that his flying service was driving him to the poorhouse. On the trip to Washington, the men witnessed the lengths to which Bob went to save money. The airstrip at Hale Airfield was gravel, but many fields on the way to the East Coast were paved over. Bob chose to land the Trimotor on the grass bordering the improved strips,

Bill Hellman (second from right) before the January 1949 flight to Washington D.C. Also pictured are (from left) Ed Eggen, Bill Dratz, and Skip Stratton. Bob Johnson is in the pilot seat of the Ford Trimotor. Courtesy Skip Stratton.

then taxi over to the hanger on the paved runway. "Don't want to wear out the tires," he told the surprised jumpers.

Bill Hellman had been ambivalent about leaving Missoula. Gerry, his wife of three years, was expecting to give birth to their first child any day. But as he wavered, Gerry had urged him to go, arguing that it was a great honor. In the end, everything worked out fine. Just after the Trimotor had taxied up to the hanger at Washington National Airport, Bill received the phone call he'd been hoping for. Gerry had delivered a healthy baby boy.

For the festivities in Washington, D.C., the Forest Service brass and the National Advertising Council proposed that the jumpers land on the Ellipse between the White House and the Washington Monument as a salute to American business for its support of the continuing forest fire prevention campaign. The agency had recently unveiled the mascot of its new fire awareness campaign: Smokey Bear, a cartoon character modeled after an orphaned bear cub that had been singed while escaping a forest fire the year before. On the day of the jump—June 28, 1949—big shots from American industry, including General Motors, had assembled at a nearby banquet hall to watch the jump on television instead of walking the few blocks to witness it in person.

In high temperatures and humidity, the jumpers had suited up. As they posed for photographs, thunderstorms appeared on the horizon. While the plane circled overhead, the ground crew set off smoke bombs to mark the landing area, but strong winds flattened the smoke across the Ellipse. When Al Cramer kicked out the drift chute, he watched it stray far from the mark. "It doesn't look good," he informed the four jumpers. "But it's now or never. They don't want to do it any other day."

Usually the jumpers leaped from 1,000 feet, but Al ordered Johnson to drop down to about 700. As the plane circled the Washington Monument, the boys waved to tourists looking out from the windows at the tip of the obelisk. On the Ellipse below, four baseball diamonds pointing into the center of the field created a geometric mosaic. The men lined up on the Trimotor floor to jump in sticks of two. Hellman was the last man out. The only hitch occurred when Bill Dratz's chute opened inside out, minimizing his steering capacity. He hovered over the edge of the Ellipse before drifting into the trees across Pennsylvania Avenue. Later, some Forest Service pencil pusher told the young men that President Harry Truman had watched the jump from the White House kitchen window.

On the ground, the men once again posed for photographs, this time with their chutes billowing out behind them in the stiff wind. Nearby, a band played and hundreds of kids cheered. The jumpers then split into pairs and climbed atop the back seats of open convertibles for a parade up Pennsylvania Avenue, escorted by a squadron of policemen on motorcycles. Still attired in their jump suits and sweating like pigs, they waited in the anteroom of the ballroom to be introduced to the banquet guests.

"Say, you boys look like you need a nice cool drink," a bartender said.

"Sure," Stratton nodded.

Just as the bartender set four Tom Collins on the bar before the jumpers, an undersecretary of agriculture, dressed in a tuxedo, approached them.

"Hey, this is the cream of American youth," he reprimanded the bartender. "They can't be drinking alcohol."

Before any of the war veterans could tell the VIP to go to hell, the bartender said, "Hell, it's only lemonade." The VIP apologized, picked up his own drink, and headed back to the banquet. Later that afternoon, when all the hoopla had ended, Hellman tried to put the trip into perspective: "Two thousand miles for a one-minute jump."

Upon his return, Bill quickly warmed to his role as a new father. Bill had met Geraldine Mather while attending Flathead County High School in Kalispell, Montana, about 120 miles north of Missoula. At first they had just hung out with each other, attending football games with the gang or swimming in nearby Flathead Lake, the largest natural body of fresh water west of the Mississippi River. But they had never talked about making a future together. When Bill cut short his senior year to join the navy, Gerry never promised to wait for him. After two years as a pharmacist mate first class in the navy, Bill transferred to the marines, trained as a combat medical corpsman, and island-hopped across the Pacific. When he came home, he asked Gerry to marry him.

Bill spent two years at Montana State University in Missoula and a year at Montana State College in Bozeman studying to become a schoolteacher. For his junior year, he transferred to the state college at Havre, Montana, out on the windy northern plains. The previous winter, he had transferred to Greeley State Teachers College in Colorado. While Bill attended classes, Gerry worked in an office to help pay the bills, even after she had become pregnant. The couple had struggled along on his ninety-dollar-a-month check from the GI Bill, living in a cute little trailer. When the vet payments arrived late, Bill and his classmate and close neighbor, Gareth Moon, would split what food they had in their pantries between the two families.

Since his dad worked for the Forest Service, Bill had no trouble getting appointed to the smoke jumpers. Once again registered at Montana State, he only needed one more semester to earn state certification to teach science and botany. He had just turned twenty-four. When he landed a teaching job, Bill planned to shop around for a real house. But the young family wasn't out of the financial woods yet. Medical bills piled up on the kitchen table next to the school bills. Things weren't desperate—but having grown up during the Depression, the couple refused to ask their parents for help.

As a squad leader, Bill jumped the bigger fires with four- or eight-person crews. Usually the bigger fires meant more overtime and more days out on the job. But sometimes it didn't work out that way. The day before, Bill had boarded a Ford Trimotor with an eight-man crew for a flight south to Yellowstone National Park. When they had landed and picked up the park ranger, their guide hadn't been able to locate all the fires, so only four men had jumped, two to a stick to each fire. When he returned to Missoula, Bill found that his name had been bumped down to the bottom of the rotation list, even though he hadn't jumped. Still, with most men still out on work projects, Chuck Pickard was the only squad leader ahead of him. And both men knew that the hot sun and afternoon winds would surely breathe life into more sleepers. During morning break, Chuck had joined Bill for a smoke on the loading dock.

"Hey, Pick," Hellman said. "You know, you're one of the best buddies a man could ever ask for."

"Sorry, Bill, I left my wallet at home today," Pick replied.

"Hey, don't insult me. I never borrow money from my friends; I only win it off them. But I don't want your money, Pick—although I could use a couple of extra bucks with that baby and all—but it would sure be nice of you if you let me jump to the top of the rotation list. You'd never forgive yourself if I had to send that kid back because we didn't have enough money to feed him, now, would you, Pick?"

"What makes you think I'm a nice guy?" Pickard asked.

"That's what everybody tells me," Bill said. "Although I can't say I've ever seen it myself. Of course, now's your chance to show me."

Pick laughed and flicked his cigarette butt into the gravel lane before heading back into the loft. His route led right by the rotation board. He hesitated, turned around, then stretched up and switched Hellman's name for his own.

"Thanks, Pick," someone said. When Pickard looked over his shoulder he saw Hellman's smiling face in the doorway.

"You'd better make sure you hit the silk this time," Pick said. "If it's another dry run, I'm not giving up another spot, even for your kid."

By 2:00 that afternoon Bill Hellman was bored. The crew on the rooftop had rolled out the new tarpaper. The early afternoon flurry of flights had petered out. Bill knew that local district crews, hungry for overtime themselves, were probably hogging all the fires that they could reach in a reasonable amount of time. He'd just wasted a day off. Still, the relentless sun scorched the mountain slopes. Maybe some thunderheads would develop this evening. Anyway, no use hanging around the base any longer. Hungry and discouraged, Bill climbed into his car and drove to his sister's house for something to eat.

"Hi, Bill," she said, as he opened the door. "You're just in time." She held out a black telephone receiver to him. "It's the jumper base."

CHAPTER NINE

Robert Jansson

Canyon Ferry Ranger Station,
Helena National Forest
August 5, 1949

John Robert "Bob" Jansson probably knew more about fighting fire than any other Forest Service worker on the Helena National Forest, which was about 120 miles east of Missoula. Jansson had discovered early on that one of the quickest ways to climb the Forest Service leadership ladder in those days was to gain experience fighting fires. Since beginning his career in 1936, he had fought more than 100 fires and had been fire boss on a project fire, a complex of fires that burned simultaneously in the same area. Jansson had also directed firefighters on numerous Class C fires, those covering more than 100 acres. Jansson had transferred to the Helena Forest in 1941 with his wife, Lois, to work for Ranger O. C. Clover, a crusty old man prone to practical joking.

Bob had met Lois while a graduate student in forestry at Montana State University in Missoula. He had been twenty-six at the time, Lois twenty-four. They celebrated their wedding in the spring of 1941 at the People's Congregational Church in Medora, North Dakota, Lois' hometown. As Bob walked down the aisle, a yellow jacket stung the tip of his thumb, causing him to jump into the air. Lois's brother, Lloyd, an usher at the ceremony, figured the groom had leaped into the air when he suddenly realized the enormity of the step he was about to take.

The next day, the newlyweds took a train to Helena. Bob left Lois at the station while he walked to the local filling station to retrieve his Model T. Along the route he suffered a minor heart attack and rested on the curb until it passed. The cause of the ailment was bacterial endocarditis, for which he took sulfa drugs. It was not his first attack, nor would it be the last. After a short spell of pain and near blackout, he recovered enough to drive the Ford back to his worried bride. The ailment made Bob a cautious man. Almost from the first, Lois jokingly described her blonde-haired husband to friends as "a man who never did anything without counting all the costs and figuring out the angles first."

With no extra housing available for district employees, the Janssons had lived in a wall tent during their first season on the Canyon Ferry District. Bob built a frame of rough lumber to support the tent. He insulated the walls with Celotex scraps, put up screening to keep out mosquitoes and flies, and laid linoleum over the ground. Jansson's mother sewed a curtained dressing room for the corner of the tent, which also doubled as a clothes closet. Later, Bob constructed a tiny shack at the back for a bedroom. He also built a desk with a bookshelf and linen closet above it as well as cupboards.

The cramped kitchen featured a three-burner kerosene stove that flared up at the slightest drop of moisture, leaving a sticky film of soot on the pans and sometimes the canvas ceiling. The cold-water tap dripped water all winter long into the sink to keep the waterline from freezing. An air tight wood stove, constantly stoked with slab wood salvaged from a nearby sawmill, kept the place cozy warm. A studio couch opened into a bed at night. A stream flowed a few yards outside the doorway of the tent. On the other side of the creek, a tall outcropping of rock blocked the wind. Old-growth ponderosa pines and Douglas firs provided summer shade for "Honeymoon Gulch."

In 1942, when Bob's faulty heart kept him out of the war, the Forest Service had assigned him to Oceanside, California, to supervise the cultivation of the gyualie plant, which produced a substitute for rubber. Bob returned to Canyon Ferry that December in time for the birth of his first child, Ruth. By the time his son, Paul, was born, O. C. Clover had retired with a disability and Bob had become ranger. A second son, Roger, had died within the first year of his birth.

With Bob's promotion, the Janssons moved into the house at the Canyon Ferry ranger station. But in 1948, the Bureau of Reclamation broke ground for a new dam about a mile up-stream and erected a village for the workers directly across from the compound. The new lake would eventually inundate the Jansson's home and the forty surrounding acres where the horses, mules, kids, and dog roamed. By August 1949, the family was preparing to move at the end of the summer.

Bob Jansson loved the wild places that lined the Missouri River. He claimed to have inspected every inch of the 300,000 acres of his district, which sat about twenty-three miles north-east of Helena. At Bob's suggestion, the Forest Service had set aside the land surrounding the Gates of the Mountains as a wild area, never to be penetrated by a road or exploited by commercial development. The paperwork on the area had come through in 1948.

Throughout the district, Bob studied aspects of different types of terrain to plan fire-suppression strategies. Under the tutelage of Henry Gisborne, the agency's premiere fire sci-entist, Bob projected how a forest fire would burn and spread in specific draws and canyons under a variety of conditions, then he considered the best strategy for fighting them. A Methodist who neither drank nor smoked, Bob could be a

stern taskmaster, working his employees on holidays and de-
manding illegal overtime.

On July 22, 1949, the federal government officially dedicated
the new dam. The celebrations were held in conjunction with
the 85th anniversary of the discovery of gold in Helena's Last
Chance Gulch and the centennial anniversary of the Department of the Interior. Many men in Helena grew beards, while
downtown store owners erected colorful false fronts on their
establishments. During the weekend celebration, a group of
children paraded down Last Chance Gulch with their dogs
pulling Radio Flyer red wagons fixed up like covered wagons.
Others, dressed in leather vests, leggings, cowboy hats, and
spurs, rode their bicycle-ponies. The Saturday Parade of
Progress and Vigilante Days took more than an hour to pass.
A military tank pulled the Forest Service float, which was cam-
ouflaged with evergreen trees. Most of the Forest Service personnel on the float had been dressed as Indians. Among them
stood a young mountain goat, a deer fawn, and an old prospec-
tor with a burro. At the head of the float a Pacific pump kept
a self-contained waterfall in perpetual motion. Helena's favorite
son, movie star Gary Cooper, led the parade with singer and
actress Dinah Shore at his side.

In the meantime, Bob Jansson, thirty miles away, rode horseback through the Gates of the Mountains, showing off his prized
wild area to five governors. Earlier in the month, Lois had followed the same trail; she described the area to her friends as
"holding its own in terms of beauty and grandeur with
Yellowstone and Glacier national parks."

But with the fire season now under way, Bob had turned his
attention to the work at hand. The previous afternoon, lookouts had reported four fires, three caused by lightning, another
by an abandoned campfire. Bob had worked the fire desk until around midnight, then slept on a cot in the office. About
an hour after midnight, a crew returning from one of the small

lightning-caused fires awakened him. After they left, he fell
back into a fitful sleep, finally abandoning his cot around 6:00
in the morning. After rinsing his face with cold water he walked
over to the cabin to breakfast with Lois and was back at work
by seven. An hour later the ranger radioed Jim Harrison at the
Meriwether Guard Station and instructed him to climb up to
the ridge between Meriwether Canyon and Mann Gulch to
check for signs of smoke. Around midmorning, after shuffling
some paper, Jansson and assistant ranger Hank Hersey drove
to the Helena airport.

"I want you to get some experience spotting smoke from the
air," Jansson told Hersey during the drive. "It's the only way to
go nowadays. I bet within ten years we blow up every lookout
there is out there. You can't escape progress." At 11:30, the two
boarded a single-engine plane, which climbed to an elevation
of 1,100 feet. To the west, the sun glinted off the copper roof
of the state capital building in the heart of Helena. To the north
reposed the Sleeping Giant, an isolated elongated set of low
rounded hills that resembled a reclining body. North of the Giant
stood the Gates of the Mountains, and beyond that, Holter Lake.
The flat plain of Helena Valley spread east about thirty miles
from the outskirts of town until it bumped into the rounded
well-timbered Big Belt Mountains. Before penetrating the deep
canyons, the Missouri River hugged the south side of the mountain range like a moat protecting the wilderness.

On their first pass over Mann Gulch and Meriwether
Canyon, Jansson spotted no sign of smoke. Half a mile downstream, the large wooden tour boat chugged through the
Gates of the Mountains. The pilot climbed to 7,000 feet for a
better view, then drifted about a mile west of Mann Gulch. The
ranger then directed the pilot to fly over Jim Harrison's usual
lookout spot.

"Do you see Harrison?" Jansson asked Hersey. The assistant
shook his head. "Me neither. Maybe he's already gone down

to report no activity. Let's go see if we can't spot the fire that
was reported around York last night."

Bob Jansson disagreed with his wife's glorious assessment
of the Gates of the Mountains wild area. He thought the small
wilderness, only 28,500 acres, lacked the grandeur of Glacier's
craggy peaks and snowcapped mountaintops. He liked it,
nonetheless, for the area sustained an intriguing and pleasing
combination of open meadows and forested slopes. He par-
ticularly enjoyed leading visitors on pack trips through
Refrigerator Canyon, one of the gateways into the wilderness
located half a dozen miles east of the tiny community of Nelson.
The trail initially squeezed through a narrow rock-walled passage flushed by a healthy creek of frigid water—the best place
to fill up a canteen. In fact, Bob always filled two canteens there
because beyond that point water grew scarce.

Once past the towering limestone cliffs, the footpath wended
through very dry Douglas fir and juniper forests occasionally
dotted by ponderosa pine, then traversed a series of humped
peaks through thick forests that offered few views of the canyon
or the surrounding mountains. The first night out, Bob always
set up a frugal camp at Bear Prairie, 6,400 feet above sea level.
Native grasses grew thick there, and in the center of the
meadow, a spring burst clear and cold from a thick growth of
brush surrounded by a ring of aspen. It seemed that every night
around the campfire, the same owl perched in the same tree
overhead at dusk. Later, bats dive-bombed in the gloaming,
often plucking insects a foot from Bob's nose. In the fall, elk
bounced their eerie bugling calls off the rock walls, and sometimes a black bear brazenly ransacked the food bags hung high
in the trees. Except for an occasional airplane headed out of
Helena, Bob never heard any industrial sounds. No chainsaws,
no trucks, no bulldozers, no steam shovels. And the stars above

shone as plentiful as the dings on the surface of a lake during a summer shower.

The second leg of the pack trip followed higher ridges with open meadows, offering panoramic vistas of Hilger Valley and the canyon of the Missouri. At the western edge of the wild area, the trail abruptly descended toward the river, leading between the sheer cliffs of Meriwether Canyon. The numerous caves in the canyon walls always fascinated Jansson. Some of the dark portholes looked big enough to harbor small colonies of humans, or at least make good outlaw hideouts. An archaeologist once told Bob that some of those caves offered evidence of prehistoric use by humans, but the scientist hadn't had enough time to do extensive excavation work in the area. Other caves looked cozy enough for mountain lion dens, still smaller ones for peregrine falcon aeries. Most, though, were too high up to explore except by the best of rock climbers. Whenever the pack animals passed the junction of the spur trail that led over into Mann Gulch, Bob began anticipating a cool swim in the Missouri.

On August 5, from the cockpit of the spotter plane, the wild area looked even more alluring than usual. After crossing the wilderness, the pilot turned back toward the Missouri River benchland above Trout Creek. Neither Jansson nor Hersey spotted any smoke in the area surrounding the tiny burg of York, nestled deep in Trout Creek Canyon, not far from Nelson. However, they did spot a little smoke from the Cave Gulch fire some distance to the south, which was already manned. The plane then headed back to Helena, touching down at about 12:25. As Bob walked across the tarmac, he glanced back at the mountains and saw a new smoke. He pointed it out to Hersey.

"Looks like the fire on the other side of the wilderness has finally warmed up," Hersey said.

"I don't think that's it," Jansson disagreed. "It's too far north." He walked into a nearby hanger to phone the supervisor's office, with Hersey dogging his heels.

"You're kidding me," Jansson said into the phone. "We just flew over there twenty minutes ago and didn't even see a ghost of a smoke." Jansson put his hand over the mouthpiece and said, "Colorado Mountain Lookout called in a fire at Section 19, Township 13 North, Range 2 West at about 12:15. Tell the pilot to refuel the plane. I want to go back and take a look." Before Jansson hung up the phone, the dispatcher told him: "Good luck. It's the thirteenth fire this season so far."

Back in the sky, the pilot headed directly toward the column of smoke that now lofted over Mann Gulch. Jansson's watch read just about 1:00. The forester estimated the fire to be about eight acres in size; it was burning entirely on the Mann Gulch side. Some charred stunted juniper trees belched out the heavy smoke. The wind, blowing downgulch, carried the smoke out of the mouth of the canyon over the river.

"It looks quiet now," Jansson said, "but it could get pretty dangerous if the wind switches and comes about from the west. That would spread the fire along the slope. My guess is there's an updraft in Mann Gulch that's holding the fire from spreading rapidly downhill. If that should decrease or if the fire eventually creeps down hill far enough to catch the main canyon draft, then we're in trouble. Mann Gulch would act like a chimney and carry the fire along up the canyon."

The men also spotted another smoke burning in the west, near York. Jansson knew there were a number of ranches in that area.

On the flight back, the ranger formed his strategy. Five years ago, he had fought a similar fire in the Mann Gulch area; the crew had reached the fire in time before it scattered downhill. He knew that if his luck did not hold this time, a blowup was highly probable. But since people lived near the York fire, not to mention valuable livestock, Jansson decided to concentrate his local forces there. When he landed, he phoned Helena National Forest supervisor Author Moir to suggest that the dispatcher request that some smoke jumpers from Missoula drop on the fire in Mann Gulch. To bolster the jumpers he would send in another fifty men with equipment and overhead, two Pacific pumps with 3,000 feet of hose, and fifty sack lunches.

"The jumpers will be able to reach the area quicker than a ground crew," he explained to Moir. The forest supervisor agreed and approved the order for the twenty-five jumpers. The order was called in about 1:30. Jansson assumed the jumpers would choose Willow Creek Mountain, which had burned over in 1926, as a landing spot. The area was about three-quarters of a mile from the ridge where the current fire burned.

CHAPTER TEN

Eldon Diettert

Missoula, Montana
August 5, 1949

Eldon Diettert closed his warm brown eyes for a second, wished for a dry lightning storm, then leaned over the table and blew out the nineteen candles as his family sang their congratulations. The cake, embellished with "Happy Birthday Smoke Jumper," was trimmed with yellow, blue, and red frosting swirls and roses.

"You've grown into a beautiful young man," said his mother, Charlotte. "I can't believe you're the little curly-haired boy who once kicked our postman."

"Oh, Mom." Eldon rolled his eyes.

"Kicked the postman?" asked sister Doris Jean. She had been born when Eldon was in the third grade. "Why would he kick the postman?"

"Because he had the most beautiful curly hair," Charlotte said. "I loved his hair so much I let it grow out until it was shoulder length, like Shirley Temple's. And the mailman would tease Eldon by calling him a little girl." A telephone rang in the living room and Charlotte Diettert continued her story as she backed out of the room. "But when El was about three years old he got sick of the taunting and one day he kicked the man in the shins, proclaiming in a very serious voice: 'I am not a little girl.'"

"You could have fooled me," said Eldon's older brother, Gerald. "I remember when I used to take him to the Saturday morning movies to see *Buster Brown and His Dog*, and every time El would break out crying because he was afraid of the dog. You always made such a fuss I had to drag you out of the theater and take you home. It was disgusting."

"You must have been hallucinating. I love dogs," said Eldon, brushing his wavy sandy-colored hair back from his face. He'd been working all morning tearing off tar paper from the roof of the parachute loft. The back of his neck itched. Although his baby face was only just beginning to take on the angled, rugged features of an outdoorsman, his six-foot frame was packed with muscle.

"Remember when Eldon went to work as a gandydancer on that section gang with the Northern Pacific?" Doris Jean asked. "We all said good-bye to this skinny little kid when he left, and this big hulk came back home at the end of the summer. You should have seen your eyes bug out when you first saw him, Gerald. I notice you didn't pick on him much after that."

Eldon had been born in Moscow, Idaho, where his dad, Reuben, taught in the University of Idaho's botany department. By 1935, the Dietterts had moved to Iowa, where Reuben enrolled in a doctorate program, earning thirty-five dollars a month teaching classes. To help out, Charlotte mopped floors, bringing in another fifteen dollars a month. To save money, the parents sent the two boys off in the summertime to the family farm in North Judson, Indiana, where doting grandparents fattened the kids on cream and whole milk. Gerald and Eldon amused themselves by jumping down from the barn loft into piles of hay and making wooden pistols with rubber bands that

shot clothespins. Their favorite targets were the barn cats.
"Someday, you two are going to turn into John Dillingers,"
Grandpa Diettert had warned them more than once.

The boys also spent time on the farm of their maternal grandparents in LaFayette, Indiana. There, they watched a tinker-
ing uncle build electrical contraptions that automatically
harnessed the mules and fed the cows. The boys also raised
pet chickens, and later they helped their grandmother chop
off the chickens' heads and pluck their feathers. Grandma
served up a couple of the birds for their last supper at the farm.

After graduating from the University of Iowa, Reuben
Diettert had moved the family to a modest cottage on Mount
Avenue in Missoula, Montana, from which he walked to his
new job at Montana State University. The boys slept in a bunk
bed in an attic room, accessible by the narrowest of stairways.
Being the oldest, Gerald claimed the lower bunk. Like many
boys of that era, the Diettert brothers built model airplanes of
balsa wood and tissue paper, mostly replicas of World War I bi-
plane fighters. When the models suffered from too many crash
landings, they would light them on fire and toss them from
the bedroom window, careful not to send the incendiary crafts
across the fence into the neighbor's garden. After school,
Eldon would practice his clarinet in the attic. When he was
done, Gerald would tackle the trombone.

Both boys contributed to the family income by working odd
jobs. During the summer, Gerald mowed eleven lawns every
week, raking in more than 200 dollars a month, matching his
dad's monthly university salary. When the grass grew too thick,
Eldon helped out by pulling the mower by a rope as Gerald
pushed. Eldon eventually inherited the business from his brother.

The boys also delivered publications like *Liberty*, *True
Confessions*, and *True Detectives* door to door. Although Gerald
found the racy publications intriguing, Eldon never bothered
to thumb through them. Instead, he often traipsed off alone
across the grassy slopes of Mount Sentinel that loomed behind

the university campus. Or he picked huckleberries in the forests in Pattee Canyon and sold them to the local markets. When he got older, Eldon also delivered groceries year round for K & W Grocery. With his spare cash he bought oil paints, drafting pencils, sketchbooks, and fly-fishing equipment.

One December, the boys had scoured Mount Sentinel for the perfect Christmas tree. They found it after climbing 2,000 feet up to the saddle between the main peaks. Gerald climbed a tall Douglas fir to chop off the top fifteen feet. The diameter at the butt end of their Christmas tree measured four inches. The boys lugged the bushy top downhill, careful not to drag it so they didn't knock off any needles. At home their dad had to saw it in half so it would fit in the living room.

On vacations the family would drive the 1936 blue Dodge sedan to Glacier National Park, 150 miles north of Missoula. Behind the car they pulled a single-wheel dual-hitch trailer stuffed with tents, food, and a campstove. On one return trip, near the southern shore of Flathead Lake, the trailer tire blew out. The parents stuffed the equipment into the backseat of the Dodge, sat the boys atop the gear, and tied the trailer to the roof of the car for the rest of the journey.

In 1947, Eldon had landed his first job with the Forest Service at Camp Nowhere, located in northern Idaho, near the mining town of Wallace. With hundreds of other youths, he had futilely fought to stop the onslaught of blister rust, a foreign disease that was decimating the western white pine population, at the time the most valuable merchantable tree species of the inland northwest. One of Eldon's mates was a Texan who liked to brag about his exploits. The quiet, even-tempered Eldon hadn't much appreciated the man's self-aggrandizement until the Texan toppled from a big log used as a bridge into the churning Coeur D'Alene River. When the man resurfaced downriver about thirty yards, he let out a whoop and screamed, "Another first for Texas!" Eldon had laughed and never resented the man's bragging again.

Like his dad, Eldon studied plants and animals. At the university he enrolled in the forestry school, but he also found a way to incorporate his other passions—painting and drawing—into his professional pursuits. During his free time at Camp Nowhere, he carried his sketchpad and paints in a backpack whenever he hiked through the woods. On each sheet, he described a bird, plant, or animal he spotted, then sketched it. By the end of the summer the manuscript was 148 pages long.

When Eldon visited home on his days off, he often spent the evenings pulling weeds in the backyard vegetable plot. Although weeding was a passion for his father and mother, Eldon had never taken to the chore. But he found some solace chatting with his backyard neighbor, Earl Cooley, one of the pioneer smoke jumpers.

"Hey, Earl. When can I come and be a smoke jumper?" Eldon would ask every time he saw Cooley.

"When you turn eighteen," Cooley would always reply.

"Hey, Earl," Eldon would then say. "Tell me again what it's like to hit the silk." And being an irrepressible storyteller, Cooley would regale the youth for hours with his tales of the woods and of fire. Cooley, a father of five daughters, eventually came to think of Eldon as a son. Another source of smoke jumper mystique was one of Eldon's boyhood chums, Jim Harrison, who lived down the block and across the street.

Eldon had finally turned eighteen in August 1948, too late to apply for a job that year. The next spring, he hand-delivered his application to Cooley at his office at Regional Headquarters in downtown Missoula. Two weeks later, Eldon received an invitation to smoke jumper training camp at Camp Menard, just as his neighbor had promised.

In July of 1949, the Dietterts, without Eldon, returned to the farm in Indiana for the first time since moving to Missoula. Eldon sent letters to them from training camp, embellishing his tales with cartoon sketches. On the first page of one letter,

Eldon Diettert at Flathead Lake, 1949. Courtesy Gerald Diettert.

he drew a smoke jumper poised in the open door of the plane, one foot resting on the step outside. "Two thousand feet down," read the caption. An arrow pointed to the bottom of the page. In the center of the next page Eldon drew a smiling jumper under full canopy, then wrote his thoughts atop the drawing in unembellished, straightforward penmanship. On the final page, a billowing chute dragged an upended jumper along the ground. Tiny birds, stars, and indecipherable marks floating around the jumper's head depicted the jumper's agitated state of mind. "Bumpy landing," read the caption.

July 5, 1949

> We've jumped four times now and by the time this gets to you, we'll have seven. It's really fun, after you get out of the plane, which is about the hardest part

of it besides hitting the ground. I landed pretty hard on the first jump and pulled a few muscles in my leg and sprained my ankle a little, and so I have to have it taped every time we jump. I could hardly walk on it the next day, but it rained and no one jumped so I didn't miss out on anything. I've jumped out of the Trimotor twice and the Travelaire once, and today we all came down to Missoula and jumped from the C-47. It's really nice, the door is big enough so you can go out standing up, so it's just one long step, but in the other two, you have to kneel down (a pretty good position—you can say your prayers) and put your foot on the little step outside the plane. I came down so easy today that it was like jumping on a feather bed.

The first jump wasn't as bad as I thought it would be. I was second out of the plane, so I didn't have time to get scared very much.

No one has gotten hurt bad yet, only a few pulled muscles and sprains. About ten injuries the first jumps, six the second, one the third, and four or five today, which isn't too bad considering about sixty guys jump each time.

We get up at five-forty-five now and start work at seven, because the air is heavier early in the morning and there isn't as much wind.

In the next letter, dated July 20, 1949, Eldon reported that "the next three jumps were pretty good."

They're more fun each time. I hit in a tree on the last two. One about three inches from the ground and another about four feet. You don't even feel any shock when you hang up in a tree, but it really makes a lot of noise and tops of trees and branches go flying all over.

We jumped on Blue Mountain, the one just west of Missoula, on the seventh jump.

"It's almost ten o'clock and I have to get up a little earlier than usual so I can get back to Ninemile in time for work in the morning, so I'll have to quit now. All I can think to write about is jumping out of airplanes anyhow.—Love, Eldon.

After completing training, Eldon had cruised timber in the Lewis and Clark National Forest east of the Continental Divide. The program offered invaluable experience for forestry students. The four jumpers chosen for the detail understood that they would be called to jump only during emergency situations. Eldon soon missed the comfortable amenities of Camp Menard and Fort Missoula, especially the showers. Once a week the men drove sixteen miles to the ranger station in White Sulphur Springs to take a hot bath.

Even so, Eldon had loved hiking through the forests to locate and mark pulp wood for timber sales. Most of the areas they canvassed were high up near the timber line at 6,000 to 7,000 feet in altitude in rugged inaccessible quiet country. He had found most of the high elevation timber pretty scrubby, but he had spotted lots of wildlife, especially deer. One day a moose and her calf had sauntered by him less than twenty yards away. When he woke in the morning, he had had to break a film of ice in the water bucket before taking a drink. And then one morning it had snowed.

"Eldon Diettert, you have to find a new job," his mother said from the doorway of the dining room. The tone of her voice said she wasn't joking. Eldon stared at her, perplexed. "They want you down at the base and we haven't even cut the cake yet," Charlotte continued. "Why don't you call them back and tell them you'll be in tomorrow instead?"

If it were anyone but his mom, Eldon would have offhand-
edly dismissed the proposal, but seeing the disappointment
in her eyes, he hesitated. He understood that things were heat-
ing up all over the Rockies. If he did skip out on this jump, it
wouldn't be long before his name rotated back to the top of
the list. But then again, rain could come tomorrow and douse
the whole season, like it had the year before.

"Now, now, Charlotte," Reuben Diettert said. "The boy's got
a job to do. They've put long hours into training him and
they're depending on him, birthday or no birthday. Besides,
by the look in his eyes, I'd guess there's nothing he'd rather
do than jump out of an airplane today, no matter how good
the company is or how good the cake tastes."

"I suppose," Charlotte murmured, attempting a smile to con-
ceal her disappointment.

"Thanks for the great party, Mom. I'll be back before you
know it." Eldon jumped from his chair and gave her a hug before rushing out of the room. "Hey Dad, can you drive me over
to the base? If I don't show up in five minutes they'll call in
the next guy on the list."

CHAPTER ELEVEN

Leonard Piper

Hale Airfield, Missoula, Montana
August 5, 1949

Leonard Piper, a 23-year-old from the backwoods of Blairsville, Pennsylvania, looked up from his work in the parachute loft at Hale Airfield when the phone rang in the foreman's office. A two-person toolkit lay on the table before him. He had just finished applying a protective layer of tape to the sharp edges of the pulaski and shovel. At nearby tables, other jumpers were sorting foodstuffs into boxes.

Usually a team of sixteen jumpers waited on call at the airfield, but today about thirty men had punched in for work. Those jumpers whose names were far down on the jump rotation sweated up on the roof, laying down new tar paper. Most of the Johnson Brothers Flying Service planes were out rounding up other jumpers, and soon even more men would be on hand on high-alert status. As well as planes. As for now, a single Doug C-47 stood outside the loft like a cat waiting for kitchen scraps at the back door of a restaurant.

The two-person fire packs Leonard assembled would be dropped from the air with cargo chutes, but not so all the equipment. The spotter in the plane would simply kick out the two-man saw,

Photos of Mann Gulch victims released by the Forest Service after the fire. Courtesy U.S. Forest Service.

bent into a circle with its teeth protected by split fire hose; the sleeping bags; the steel five-gallon water jug, which sometimes erupted on impact; and the two-man food packs, each containing a three-day food supply consisting mostly of C-rations. If a chute got hung in a tree, the spotter would also free-drop a pair of climbing spurs during the plane's final pass. When they were strapped to the inside arches of a pair of boots, the spurs stuck out a few inches beyond the soles, allowing a jumper to jab the sharp edges into the trunk of a tree for a bow-legged climb to retrieve the chute. Earlier in the day, Leonard had packed eight-person toolboxes that included a pulaski and shovel for each man.

In an adjoining room, men were picking leaves and twigs out of nylon chutes recently returned from fires. With a pulley, they would haul the chutes up into the rafters of the tower to look for holes or frayed shroud lines. If the chutes needed mending, they would stitch them on industrial-sized sewing machines. After inspection, experienced jumpers would lay out the chutes on long triangular tables and meticulously fold and stuff them back into packs. When they finished, they would attach a label to the pack with their initials, which held them accountable for their work.

Leonard enjoyed everything about smoke jumping except this infernal waiting. Sometimes it reminded him of the service, where "hurry up and wait" was the standing order of the day. But when the order to move would finally arrive, the bosses would leave little time to execute them. Fifteen minutes. That's how much time he'd have to suit up, stow the gear, and hustle onto the waiting plane after a fire call. If they had some distance to cover, they would dress in the plane en route to the fire. Leonard would have loved to take his guitar along to serenade the guys on a long flight. Not that they would have heard a single note above the drone of the engines and the sound of the rushing wind coming through the open jump door. But it would be a kick, nonetheless. But who could he trust to bring his beloved instrument back after he jumped? Earl Cooley, who sometimes spotted for the men? Earl would most likely kick the guitar out the door after him, without a cargo chute. The smoke jumper brass didn't put up with much nonsense.

In the foreman's office, Leonard saw Jack Nash hand the phone to Fred Brauer. Maybe he'd get to do some real work today after all, he thought.

Leonard had grown up with five brothers and three sisters in a farming community. They had often helped neighbors harvest wheat and oats. As horses slowly dragged a large stationary tractor-driven thresher to the next farm, Leonard joined the other workers in the fields to pitch grain stalks onto wagons. When the thresher was in place, they forked the grain from the wagon into the machine that separated the seeds from the straw.

When not at school or work, Leonard explored the woods or trapped animals near the farm on Chestnut Ridge. At age ten, he and his brother, Linely, who was two years younger, had spent weeks following an eccentric old man through the forest after hearing rumors that the man had taken money from the corpses of drowning victims of the Johnstown, Pennsylvania, flood and buried the treasure. Another time, the two boys had found a mound of rocks some farmer had most likely lugged off his fields. But the two boys convinced each other they had discovered an Indian grave containing gold. For weeks they dug under the mound until they had excavated a hole big enough to hold a Model T. They might have dug their way to China if their father hadn't happened upon the dig and ordered them to fill it in before some hapless cow fell in.

Another brother, Donald, had the distinction of acting as a stunt man for Leonard. After watching a western film in which a cowboy rescued his pal by scooping him up onto his galloping horse, Leonard had practiced the maneuver with Donald until they perfected the stunt. The curious boy had also set a small creek on fire to see if it was really true that gasoline could burn on water.

In most respects, Leonard, a member of the Future Farmers of America, had a reserved personality, but he hadn't been too shy to participate in the senior class play. The sleepy-eyed young man with a pleasant smile had landed the role of the father in a play titled *Meet the Folks*. In his scrapbook, Leonard had pasted a black-and-white still taken during rehearsals. In center stage, a short, boyish-looking schoolmate, who played Leonard's son, sits in a plush armchair, his bare feet dangling in a washbasin. To the right, a maid pours water from a kettle into a pan. Leonard's thespian wife stands to the left of the chair, looking very attractive with her hair up. She wears a knee-length belted dress with wide lapels. Leonard stands next to her wearing a tie and a double-breasted pinstriped suit. He holds his hands at his side, just as the drama coach instructed, intently watching the maid pour the water.

After high school, Leonard enlisted in the navy for an eighteen-month stint. After being discharged in 1947, he enrolled at the university in Missoula to study forestry. Leonard's sister, Thelma, lived in Helena, and he often visited her during the summer. As usual, Leonard kept his own counsel before joining the smoke jumpers, never telling anyone in his family about his plans. When Leonard drove to Helena to deposit his possessions in Thelma's keeping, her husband, Lloyd McDonald, mentioned that the job might be dangerous. Leonard simply told him that it was what he wanted to do.

Leonard hadn't been home to Pennsylvania since moving west, but he planned to visit the family farm at the end of the summer if an early snow or prolonged spell of rain brought a premature halt to the fire season, leaving him enough time to take the train there and back before the fall quarter started.

In the foreman's office, Jack Nash handed the phone to smoke jumper operation chief Fred Brauer. That usually meant something big was up, since Fred always wanted to get the particulars of any large fire from the source. Not that he didn't trust Jack to get the correct information; Fred just felt he got a better feel about a situation while listening to the voice of a person closer to the action. Leonard and a few other jumpers drifted toward the doorway to eavesdrop. Brauer, the receiver glued to his ear, listened intently and jotted down notes. When he spoke, his voice boomed through the loft.

"You know we don't like taking on the big jobs when ignitions start popping up all over creation," Fred said. "We should stick to the smaller fires to keep them from getting bigger. . . .

You think a crew could knock it down, eh? Twenty-five men? No can do. The only plane we have left here is the Doug, and that only carries sixteen men, plus their gear."

Leonard rushed back to his station to clear the table and put the tools back in their rack.

In the next instant, Brauer stepped out of his office and roared out the names: "Sylvia, Navon, Thompson—Silas and Newton, Reba, Sherman, McVey, Piper, Sallee, Thol, Rumsey, Diettert."

"Diettert's having a birthday party," someone shouted.

"I'm already dialing his number," Nash said.

"Is Hellman still around?" Brauer asked.

"He went over to his sister's," Nash said. "I'll buzz him, too."

"Stratton—that's Merle, not Skip," Brauer continued. "Someone round up Wag Dodge and tell him he's foreman. Jack, you go along and kick out the cargo. Your limousine is waiting outside the door, ladies."

CHAPTER TWELVE

Merle Stratton

Hale Airfield, Missoula, Montana
August 5, 1949

Merle Stratton grabbed a bulging canvas sack and jogged out to the tarmac. Besides his chute and jump gear, the sack contained two wooden clack boards. After the fire he would strap his gear to the boards and lug the 150 pounds to the nearest trail. After the men finished loading the equipment and pushing it toward the front of the Doug, they began to board. Rookies Walt Rumsey and Bob Sallee climbed aboard first and crawled forward to sit on the gear. Next came David Navon, another rookie but an experienced paratrooper. Stratton was one of the last aboard. He sucked in his gut and held his head high as he waddled down the aisle and dropped down on a fire pack. He stretched out his legs and tried to look nonchalant, but he was nervous as hell. He caught a few of the jumpers giving him sideways glances, but he did not blame them. "It's not going to happen this time," he felt like shouting out.

During his last flight, in a single-engine Travelaire, Merle had doubled over with stomach cramps and then vomited out his guts. He had later passed on that jump. When the pain persisted after the plane returned to the base, Fred Brauer had

driven him to St. Patrick Hospital, fearful that the jumper was
suffering from an attack of appendicitis. The next day the doctors had released Merle, telling him that airsickness must have
caused the unrelenting pain in his gut. The prognosis hadn't
been encouraging.

"It's just like getting seasick," the doctor had told him.
"Some people don't, some do. Some sailors get over it after a
few weeks at sea. But I don't think we can afford to keep you
airborne for that long. Of course, after a prolonged shore leave,
it often returns. The only advice I can offer is to try it one more
time and if you vomit again, hang up your chute. You'll just
keep making yourself miserable—not to mention everyone else
on the plane."

As soon as Merle sat down in the Doug, he realized he'd
forgotten to pick up one of the half-gallon cardboard ice
cream containers the jumpers kept on hand in case of airsickness. Too embarrassed to ask the others to pass one down,
Merle reassured himself he'd be okay this time. "Mind over
matter," he murmured. Plus, he had skipped breakfast and
lunch. How could he get sick with nothing in his stomach?

Merle had not experienced the problem his first year as a
smoke jumper. Nor when he flew around the South Pacific in
planes. The little Travelaire had caused the problem, Merle
assured himself. "Things will be different in the big plane," he
thought as pilot Ken Huber swung the Doug onto the gravel
runway and pointed her toward the south end of Hale Airfield.
Before the war, Huber, a native of eastern Montana, had worked
at Camp Stonybrook, another CCC camp located near the
Ninemile Remount Depot and Camp Menard. He had learned
how to fly in the service and landed a job with Johnson Brothers
Flying Service when he returned home.

Merle glanced out the open jump door, only ten feet to his
right, determined to enjoy the flight. Wag Dodge, the foreman,
sat right next to the door, holding on to a cargo strap and star-

ing out of the plane. Beside Dodge sat Bill Hellman, who was talking to Henry Thol, helping keep the rookie calm. As the plane turned around, the pilot gunned the engines and the heavily loaded craft slowly picked up speed. The men leaned their bodies slightly toward the cockpit to keep balanced in their seats. Then the rattling of the tires stopped and the plane rose, dipped, and then rose again. The men working on the roof of the parachute loft waved as the plane roared overhead.

Over downtown Missoula, Ken Huber sharply banked the plane east to follow the Clark Fork River through Hellgate Canyon. Merle felt fine. Then came the steady climb in altitude up the Blackfoot River Valley. Funny how a little thing like an upset stomach could ruin a good thing.

Merle had first heard about smoke jumping from his roommate, Chuck Muehlethaler, at the University of Idaho in Moscow. At five feet ten and 140 pounds, Merle had had no trouble meeting the physical requirements. He thought that firefighting experience might help round out his education in forest management.

Hailing from Worley, Idaho (population 300), in the Idaho Panhandle, Merle had honed his outdoor skills hunting and fishing in the mountains east of town. Westward stretched the Palouse Prairie that had mostly been plowed under and replanted with wheat. The Stratton cottage, about half a mile outside town, had no electricity or telephone. Each day, school buses fanned out across the county's dirt roads to pick up the farm kids and bring them to the Worley High School. Merle's dad worked as a section foreman for the Milwaukee Railroad that connected Chicago with Seattle.

There had been little for a teenager to do in the town except rollerskate in the dance hall. After delivering the evening *Spokane Daily Chronicle* to about forty households, Merle would usually work on old cars with his friends. They would often pile into a '28 Chevy, whose top they had cut off, to cruise Worley's main street, honking the horn at any young women they passed. One evening at the roller rink, Merle met a Canadian girl with whom he corresponded after joining the army.

During the war, Merle had flown to and from airstrips cut from the jungles of India and Burma to load ammunition onto British planes. While in India, he had lived in a grass *basha* constructed by the locals. In other places, the soldiers had sought shelter from the summer monsoons in regulation tents. Three times a day, Merle forced down a dose of quinine to protect against malaria. And every full moon, the men stayed up to keep watch for Moonlight Charlie—Japanese fighter planes that searched out and strafed the airstrips under the lunar light. Witnessing firsthand the living conditions of the poor on the subcontinent, Merle had realized how fortunate he was, even though his family at home still lived without many modern amenities.

After his homecoming in 1946, Merle had continued to write to the Canadian woman, but no romance had evolved. In Missoula, he hooked up with a pretty nurse at one of the dances the nursing students organized in the recreation room of their dorm. But Merle wasn't serious about any particular woman. Next year he planned to graduate with a degree in forestry, and then he'd take his time about deciding what to do. Life was just beginning for him.

Merle's first mistake that day was to look out the open door of the Doug. As the air became more turbulent, he noticed the cross-section of the tail begin to slew from side to side, and his brain followed suit. The next moment, the plane hit a downdraft and the bottom of Merle's stomach seemed to fall out. He wasn't the only one starting to squirm. Another jumper later described the flight as "the roughest I ever took." Still,

Merle held on. Not eating lunch had been a good tactic. He was determined to make it out the door this time.

Merle's first bout with airsickness had frightened him on two accounts. At first he had feared he was going to die. Then, after he had emptied his gut and continued to gag with the dry heaves, he had feared that he would never die. Now, as the big plane continued to rock and roll, Merle foolishly continued staring out the open door, trying to concentrate on the horizon. Sometimes the view of the mountain ridges dipped below the cross-tail and then came back into view as the plane rolled the other way. He might as well have been on a boat in ocean swells.

The other jumpers ignored Merle as best they could, but they couldn't avoid the underlying tension. Merle Stratton was going to puke and they knew it. They just didn't know when. Get it over with, some thought. Wait till I'm at the door, others silently pleaded. Someone should pass him a bucket. Wag Dodge walked up aisle with the order to suit up. When he got to Merle, he dipped to one knee.

"How're you feeling?" Wag asked.

"Fine," Merle said. "I think I'm over it. I think I'll get to jump this time."

Wag patted Merle on the knee. "Good man. Just hold on. We'll be there in no time. Better suit up now." As Dodge stood up he pointed both thumbs up and then turned back toward the cockpit. When Merle began to gag, Wag practically sprinted back to the cockpit where he wouldn't smell or hear anything.

Without a carton, Merle aimed the bile into his helmet. Not much came out, but the gagging mercilessly continued. The dry heaves sounded like a man suffering a coughing fit. Merle slumped down, half lying on his side, caressing his helmet beneath him like a man would a snuggling cat. The faces of the other jumpers turned green and they struggled to hold down their own lunches. A few moments later Wag came and knelt beside Merle and put his hand on the jumper's shoulder.

"You'd better pack it in for today," he said. "Why don't you go lie down at the front of the plane so you won't be in the way?"

Merle rolled his head like a drunken man. "Sorry, boss," he said. "It looks like my jumping days are over."

"Worse things could happen," Wag answered.

Two hours later, after the Doug had delivered its jumpers and returned to Hale Airfield, Merle Stratton staggered down the steps of the plane and dropped down onto the steady ground. After a while the insides of his head stopped whirling like a merry-go-round. When he felt better, he gingerly walked into the loft, stored his gear, and located Fred Brauer in the dispatch office.

"Sorry, Fred," he said. "My gear is in my locker and I'm heading home tonight." After the two men shook hands, Merle gathered his personal belongings, got in his car, and drove west toward Worley, Idaho.

CHAPTER THIRTEEN

Henry Thol

*Aboard the Doug C-47 en route to Mann Gulch
August 5, 1949*

Henry Thol Jr., an eighteen-year-old from Kalispell, Montana, rolled down the long sleeves of his blue work shirt and checked the pockets of his Kant Bust'em Frisco jeans for any screwdriver or pair of pliers he might have stuffed in his back pockets, something he should have done before boarding the C-47 with the rest of the jumpers for the flight to Mann Gulch. Then he reached down and tied his boots. The sturdy eight-inch-high White boots, handcrafted in Spokane, Washington, were a gift from his parents. All the professional loggers in the Pacific Northwest wore the brand, only they caulked theirs by inserting little steel studs across the soles to give them traction when they walked across the trunks of freshly fallen trees. A handful of the smoke jumpers also caulked their boots, but they had to wear pieces of fire hose stuck over the studs so they wouldn't pockmark the wooden floors of the buildings around the base.

The frayed edges of Henry's pantlegs came down only slightly below the tops of his boots. It was an old logger's trick his father had taught him on their first hunting trip. "Trim the

The Douglas C-47. Courtesy U.S. Forest Service.

edge of your pant leg and slit it a bit so that broken branches and snubs can't catch your cuff and trip you up." Henry's mother hadn't appreciated that fact that the two of them had ruined his brand-new jeans.

Henry's hands shook with anticipation as he wrapped a girdle around his midsection, a device that would protect his gut if he crashed through tree branches. Next, he pulled on heavy canvas jump pants with a reinforced stirrup crotch. "Remember to keep your legs together if you're coming down through a tree," the instructors often said. "Otherwise you might be joining the Girl Scouts."

A large bulging pocket sewn onto the right leg of the jump pants contained seventy-five feet of tightly coiled nylon rope, just in case he needed to let himself down if he draped his chute over the crown of a tree. At training he had turned to fellow jumper Starr Jenkins and asked him how seventy-five feet of rope would get him down from the top of a 200-foot Douglas fir. Jenkins told him he could always tie on his reserve chute and its risers to extend the length, then his chute harness, then his shirt and pants and underwear and bootlaces. "And then you can slide the rest of the way down on bubblegum and sheer guts," Starr said. Henry had laughed so hard that the instructor stopped his lecture and stared at him. "Would you like to share the joke with everyone?" he asked. Henry apologized and repeated Starr's remarks and everyone laughed except the instructor. "That's very funny," he finally said. "But to begin with, that's my joke."

Onto his left leg, Henry strapped a small canvas sack crammed with personal gear—a bar of soap, a toothbrush, clean socks, underwear, and a pair of dungarees. Henry struggled a bit pulling on the stout canvas jump jacket with the felt-padded elbows and high collar that would protect his neck from stubs of broken branches. The heavy clothing and a touch of the nerves soon got him sweating. He stood up and slipped on the sturdy chute harness. Fully outfitted, Henry wore seventy pounds of gear that was worth 600 dollars.

Henry had dreamed of this moment ever since he'd first heard of smoke jumpers from his father, a retired Forest Service ranger from Kalispell. In high school, Henry had worked as a fire guard at the Condon Ranger District for two summers. Actually, he had mostly functioned as a go-fer for the camp cook. In 1948, he had worked around the jumper base in Missoula, helping out the cook and cutting grass and brushing off the pool tables at the fort. His father had informed him that there may have been better-paying jobs in the world, and there certainly were a lot of easier jobs, but he couldn't do any better in life than work for the Forest Service. "The Forest Service is a world-class organization," Henry Thol Sr. often reminded his son.

When training camp first started at Camp Menard, Henry had not felt confident that he could make the grade. In a letter home he said "Time will tell." But two weeks later, during a week-end visit to Kalispell, he proudly described his successful first jump to his mother. Then he added that "some of the boys did-n't make the cut. They did all right on jumping, but they were too poor with the tools. They needed additional training."

Later that evening, when his father asked how he was get-ting along, Henry Jr. answered, "Oh, fine."

"Are your instructors good?" Henry Sr. asked. "Have they had any fire experience? Do they know what they're talking about?"

"Oh Dad, they know more than you do," the son teased.

"That's quite a statement," the proud forester replied, but he let it go.

Two days before, Henry had boarded a Ford Trimotor for a flight south to Yellowstone National Park with several other jumpers. Neither Thol, Leonard Piper, Robert Bennett, nor Bill Hellman had gotten to jump, but the other four had lucked out. Those fires had been small, though, and were hardly puffing when the plane flew over, and the men were probably hiking out already. Henry had reckoned that with a little luck, his fire would take at least a few days to contain and mop up, providing a lot of overtime.

But even though he hadn't jumped at Yellowstone, Henry had enjoyed the flight in the Trimotor with its loud uncowled engines, the external control cables that slapped against the corrugated aluminum sides in the wind, the truck tires mounted on huge solid wheels, the large square windows like those on a streetcar, the thick wings, and the fuselage cut square at the bottom. The men referred to it by various nick-names: Heap, Tin Goose, Flying Quonset Hut, and Old Ironsides. But the light ship could maneuver in and out of canyons to land on tiny airstrips. The three-foot-wide wing en-abled tremendous lift and extended glide when the engines failed. Henry liked looking out the wide windows. He knew it would be more difficult to sightsee in the Doug with the bucket seats backed against the sides.

The Trimotor had taken off from Hale Airfield in a northerly direction, buzzing downtown Missoula. Out the starboard window, the fifty-foot "M" composed of white-painted rocks that was situated about a third of the way up the flank of Mount Sentinel had stared him right in the face. As the air had rushed through the open door, the men had quickly put on their jumpsuits to keep warm. About forty-five minutes later, the plane passed over Georgetown Lake; and then Henry spotted the big stack of the Anaconda Company smelter in the town with the same name, just west of "Butte America," the copper-mining capital of the world. As the plane continued southeast, the drier mountain ranges supported less timber. Meadows dotted some of the more rounded peaks. Rocky ridges stood bare of vegetation. In the occasional valley, patterns of irrigated green farmland stood out amid the high sagebrush prairie. When the Trimotor flew over Hebgen Reservoir, about two hours after leaving the base, the men knew they were close to West Yellowstone. Counting his training jumps, Henry had ridden in a plane eight times, but as the Trimotor slowly descended to the grassy field outside West Yellowstone, Henry realized that he'd never landed in a plane before. He felt more nervous than he had when he made his first jump.

At the airport, a ranger informed the jumpers that a ground crew had already attacked one of the fires. Bill Hellman and Robert Bennett, last on the rotation, decided to wait at West Yellowstone, and Hellman loaned his harness and reserve chute to the ranger, who guided the pilot to the fires.

Starr Jenkins, who had snapped photographs the whole trip, leaned across to Thol and said, "I want to jump last so I can take some pictures of you guys going out the door," but when the spotter ordered Jenkins to get up front for the first stick with Kermit Cole, he didn't refuse. Later, before Starr jumped, he had turned to Henry and wished him well on his first jump. But the ranger never located the other smoke, and the four remaining jumpers had felt a bit deflated during the long ride home.

Henry pulled on his leather gloves just to make sure he didn't leave them behind and then pulled on the regulation leather football helmet. Airholes were drilled in the crown and ear-holes in the sides, and it was equipped with a sponge-like chin cup. He then flipped up the hinged wire-mesh facemask. Before he jumped he would attach the two small straps to buckles behind the earholes of the helmet. Henry Thol was raring to go.

"Jesus, Thol. We've got to get to the fire before we jump," said David Navon, an ex-paratrooper who was one of the oldest jumpers.

"I just don't want to leave anything behind," Thol said.

"Can't be too careful in this business." Navon slapped him on the back. "But are you sure you don't want to put on your parachute, too?"

Thol's face turned crimson.

"Here, let me give you a hand," Navon said. The former paratrooper tugged and pulled at the straps on Henry's harness, then clipped on the backpack containing the main chute, which was twenty-eight feet long. Then he turned the teenager about and attached the drab olive bundle with the smaller reserve chute to Henry's chest.

"Now you take care of me," Navon said, turning about. Henry was flattered and flustered that the paratrooper trusted him with his chute.

"You got your knife ready?" Navon asked. Henry slid the sheathed knife into place at the top of the reserve chute.

"Now when are you going to use that?" Navon asked.

"If a shroud line goes over the top of my canopy," Henry answered.

"And how will you know when that happens?"

"I'll either feel it or look up to see my chute looking like Mae West's chest."

"And how many lines can you cut without causing your chute to fall faster?"

"Three," Henry answered.

Dave reached out and patted him on the shoulder. "You'll be just fine," he said. A few moments later, Wag Dodge assembled the men.

"We're heading over to the Lewis and Clark National Forest on the east side of the Divide near Helena," Wag explained. "They reported the fire at about fifty acres, burning atop a ridge in a place called Mann Gulch. Hopefully we'll have it contained tonight, and then we'll mop up tomorrow and sit on it for a while. We'll be jumping in four sticks. Since Stratton won't be joining us, three men in the last stick. I'll jump first, then you others can jockey for position. Try to mix the experienced jumpers in with the rookies. Elmer Bloom will be shooting some footage for some training films. So everyone say cheese before you leap. Any questions?"

Henry turned to Navon and smiled, but the old paratrooper had turned to another jumper to check his gear.

CHAPTER FOURTEEN

Earl Cooley

*Aboard the Doug C-47 en route to Mann Gulch
August 5, 1949*

When Earl Cooley had gotten the call in the dispatcher's office at Hale Airfield, he had been eager to get into the air again. Ever since he had transferred to the personnel department, he hadn't gotten to jump. Plus, Fred Brauer rarely called on him to fill in as a spotter—only when the shortage of men was dire, as now. Before Earl had headed to the plane, Fred Stillings, head of aerial operations in Region 1, called to ask him to bring him back information about the fire. "We're trying to get a handle on what's going on out there," he had said. Earl had been the last to boost himself into the plane. After the Doug gained altitude, he moved among the jumpers, inspecting chute packs and harnesses. When he stopped by Eldon Diettert, he asked the neighborhood kid how he was getting along.

"Great," Eldon said. "I'd just blown out the candles on my birthday cake when Nash phoned me."

"You should have stayed home and enjoyed the party," Earl said. "You could have gotten back to the top of the rotation pretty quick."

"No way I'm going to miss this," Eldon said. "This is the best birthday present anyone could ask for."

"You nervous?" Earl asked.

"Yeah, a little," Eldon said.

"Good. You shouldn't get too relaxed in this profession."

"Hey, Earl. When you get back, could you please let my mother know where I am?"

Earl Cooley had been one of the first men to ever parachute to a fire, but due to organizational politics, he'd been relegated to the background. Earl bided his time in the personnel office, interviewing jumpers and rating their performances for the annual report. If they showed any signs of trouble, he forced them back in line—or else. In 1946, he'd fired thirty-three men between the end of training in July and the eighth of August. "Adventurers, wanderers, Montanans, strangers, we get 'em all," he had once said. In a few years, when he reached his fortieth birthday, his jumping days would officially end. Then he planned to formally request a transfer to a ranger district, where he would finish out his career.

Cooley had been born on a prairie homestead near Hardin, Montana, with 1,200 acres of bottomland along Sarpy Creek. When his father was not reaping or sowing, he ran the post office, which had the area's only telephone. The living had been good, with plenty of food on the table and a vein of coal free for the digging on the nearby prairie. But following the depression of 1919, the farm had gone bust and the Cooleys had moved to Corvallis in the Bitterroot Valley, about thirty miles south of Missoula. At first Cooley worked on local ranches for a dollar a day in the summer; in the winter he received fifteen bucks a month plus board. But the adventurous young man found the surrounding mountains and forests irresistible, and he eventually landed a job with the Forest Service as a lookout at Moose Creek Ranger Station in Idaho. During winters

Earl had attended the Forestry School at Montana State University.

Back in those days, there were two ways of fighting fires. After spotting a nearby lightning strike, Earl would shoulder a shovel and pulaski and hike to it. Or, if the fire burned too far from the lookout, the district ranger would dispatch a few men to the scene. If a fire took off, crews of men reinforced them while mule teams from Ninemile kept them supplied.

In 1939, Earl had signed on with the experimental smoke jumper program. He survived his jumps at the training camp at Seeley Lake that spring, then moved with the crew on July 10th to the Moose Creek airstrip, where the pioneer jumpers erected the first permanent parachute loft, which included a tower tall enough to suspend a 30-foot chute. The following year, on July 12, Earl Cooley and Rufus Robinson jumped into history when they parachuted to a small fire burning up Martin Creek on the Nez Perce Forest. Cooley was second man out the door, and he almost beat Robinson down when his shroud lines tangled and twisted behind his neck. The chute stretched out but did not open, slipping into a streamer that had let Cooley down at almost maximum speed. With only a few hundred feet to the ground, Earl had looked down for his emergency chute handle. That movement took the pressure off the knotted lines and the chute risers unwound, spinning Earl around until the chute fully inflated, just in time for Earl to safely land.

Despite the dramatic plummet, the smoke jumper program had continued. That first summer the smoke jumpers earned their keep, extinguishing nine fires in infancy and saving the agency money. For example, two jumpers had reached the Robbins Gulch fire in fifty minutes, operating at a cost of 350 dollars. Officials estimated that a ground crew would have consumed twenty-four hours in travel, giving the fire time to expand, escalating the costs to 10,000 dollars. The total cost of the smoke jumper program that first season, including per-

Earl Cooley (right) with Rufus Robinson (left) and trainer Frank Derry (center), ca. 1940. Courtesy Earl Cooley.

sonnel, depreciation on equipment, and flying, had tallied in at about 9,000 dollars. Pencil pushers estimated that suppression costs for the nine fires controlled by jumpers would have cost more than 32,000 dollars if ground crews had been used.

The agency expanded the experimental program until World War II. In the spring of 1942, four squads of men had mustered for work, but most of the veteran jumpers enlisted in the service. Of the thirty-three recruits, only five had experienced jumping. Plus, parachutes had become scarce as the Eagle Parachute Company began manufacturing military

chutes. To maintain the program, the smoke jumpers had man-
aged to obtain some chutes that had been rejected for minor
flaws.

Cooley, then thirty-two years old and married with two children, received a deferment from the draft after a Forest Service
official told the draft board that Cooley was "an essential man
and occupies a key position with the Forest Service." Believing
his work with the agency was of national importance, Cooley
did not enlist in the armed services. But most of the others
did. For the 1943 season, only five jumpers remained in town.
When a heavy recruitment program produced only four men
with minor physical defects that had kept them out of the army,
the agency prepared to mothball the program until the end
of the war. About that same time, a young conscientious objector wrote to the Forest Service suggesting that the agency
classify smoke jumping as an alternative service for men in
Civilian Public Service. When the agency agreed, conchies from
across the country applied. Earl Cooley stayed on to help train
and supervise more than 250 conscientious objectors during
the war years. By the time the war ended, the Forest Service
had declared the smoke jumping experiment a success and
designated it a permanent part of operations.

Some returning vets had been dismayed to discover that conscientious objectors had filled their jump boots, and a few held
a grudge against Earl as well for not enlisting in the service.
Earl's time as a supervisor at the jumper base proved short lived.
Some of the vets had not appreciated his consensus style of
management. In the service they had grown used to giving and
taking orders. They felt that the program needed a stronger
leader. Eventually Earl transferred to the personnel department, where he was available for fire duty when the base was
shorthanded. His official title was project administrative assistant, and in the spring he oversaw the fire training in rookie
camp. Up to that point in his career, Cooley had made forty-

nine fire jumps. He had also observed hundreds of fires from the air but only two that had burned on the eastern side of the Continental Divide.

After checking Eldon Diettert's gear, Cooley turned to another rookie, Henry Thol Jr. Earl had met the jug-eared kid the summer before when he'd helped out around the base. Henry's chutes passed muster and Cooley slung the static line over Henry's shoulder.

"Remember, don't hook up your static line with it running under your arm, or your chute will likely dislocate your shoulder when it pops open," Earl said.

"I know. Over the shoulder. Over the shoulder," Henry repeated. "Navon already reminded me half a dozen times."

Earl looked out the window to see where they were. Ken Huber had left the Blackfoot River Valley and cut over the Garnet Range, then across another lonesome mountain valley near Helmsville. When Earl spotted the railroad tracks at the agricultural town of Avon he knew it was just a hop, skip, and a jump to the tunnel that bored beneath the Continental Divide at Mullan Pass. Beyond that, Helena nestled in a tight valley backed up against the eastern front of the Rocky Mountains. As the plane flew over the Helena airport, Silas Thompson yelled out that he spotted the fire. Cooley looked in the direction of the Little Belt Mountains, about twenty miles to the northeast, and saw two columns of smoke. After a brief discussion with Huber and co-pilot Frank Small, he determined which was the Mann Gulch smoke by using the coordinates forwarded from the dispatcher—Section 19, Township 13 North, Range 2 West. When he located it on the map he shouted to Huber: "When you hit the river follow it north. She'll be waiting for us." Cooley then slipped on his jump harness and attached a reserve chute to his chest. He carefully stepped over the supine body of Merle Stratton and then moved back through the fuselage of the plane. The men eyed him with anticipation as he passed.

"We almost there, Earl?" Henry Thol shouted. Henry had taken off his helmet and his brow was beaded with sweat.

"Just about," Earl said.

Foreman Wag Dodge and assistant spotter Jack Nash joined Earl at the open door. A safety strap was strung across the doorway. Earl put on his safety goggles and lay down on the floor of the plane and gripped the door brace. It was the only position from which he could see underneath the wing. As the airstream tore at his shirt he felt cool for the first time that day. Nash and Dodge lay down beside him. Earl checked his watch when they made the first pass over the fire—3:10 PM.

"I'd say it's about fifty, maybe sixty acres," Earl shouted above the rushing air. Wag nodded in agreement. The fire burned atop a ridge that separated a gentle funnel-shaped gulch to the north and a steep walled canyon to the south. The fire slowly burned downhill in thinly vegetated rocky soil. The loft of the smoke blew in a northeasterly direction. Neither of the men noticed any indication that embers of the fire had spotted ahead or that the flames had climbed into the crowns of the trees. Dodge and Cooley conjectured that the fire would sit still as temperatures cooled. They also agreed a crew might be able to dig a fire line around the area through the night before the fire began to reawaken the next afternoon.

"I think it's run its course," Earl shouted. "It'll probably just keep creeping downhill against the wind toward the bottom of the gulch."

Earl pointed at a sparsely timbered area on the ridge ahead of the fire as a possible jump spot, but Wag shook his head. "The wind's carrying the smoke over that spot," he shouted. "Plus, it might blow them past the ridge into the canyon." Cooley agreed.

Cooley understood that if there was wind turbulence this high up, there would be even more on the ground; the wind was probably rising from one side of the ridge and blowing down the other. Through the microphone on his headset, Earl asked Ken Huber to buzz the gulch again. On the next pass, the foreman and the spotter agreed on an open grassy area near the head of the gulch. There, the slope gradually led off into the bottom, allowing for a fairly level landing spot. It lay about half a mile from the fire and about 500 feet below the fire's outer ring. The area was also clear of smoke.

As the plane passed over the jump site, Cooley counted to five and then released the small white flare chute. Ken Huber circled again so Earl could keep the chute in sight. Cooley knew the small weighted chute could hit two or three wind drifts before reaching the ground. He also knew that while an upper-story wind could blow it north, a lower wind could push it back in the opposite direction. This time the chute drifted about 300 to 400 yards straight up the gulch. Earl estimated that the winds were holding steady at about fifteen miles per hour. If winds picked up to twenty miles per hour, he would abort the jump and direct Huber to land at the Helena airport. In fact, the last time he had spotted for a jump east of the Divide, on the Benchmark fire, the wind had blown so strongly that he had aborted the mission.

On the next pass, Huber brought the plane down the gulch, directly into the wind, and Earl kicked out another drift chute a quarter-mile after they passed over the jump spot. This one drifted up canyon and landed just to the side of the landing spot. As Earl pulled his head back into the open door, the pilot's voice crackled over the headphones. "Say, Earl. The air's sucking us into the gulch. I'm going to climb and drop the men from above the ridge, at 1,200 feet. I can't get them any lower. And we'll drop the cargo from there too."

Cooley bit his lip. Although Huber had flown for Johnson Brothers Flying Service for four years and had shuttled paratroopers during the war, he hadn't quite adjusted to mountain flying. Cooley knew that if Bob Johnson had been along, he would have fought the winds to give the men as easy a landing as possible. Moreover, he'd probably have scraped the tops of the trees with the plane's tires when he dropped the cargo, laying the packages right in the jumpers' arms. If they dropped the cargo from the higher altitude, the goods would drift all over the place. But he couldn't argue with the pilot. The important thing was to get everyone down on the ground without injury and then get the crew back home safely. When Earl passed the information on to Wag, the foreman shrugged. Earl stood up and moved back down the fuselage to tell the men to prepare to jump.

"Damn, Earl," Navon shouted. "Can't you find us a more interesting fire? This is going to be one hell of a boring mop-up job."

"Well, I guess we can all turn around and go home and hang around the base if you don't feel like working today," Earl chuckled.

CHAPTER FIFTEEN

Jim Harrison

Meriwether Campground
August 5, 1949

Fireguard Jim Harrison, his shirt soaked with sweat, jogged up the trail that switchbacked up the 1,500-foot walls of Meriwether Canyon. At other times he would have dallied to explore the shallow caves that pockmarked the limestone, but today he had an urgent mission. The district ranger expected him to radio in his fire report by 3:00 in the afternoon. If he lucked out and spotted a fire in the area, Jim could anticipate becoming a crew foreman.

The tall Douglas fir and western larch that crowded the canyon floor thinned as Jim ascended the rock wall. Eventually the dramatic cliffs gave way to a rounded top that supported a different type of forest, a drier ecosystem dominated by ponderosa pines with Douglas firs in the understory. As he neared the ridge top, Jim felt uplifted despite the physical exertion. It always happened when fire was about. No matter how tired he felt from a day of menial chores, the smell of smoke exhilarated him and turned an exhausted frown into a smile. Fire seemed to have a positive effect on most firefighters. Whenever he worked on a crew, smoke inspired men to lay aside their grudges, knowing that they would need to work as a team. The purpose of life became clear and understandable—to put down an evil foe. Jim Harrison agreed with a jumper who once said that fighting fire was the moral equivalent of war. But it was even better, because young men got to display their courage, determination, and stamina without hurting anyone. And not getting hurt in return—usually.

Jim clutched a pulaski in one hand, a shovel in the other. His canteen strap hung around his neck and under an arm. He hoped that if he spotted a small fire, he could quickly ring it with a fire line and then radio in that he had everything under control. He'd show those smoke jumpers how expendable they were. He chuckled to think how his allegiance had so quickly shifted to the side of the groundpounders. Now whenever a fellow groundpounder groused "Who needs those harebrained smoke jumpers?" Jim always nodded in agreement.

One old-timer who had manned a lookout during the war liked to tell the story about a smoke he had spotted about a mile from his tower. The man phoned the dispatcher and said he would hike over and put it out himself. "Hell, if I had drunk a can of beer before I started walking, I probably could have pissed it out," the man told Jim. "But they said, 'No, we're going to send in the jumpers.' Who was I to argue with them? Anyway, a couple of hours later I hear the plane come rumbling up the valley. Who knows how many dollars it cost to fly that heap all the way from Missoula? Then it passes over the smoke a couple of times, and drops some pretty colored ribbons. Then I see two white mushrooms pop open behind the plane and the parachutes start floating down to earth. Wouldn't you know it, those boys landed about fifty feet from the lookout. I walked over to say hello and they explained that they couldn't find any safer landing spot. So they ended up making the same hike I would have. The fire was about as big as a barbecue pit and they put it out in no time. Then, to add in-

sult to injury, they hiked back over to the lookout for supper.
I did 'em right with grub, 'cause it wasn't their mule-brained
logic that set up the whole fiasco. And they were nice enough
boys, even though they were conchies. A couple of Hutterite
farm boys.

"When I met one of those boys later that summer, he told me
it had taken them two whole days to get back to Missoula. First
they had to hike out to the trailhead where a truck picked them
up and carried them back to the ranger station. From there they
took a bus into Helena where they slept in a hotel. The next
day they caught the train back to Missoula. Now you explain to
me how those guys are supposed to be saving us money?"

A year ago, Jim might have defended the jumpers by pointing out the fact that the jump occurred during the war when
the program was still considered an experiment and the brass
wanted to try out the new harebrained idea as often as possible. But this time Jim just nodded in agreement. "It's a funny
way to run an outfit," he said.

By the time Jim reached the ridge top, the temperature had
topped 90 degrees. A slight breeze blew from the north at about
six to eight miles per hour. Jim gulped down some water from
the half-gallon canteen. Then he smelled the smoke.

Jim was familiar with the view into Mann Gulch. The two-
and-a-half-mile-long funnel-shaped drainage doglegged and
then narrowed to a hundred yards before emptying into the
Missouri River. The south ridge, where he stood, was the high-
est flank. He looked down onto a mature stand of ponderosa
pine and Douglas fir in the bottom, where a distinct moisture
gradient also provided for heavy undergrowth. Jim had once
started hiking up the gulch from the river but had quickly
turned back after tiring of fighting his way through thick
stands of juvenile trees. About halfway up on the south-facing
slope, directly opposite him, the summer sun superheated the

ground, killing any young trees that took seed there. From that point on, only grasses and forbs survived the harsh conditions. At the very top, a wall of rimrock capped the ridge, its bold face standing as high as twenty feet in places and as low as knee-high in others.

The Gates of the Mountains formed as part of a geological structure called the Disturbed Belt that included northwestern Montana, western Alberta, and eastern British Columbia. It was also part of the much larger Overthrust Belt that stretched from British Columbia to central Mexico. One hundred and fifty million years ago, the area had been under an inland ocean that gradually deposited deep layers of rocks, limestone, and sandstone. When the western continent had risen from the waters, great slabs of the sedimentary layers had slid over each other inland or eastward and then rose almost vertically into the sky. Like the more dramatic Rocky Mountain Front to the north, the Gates of the Mountains had folded, cracked, and crumbled into place. An arch had once connected the north and south ridges of Mann Gulch along the riverbank, but it had fallen long ago.

As he walked into the ground-hugging smoke, Jim heard the crackling of flames. Fifty yards later, he stepped into a blackened area where short tongues of flame slowly ate at the grasses beneath the trees. Here and there he passed a charred crisp skeleton of a torched sapling, but for the most part, the fire crept slowly but steadily through the pine needles, grass, and thick duff. Sticking to the burn area, Jim tried to estimate the fire's size. Ten, twenty, thirty acres? He'd never been able to figure out exactly just how far an acre extended. But he did know one thing. He wasn't going to be able to report to Ranger Jansson that he had contained this fire single-handedly. Still, he could begin to anchor the southern perimeter of the fire to prevent it from spilling over into Meriwether Canyon. That could easily happen if the updrafts from the canyon bottom subsided.

Jim returned to the trail, hung his canteen and knapsack on the limb of a tree, slipped on his leather gloves, and grabbed the pulaski. First he chopped down a couple of saplings with the axe blade, then flipped the tool head over and began digging fire line with the mattock head. It took half a dozen swipes to clear away the litter, remove the grass and roots, and dig down into mineral soil that wouldn't burn. It would have been easier with a twelve- or sixteen-man crew using the caterpillar method, each man taking a swipe or two as he continually moved along. By the time the last man passed the spot where the first man had started, the mineral soil would be exposed. A caterpillar line could encircle an acre of fire in no time.

As his body fell into the familiar rhythm, Jim still entertained visions of lining this fire by himself. Strike, pull. Strike, pull. Every once in a while, flip the tool head and chop out a root. Just leave the fallen logs for now and get them later. It would take hours for the fire to burn through them across the line anyway. Leave them for the reinforcements. Strike, pull. Strike, pull. Sweat glistened on his forehead, and Jim rolled up the sleeves of his cotton shirt. Clink. Clink. Damn, he hated digging in rocky soil. In other places, the duff ran deep and his fire line resembled a small trench. Jim jumped when a small tree crowned with a startling whoosh. He didn't like the ripping sound of fire racing out of control. He'd rather it continue to crackle, just like it did in the fire pit back at camp. Strike, pull. Strike, pull. The back of his mouth felt like sandpaper. The faster he got this line dug, the quicker he'd be out of here. He'd have company by this evening, plenty of guys to share supper and shoot the breeze with.

Maybe they'd even send some jumpers over. That would be sweet, but he doubted it. The district liked to man these big fires with locals. As he ruminated, he mechanically swung his pulaski. He'd just get this side of the fire cut off and then he'd go down and radio for help. Maybe, if he helped mop up the

fire for a few days, he'd get some R and R in Missoula. With
the money he made from overtime, he could take out that cute
nursing student he'd met last time he went home. This was
good work, he thought. One day of this and he'd be back in
shape. No more soft muscles for Jim Harrison.

When his forearm cramped, Jim stopped digging, straightened his frame, and looked down his line. Suddenly, he felt
overwhelmed. The line stretched only about thirty yards. It
didn't look like much compared to the remaining circle of fire.
He walked over to his canteen and took a swig of water.
Although it was too early for the scheduled report, he decided
to run down to the campground and call in anyway. The fire
wasn't going anywhere, and the quicker a crew arrived, the
quicker they would contain it. After stashing his tools just off
the trail below the lip of the ridge, Jim raced down the hill.

As Jim approached the bottom of Meriwether Canyon,
Harvey Jensen was tying up his tour boat to the small wharf
and helping his passengers disembark. About twenty minutes
earlier he had spotted the smoke emanating from top of the
ridge. When he didn't spot Jim at the boat landing, Jensen had
assumed Harrison knew about the fire. About 12:15, he'd
hiked up to the fireguard cabin to talk with Jim but hadn't
found him at home. But as Jensen headed back to the boat,
Jim came jogging down the trail.

"Got a fire up on the ridge," Jim said. "And a pretty big one,
too."

"Yeah, I know. I just came up to tell you about it."

Jim banged open the cabin door and picked up the radio
mike, but he couldn't get through to the Canyon Ferry Ranger
Station. Since no one had scheduled a transmission for that
time, the radio at Canyon Ferry was turned off. Ranger Bob
Jansson feared that with only one radio in the district and no
technical support, the radio would break down with constant

use. Moreover, it was the lunch hour and the dispatcher, Schmitt, had left his station for the cookhouse.

Jim tried to reach the dispatcher in Missoula. Missoula would transfer the message by long-distance phone call to Helena. But Jim's timing was off again. During fire season, the Missoula radio monitored only the first five minutes of every fifteen minutes of the hour on all frequencies. Plus, the radio happened to be down for repairs. Jim did come in loud and clear at the Ninemile Remount Depot, but they broadcast over a different frequency so could not talk back to him. Frustrated, Jim hung up the mike.

"I'm going back up there," he told Harvey. But before he left, Jim jotted a note on a piece of paper and tacked it to the cabin door. It read: "I'll be back down at three-thirty. Gone to fight fire—Jim."

"Well, what are you going to do up there all by your lonesome, if the fire's as big as you say? You'd better wait for help," said Harvey.

"I've already started a line to keep it out of Meriwether. I think I can get that done by myself. I never should have come down here to make an early call. I could have had half that line dug by now."

After grabbing a spare canteen, Jim sprinted up the path again. Two teenage girls stepped out of his way.

"Good morning," they said. "What's the big hurry?"

"Got a fire to fight," Jim said, his heart pumping with pride. "Hope you enjoy your stay at Meriwether."

CHAPTER SIXTEEN

Marvin Sherman

In the Doug C-47, circling Mann Gulch
August 5, 1949

Twenty-one-year-old Marvin Lester "Dick" Sherman stretched the leather straps of his helmet under his chin and threaded them through the buckles on the collar of his jump jacket. From his seat along the side of the Doug, he nervously glanced at the open door. He'd never gotten used to parachuting. "I nearly die every time I jump," he had once confided to his friend, Ross Middlemist, at the Lolo Ranger Station. In the doorway, Earl Cooley, goggles on, sprawled on his belly peering at the ground. Every few moments he shouted instructions into his microphone to help pilot Ken Huber position the plane over the jump site. Foreman Wag Dodge crouched just inside the door above Cooley, looking back at the men. When Dodge gave the signal for first stick to line up behind him, Marvin scrambled to his feet and bumped into Walt Rumsey, who had been sitting in the seat opposite him. David Navon and Bill Hellman stood in front of them. With Wag Dodge the first man out, the first stick needed only three more jumpers.

"Go ahead." Marvin gestured with his hand. "Age before beauty."

"Any day," Rumsey said. "I'll save you a good seat below."

Marvin Sherman, a shy freckle-faced kid from Darby, Montana, sat back down. He wasn't in any hurry. In fact, he almost wished he could fly back to the base with Merle Stratton, who lay in a fetal position just outside the cockpit. He'd give anything for the pilot to turn about and head back to Missoula, where his girlfriend waited.

Mary Ellen had brown hair and was tall and slender. When she wore high heels, she stood eye to eye with him. Marvin spent his spare time at Mary Ellen's family's modest home in Missoula, a long narrow house that had been built early in the century by the Northern Pacific Railroad for its workers. The narrow side of the house, which had no windows, faced the street. It was sided with fake brick shingles. In good weather, he and Mary Ellen would sit on the front stoop for hours. Just last Easter, he'd asked her to marry him. Before church that morning, Mary Ellen's mother had coaxed them to pose for some photographs by the side of the house. As he posed in his double-breasted suit, his heart swelled when Mary Ellen linked her arm through his. She wore a stylish pleated skirt that hung just below the knees and a saucer-shaped hat atop her dark curly hair. In a way, Marvin already felt married. He pitied the guys who chased after nursing students or college coeds on their days off at the park downtown. There was nothing like a steady girl to make a man feel fulfilled.

Later that Easter Sunday, after an early dinner of fresh ham from a pig Marvin had helped butcher at Cousin Ray's ranch up the Bitterroot Valley, Mary Ellen grabbed the camera again to take some more photographs. By this time Marvin had changed to jeans and rolled up the cuffs of his pants. He pushed his bill cap far back on his head and then lit a butt, just like a Hollywood actor. A black kitten vied for his attention.

"Hey, why don't we drive out to cousin Ray's and take the horses out for a ride?" he asked as the shutter clicked. As usual, Mary Ellen conceded to his wishes.

As the couple headed out the south end of town, they passed Hale Airfield where the fleet of Trimotors and Dougs stood at attention outside the hangers. Not much air traffic on the holiday. Just down the road at the far end of the airstrip, a bunch of cars jammed the parking lot of a tavern. But after that, the couple had the road to themselves. As the valley narrowed, the road hugged the banks of the Bitterroot River. On the rounded grassy covered hills across the river they spotted a herd of horses used as bucking broncos on the rodeo circuit.

"I saw my first buttercup yesterday," Mary Ellen said.

"Where?"

"At the base of Mount Sentinel."

"You got me beat," Marvin smiled. "I haven't seen one yet."

A few miles down the road, the cramped river valley opened up to the south at the small roadside burg of Lolo. A half-mile beyond the town, the dramatic wall of the Bitterroot Mountains lined the west side of the valley, anchored at the near end by the snow-capped summit of Lolo Peak. On the eastern side of the agricultural valley stood the rounded and wooded Sapphire Mountains. Only about fifty years earlier, the last remnants of a band of Salish Indians had abandoned their ancestral home in the Bitterroot Valley and moved sixty miles north to the Flathead Indian Reservation. On October 16, 1891, Chief Charlo had led a mile-long procession consisting of horses, wagons, and 200 people through downtown Missoula. For the march down Higgins Avenue, the Indians had donned their finest apparel and painted their faces. Even in 1949, fifty years after their withdrawal, Indians still camped in teepees outside the city limits whenever they came to Missoula to buy supplies or to dig bitterroots south of town in the late spring.

At a juncture just outside Lolo, a gravel road headed west up to a pass and then descended into Idaho. Lewis and Clark had followed the same route in 1805, describing it as the toughest country they encountered on their cross-country jaunt. Marvin pointed out the window.

"Mormon Peak," he said. "That's where my lookout was."

In reality, Mormon Peak was a foothill standing about 1,000 feet below the top of Lolo Peak. The lookout, perched atop a 40-foot tower, offered a view directly into the town of Lolo as well as up the Lolo Creek valley, where many timber companies owned land. Another lookout, clearly visible from Mormon Peak, stood atop Blue Mountain, about five miles away. During his last summer on the mountain, Marvin had become good friends with another teenager, Tom Maggee, whose family owned a ranch on Lolo Creek. Tom had met Marvin through his two teenage sisters and some other boys the girls had attracted. Marvin and Tom had soon became fast friends. The local ranger paid Tom ten dollars to check the phone line and deliver some supplies to Marvin via horseback. Tom often talked his folks into buying them a case of beer for the visit. The two young men would drink the warm beer as they cleared the trail and maintained the phone lines. After accumulating a few empties, they would dig deep holes to hide the evidence. In the evenings, the boys would longingly look down upon the Rockaway, the dance hall in Lolo, and silently wish they were fox-trotting and jitterbugging with the ranch girls. But when their talk turned to the subject of pretty girls, Marvin would say, "Hell, we're already in heaven; why do you want to go down there?"

The sight of Mormon Peak brought other memories to mind. "Sometimes, the ranger let me keep the district's two burros at the lookout," Marvin told Mary Ellen. "Their names were Gene and Genny. Genny could pack only twenty gallons of water, but Gene could carry thirty gallons. When I didn't have the burros, I had to strap on a five-gallon backpack and two water sacks that held a gallon each and hike down one and a half miles to the head of Mormon Creek to fill them up, and then back up again, every two days."

Marvin had known his cousin Ray Belston would get a kick to see them at the ranch. Ever since he had gotten serious about

Mary Ellen, Ray Belston had harassed him for not coming out
to check the trap lines for mink and muskrat or go fishing with
him along the Bitterroot and Big Hole rivers. But at least
Marvin still helped out with the branding of the calves in the
spring, putting up the hay in the summer, and breaking horses.
Ray had also frequently visited Marvin at the lookout. But those
had been the days before the war had ended.

A tap on the shoulder brought Marvin out of his reverie. "I
guess we're next," shouted Henry Thol. Marvin looked to the
rear of the plane to see Wag Dodge, the first in line for the
four-man stick, standing at the doorway, waiting for Cooley to
slap the back of his calf.

"Yeah, looks that way, don't it?" Marvin said as he pulled the
protective wire mask down over his face. Just think of the
money, Marvin told himself. This winter Mary Ellen and he
would be married. He'd invite all the jumpers to the wedding.
They were great guys, but they just couldn't hold a candle to
Mary Ellen. And soon he'd have kids too. It wouldn't be fair
to leave Mary Ellen alone. No. This was going to be his one
and only season as a smoke jumper.

Staring out through the mesh of the protective face mask
Marvin tensed as the familiar fear began to take hold of him.
It was no time to be thinking of Mary Ellen. He couldn't quit
now. Maybe when he got home, if he could only find work that
paid as well. But these were things to consider another time,
he thought, as he listened to the wind rushing by the open
door of the Doug.

CHAPTER SEVENTEEN

David Navon

*In the Doug C-47, circling Mann Gulch
August 5, 1949*

David Navon felt foreman Wag Dodge tug on the chute pack on his back, then on the quick-release harness. Navon then turned around so Dodge could check the reserve chute on his chest.

"You know the routine. Keep your static line over your right shoulder. Watch out for that first step. It's a long one."

Wag patted David on the shoulder and then examined the next man in the four-man stick. Walt Rumsey, feeling a bit nauseous, had worked his way to the rear of the plane so he could get out before he got sick. When Wag got back to the open door, Navon watched co-spotter Jack Nash clip Wag's twelve-foot static line to the cable that ran along the ceiling of the plane. Then Nash checked Wag's gear one last time.

One could never be too careful in this business, David thought. Although he was a rookie smoke jumper, David had hit the silk plenty of times in training for World War II. Only on this jump he didn't have to worry about German soldiers trying to send a bullet up his rear end. Attached to the 82nd Airborne Division, David had survived two combat jumps—one during the Normandy invasion, the other with Operation Market Garden near Nijmegen, Holland. During that operation he was wounded. After recovering in England, David returned to his division in time to partake in the Battle of the Bulge, where his division was surrounded in Bastogne. After the war he transferred to the 101st Airborne and served in Berlin.

The previous week, David had written to his younger sister, Anita, back in Modesto, California, to explain that he'd only taken the smoke jumper job to earn some extra money. With any luck, this fire season could turn out to be a thousand-dollar summer. The week before, he'd sent fifty bucks to Anita to add to her European travel fund. He wanted his kid sister to have as many opportunities as he had had to travel the world.

At twenty-eight, David was one of the oldest seasonal jumpers. The younger guys used to kid him about his receding hairline and widow's peak. He now combed the long strands of hair atop his head straight back and instructed the barber to just trim around the ears. Still, he cut a dashing figure, especially with his alert dark eyes. He had no trouble striking up conversations with the ladies who patronized the bars in downtown Missoula. But maybe it was time to consider settling down. After all, he'd been on the move most of his life. He didn't regret a single moment of the adventure, but once in a while he felt a longing for something he couldn't quite articulate. Now, he felt, was the time to establish himself, especially in a career in forestry.

David was born in Argentina where his dad, an immigrant American citizen, sold farm machinery for International Harvester out of Chicago. Later, the family moved back to the United States and settled on a farm in California's Central Valley. When David's dad lost the farm during the Depression, the Navons moved to Modesto, where David graduated from high school in 1938. Seeking some adventure, he crewed on a Swedish freighter for a year and worked his way around the

David Navon (second from left) at Camp Menard, near Huson, Montana. Courtesy U.S. Forest Service.

world. In 1939, he entered Modesto Junior College and joined the National Guard to earn some extra cash and get some military experience. The draft called in 1941. A year later, already a second lieutenant, David volunteered for paratrooper training with the 82nd Airborne Division. In March 1946, with the rank of first lieutenant, he was honorably discharged.

But David had not lost his wanderlust. After a year of studying forestry at the University of California, Berkeley, he traveled to Scotland to attend the University of Aberdeen. In Britain, he visited the major museums and wrote long letters home. He always posted the letters with beautiful stamps, which his sister and father added to the family stamp collection.

When he returned to Berkeley, David had finished his degree work in a class of about sixty men, most of whom were war veterans. The serious-minded men, many of whom were

married and already fathers, often challenged teachers who
had not fought in war, confident that their life and world experience had given them insight beyond the limits of books.

While he was an undergraduate, David and classmate Myron
McFarland had purchased a war surplus jeep at an auction in
Oakland. When the vehicle arrived in a crate, the two hired a
mechanic to help them assemble it. They each paid half the ex-
penses and traded the vehicle back and forth every other week,
executing the swap every Sunday after lunch. The only rule was
that neither could ask the other to borrow the vehicle. Just before graduation, McFarland had bought out David's share before David headed back to Europe to visit the sites of the battles
he had fought in. David later sent a tea set from Europe to
McFarland as a wedding present. The two men had plans to meet
five years hence when the close-knit class of '48 gathered for a
reunion.

With a forestry degree in hand, David was ready to jump into
a new career. Curious about different types of ecosystems, he
planned to return to Berkeley to get another degree, this time
in range management. That degree, he reasoned, would enhance
his qualifications to nail down a permanent position with the
Forest Service or some other land-management agency. As evidence of his zeal to continually learn, David had driven 200 miles
on his one day off in the summer of '49, all the way from the
Bitterroot Valley to the Powell Ranger Station in Idaho, just to
see some of the last remaining stands of western white pine trees.
An exotic disease, blister rust, was killing off the species that had
supported a thriving lumber and matchstick industry in the
Idaho Panhandle and western Montana. Fellow smoke jumpers
Starr Jenkins, Short Hall, and Jock Fleming had joined him for
the outing. David had been the first to spot one of the survivors.

Of course, like many people, David sometimes dreamed big.
He had once confided to Jenkins that he wanted to persuade
an owner of an island off the California coast to let him stock

the real estate with exotic big game and manage it as a preserve where wealthy "big white hunters" could come "on safari" to bag their lion, tiger, kodiak bear, or rhino. He still held onto the scheme.

As David stood in line with the first four-man stick of jumpers, he felt a poke in his back. "So did you get stuck in that snowstorm last winter in LA?" asked Walt Rumsey. David didn't like to be distracted so close to a jump, but he recognized that the rookie was probably experiencing the jitters.

"Yeah, it was great," he shouted over his shoulder without making eye contract. "It was the first time since they started keeping records of the weather there that snow blanketed Los Angeles and San Diego. It killed off a lot of the citrus trees, but the kids sure had fun. Cars crashed all over the place and people were still walking around in shorts and stuff. It was crazy. I hear it was really bad throughout the West, with a lot of cattle starving. How'd your family do in Nebraska?"

But David wasn't really listening to Walt's answer. He had one eye on Earl Cooley, who was lying on the floor of the plane, looking out the jump door, and talking into his microphone. Five seconds later, Cooley got to his knees and slammed Wag Dodge on the back of the leg and Wag crow-hopped out of the doorway. Hellman followed two seconds later with a big shout. Rumsey followed silently. As David crowded into the doorway he shouted down to Cooley, "Hi, Earl."

"Get the hell out of here," Earl shouted back, slapping him on the back of the leg to hurry him out. Then Cooley shouted "Jumpers out!" into the microphone.

David folded his arms across his chest, gripped the rip cord of the reserve chute, and stepped out left foot first so that the cyclone created by the tailwind of the plane wouldn't throw him face first into the plane's tail. His stomach jumped up toward his diaphragm during the free fall—one second—two seconds—three seconds—before the whomp of the opening chute abruptly checked his descent and sent his feet looping above his head. He groaned, gravity righted his body, and he looked up to see the gorgeous white canopy in full blossom against the blue sky, no lines tangled.

The same strange feeling that had overwhelmed him during his first training jump in the army overtook him again. In fact, he had experienced it every time he had ever jumped, even in the thick of battle. Hanging suspended above a world with only the wind in his ears, David felt as if he were floating through heaven. No danger lurked up here; it all waited below. The biggest fix he'd gotten into as a smoke jumper had been when a horny bull moose had chased him up a tree while he was cruising timber in the forests surrounding Seeley Lake. For a fleeting moment David wished he could sustain the feeling forever, but he knew better than to daydream during a descent.

Below him, Dodge and Hellman were pulling on the lines of their chutes to bank and angle toward the grassy steppe near the head of the gulch. Glancing above, David saw Rumsey's chute fully open. Looking down again, David could not see much fire on the smoky ridge. No crowning, and the flames didn't seem to be in a hurry to get anywhere. Then a blast of air buffeted his canopy and David pulled on his risers but couldn't get his chute to respond. A stiff wind quickly blew him toward an abrupt slope of bare rock directly beneath the fire. Realizing it was not the greatest of landing spots, David grabbed three of the fourteen lines that stretched from the chute to the right shoulder of his harness and began pulling himself up, hand over hand, toward the canopy bubble, as if he were climbing a rope at training camp. As he ascended the lines, the parachute bubble turned over on its side and began dumping out air. The higher he climbed, the more the canopy sagged, until it started flapping. With half the chute collapsed, David fell like a stone and began to twirl around. At 500 feet he eased the slip and steadily backed down the lines. Under full canopy again, David was able to angle toward the landing spot like a gull honing in on a free meal at a California beach. He'd learned the slip technique in the military, a maneuver that allowed him to descend more quickly and keep on course.

Below, Dodge hit the ground hard and fell forward. Then Hellman pulled up, hit and flopped on his side like a sack of potatoes. As the earth rushed toward Navon, he held his feet together and relaxed his body. Out of the corner of his eye he saw Hellman kneeling on the ground about twenty yards away, watching. Navon pulled back on his risers to brake the momentum of the chute. For a moment, he seemed to gracefully step onto the ground as if he were reaching the bottom step of a steep staircase. But just as it seemed he would stay upright and walk forward, his left foot turned over on a rock hidden in the grass and David stumbled to his knees and fell face first.

"Now that was graceful," Hellman laughed once he realized David wasn't hurt.

"Why show off?" Navon replied, scrambling to his feet and blushing a bit. "No one down here to impress."

Both men quickly looked up at Rumsey. The kid had missed the turbulent winds and was floating in slightly downhill from them, about thirty yards off the mark. With Rumsey safely on the ground, David gathered in the shroud lines of his billowing chute as if he were struggling with a wild stallion at the end of a lasso. When he reached the half-inflated canopy he beat the air out of it, punched it into a large ball, and stepped out of his harness. He stuffed the nylon parachute into his gear sack. Later followed his jump suit. No mule pickup this time, he thought. Just a short two-mile hike downhill with the clack boards on his back to the Missouri River and then an enjoyable boat ride to a waiting vehicle. Then David noticed that Wag Dodge hadn't gotten to his feet yet. Walter Rumsey was helping Wag shrug off his jump suit.

"Damn, my elbow aches like blazes," Wag said.

When Dodge bent his elbow the men saw a puncture wound. "Jeez, Wag," Rumsey said. "I can see the bone. But it's not bleeding too much." Rumsey took out his first aid kit and began dressing the foreman's wound. Meanwhile the Doug rumbled overhead, ejecting the second stick of jumpers. Four more white mushrooms blossomed against the blue sky.

"Everyone looks OK," Dodge said, studying the jumpers as Rumsey tied off the bandage on his elbow.

"Going smooth as silk," Hellman replied.

When they had descended a thousand feet, the turbulent air sent two jumpers drifting together.

"Don't get tangled, boys," Dodge muttered.

They did, but fortunately the men floated at the same level so one did not crumple the other's chute. Both canopies remained inflated. After a while, Dodge and the others heard the two men cussing each other.

"Sounds like Diettert and Newt Thompson," David said.

"What the hell are they doing up there?" Hellman said. "Making out?"

Walt Rumsey shook his head and turned away. "I can't watch this," he said.

At the last second Diettert and Thompson swung away from each other and their chutes drifted apart. They both hit the ground with perfect rolls, although they were about fifty yards off the landing spot. Along with Stan Reba and Bob Sallee, the second stick soon joined the others.

"How long you guys been going steady?" David greeted Diettert and Thompson.

"I heard they got a tandem bike at the base. You guys might want to try that out too," Rumsey chimed in. The two young men were happy just to be on the ground alive and uninjured and the insults washed over them. They laughed and put their arms around each other's waists.

Four-man stick. Courtesy Merle Stratton.

"I'll stay with you forever, darling," Diettert said in a falsetto voice.

"I'm yours as well," Thompson replied.

The third stick delivered Joe Sylvia, Marvin Sherman, Henry Thol, and Silas Thompson. And the last, Robert Bennett, Phil McVey, and Leonard Piper.

When all had reached the ground safely, Dodge laid out orange streamers in a double "L" pattern. On the next run Earl Cooley and Jack Nash kicked out the cargo chutes and the free-falling gear. Then the Doug, now lightened of its burden, circled one last time to check for a distress signal before heading back to Missoula at about twice the speed it had arrived.

"It's a great day to fight fire," someone said as the men scattered to retrieve the supplies.

CHAPTER EIGHTEEN

Robert Bennett

Mann Gulch
August 5, 1949

Robert Bennett shrugged off his jump suit, stuffed it into his equipment sack, and added it to the growing pile of bags. After the last of the cargo chutes hit the ground, he rounded up the boxes, water jugs, and sleeping bags, briefly stopping to watch the silver Doug pass overhead one last time on its trip home. Then he spotted a smaller plane buzzing the north side of the gulch.

"Must be the local fire spotter," someone said.

Robert headed downhill toward a piece of equipment whose parachute had not opened. He went about 400 yards before reaching the crumpled package that had been stopped by a jagged rock. Then Robert recognized the forty-pound radio. The box containing the bulky contraption had tipped over on its side as Jack Nash kicked it out of the plane, allowing the static line to wrap around it. Unlike a jumper's static line, which attached to a cable running along the ceiling of the plane, the static lines for cargo fastened onto one of the plane's seats. From constant use, the line had frayed. As the weight of the radio pulled it tight, the line had snapped apart before it opened the chute. Robert hefted the smashed frame onto his shoulder and rejoined the crew.

"At least we don't have to lug this damn thing around," he said when he reached the foreman.

"The ground crew should have one with them," Wag Dodge said. "And maps, I hope. We're so short on maps they didn't give me one. Those guys ought to be around here somewhere."

It took the crew almost an hour to gather the various pieces of cargo, including the free-falling bedrolls that had bounced far down the hill. After they piled the gear in one spot, the men heard a shout from the south flank of the gulch, opposite their position. The voice sounded as if it emanated from a position below the fire. All turned and stared up at the smoky hillside, but no one could distinguish any figures on the slope.

"The groundpounders must be up there somewhere," Wag said to his squad leader, Bill Hellman. "I'll track them down while I'm reconning the fire. Let the men chow down, then get them tooled up and follow my trail. And make sure they fill up their canteens with water from the jugs. It's as hot as Hades here."

"Okay, you heard the man. Break out the refreshments," Hellman shouted.

With the axe head of a pulaski, Robert Bennett carefully pried open the long rectangular food box.

"What's on the menu today?" asked Henry Thol.

"Brown bread," Bennett said, pulling out a can marked with the B&M logo and tossing it to the youth.

"Ugh," replied a chorus of voices.

"Then how about baked beans?" Bennett said cheerfully, pulling out another can with the same logo.

"Get to the serious stuff, will ya? I'm hungry," sang out Joe Sylvia.

"Hardtack, fruit cocktail, peaches, ham . . ."

"Now, you're talking," David Navon said as he plucked the can of smoked ham from Bennett.

"Hey, I thought you kosher guys didn't eat pork," someone said.

"Only when we're stranded in the woods 3,000 miles from nowhere," Navon said. "Otherwise, we follow the Donner diet. I don't think you guys would appreciate that."

"Scrambled eggs, butter, potatoes—the little red ones without the skins—carrots, Brussels sprouts . . ." announced Bennett, as he continued to empty the contents of the food box onto the ground.

"Toss that last one into the fire," Newton Thompson said.

"And finally—the good stuff—coffee, evaporated milk, and hot chocolate."

"No time for that now," Hellman warned. "Just divvy up that ham and the peaches and let's get to work. That fire isn't going to go out on its own. And while we're on the subject of food, who wants to come back tomorrow morning to cook breakfast? You can consider this your supper."

As if they were a multiheaded hydra, all the men simultaneously turned toward the big-eared baby-faced Henry Thol.

"Aw, c'mon," Henry whined. "Not me. Heck, I'm just as old as Diettert. Why not him?"

"You know how to boil water, Diettert?" Hellman asked.

"No, sir," Diettert said.

"Then the jobs all yours, Henry," Hellman said.

"I don't mind doing the cooking," Bennett spoke up.

"Then it looks as though you're off the hook, Henry," Hellman said.

Conversation trailed off as the men concentrated on their food. Bennett, a second-year jumper from Paris, Tennessee, took a seat on the slope slightly below the others, where he had a clear view of the fire to the south. Robert wiped the sweat from his broad forehead and brushed back his short brown hair.

A shy, reserved youth most of his life, Robert's solemn eyes often conveyed a serious, businesslike aura. But among the jumpers, he felt free to express himself, as if his opinion weighed just as much as the next man's. The camaraderie reminded him of the friendships he had enjoyed with his childhood pals, playing hide-and-seek, red rover, and tag. Or later as a teenager, when he had played center on the high school football team. As he gazed up at the flank of the fire, about half a mile across the gulch, Robert bent his knees and rested a hunk of ham on his kneecaps as he slurped sugar water from a can of pears. He noticed that the fire had crept a bit across the top of the ridge since their arrival.

Robert didn't really like to cook, but he didn't mind taking on responsibility. And from experience, he knew that a minimal amount of culinary skill was enough to please the jumpers. Anything heated to a lukewarm temperature that had some chew to it passed muster, especially if there was plenty of strong black coffee to wash it down.

Besides, it was pretty obvious to Robert that Henry Thol, the rookie fresh out of high school, was tired of getting picked on. He had assumed responsibility for the task as a small gesture of friendship. Being good-natured was his trademark. Upon graduating from E. W. Grove High School, he had bequeathed his art of always being a good sport to a friend in the junior class, Billy Ray Balch. The editor of *The Tower*, the yearbook for the graduating class of 1945, had noted that Robert's favorite expression was "Pardon me."

But Robert was no saint, by a long shot, as his brother and sisters could attest. He was still known as the brother who almost burned down the family garage while experimenting with matches. And the one who had dropped a piece of tobacco into his sister Jeanne's eye, just to see what would happen. Not to mention shooting his younger sister, Joyce, in the back with a bb pellet, although her earsplitting scream rattled his nerves so much that he had immediately begged her forgiveness. When he was home, Robert still worshipped at the First Christian Church in Paris, Tennessee, where he had also attended Sunday school.

After high school, Robert had joined the 29th General Medical Corps, serving with the occupation forces in Japan. He ended his military service in Korea, with an honorable discharge on Christmas Day, 1946, with the rank of staff sergeant. The next fall, he pursued his childhood dream of becoming a forest ranger by enrolling in the school of forestry in Missoula. And during the summer of '48 he signed up with the smoke jumpers to earn some extra cash.

Three days ago, Robert had been working with a dozen other jumpers at Sullivan Lake Ranger Station in eastern Washington, about 200 miles northwest of Missoula on the Kaniksu National Forest. On the flight there, the Doug had followed the Clark Fork River into the narrowest part of the Idaho Panhandle—which was about forty-five miles wide—and had flown directly over Lake Pend d'Oreille and Priest Lake before crossing into the northeast corner of Washington, only twenty miles from Canadian border. The ten-mile-long blue ellipse of Sullivan Lake sparkled at the bottom of a trough between two mountain ranges. A ten-mile paved road connected the ranger station to the lonely outpost of Metaline Falls. The town overlooked the Pend d'Oreille River, a few miles upstream from where it veered into Canada before swooping back south to flush into the Columbia River.

The jumpers had shared a bunkhouse at Sullivan Lake. The cook had provided breakfast and dinner, but the men had to make their own sack lunches from the "makings" table after breakfast. "Whatever you take to the job you've got to carry out," the ranger told them. "And no littering up on the job site or the roadsides." He also warned the men about bears that frequented the garbage pit located just outside of town. Then he gave them their new job title: "brush pilots." Throughout the ensuing weeks, Bennett and the others gathered slash left over from logging operations into giant piles that would be burned after the year's first snowfall.

During their time off, Bennett and his buddies, including Henry Thol and Leonard Piper, took a bus into Metaline Falls or visited the nearby county beach, where the local girls hung out. While in town, though, they had to call it an early night since the last return bus left at 10:00. "If you miss that one," the ranger warned them, "it's a ten-mile walk, if you don't lose the road in the dark. Or meet a bear. Or step on a porcupine or a skunk. Lots of animals out at night around here. And they seem to like to use that road. And you're expected to get enough sleep to be able to work hard the next day. Got that?"

One afternoon, Robert, Short Hall, Red Anderson, and Starr Jenkins hiked seven miles up to a nearby lookout. The square cabin sat atop a wooden tower. George Sand, who manned the tower, had identified the dim ridges of Idaho to the east and the rumpled mountains of Canada to the north for the boys. Directly below, a sliver of Sullivan Lake glimmered amid the thick timber. After listening to George explain how the fire finder worked, the men had departed. Their ascent took three hours, but they ran back down the precarious trail in exactly one hour. Back at the station, the ranger had given them the good news: the Douglas C-47 would pick them up the next morning to haul them back to Missoula.

Now, here he was, finally on a fire. A gust of wind blowing up the canyon chased bits of wrapping paper from his feet. "What time you think you'll want supper ready?" he asked Bill Hellman, who was picking red cherries from a can of fruit cocktail.

"Depends on whether we hook up with that ground crew or not. If they can get a quarter of the fire lined throughout the night, then we'll get the rest done by four AM or so. If not, then it's going to take more than a day to contain this thing and we'll be ready for a break anyway. And I'm sure everyone will be complaining about how hungry they are. Why don't you plan to head on down about three or four in the morning to get a fire going?" One good thing about volunteering to cook, Robert thought; you always got to munch a little beforehand as you prepared the meal.

Hellman threw his can into the grass. "Guess you girls had better tool up," he said. "Navon and Sallee, grab the crosscut saws. Rumsey, you take the water can. The rest of you know the drill: pulaski in one hand, shovel in the other. We'll walk single file and follow Wag's trail and skirt up the slope toward the far edge of the fire. With the winds blowing up-canyon now, I suspect that's the best anchor point. Keep an eye open for tumbling rocks or logs and sing out 'roller' if you see or hear something coming down on us. Let's head out."

Before Hellman was ten steps away all the men had fallen in behind him, chucking their cans into the grass as they rose. Bennett checked his watch: 4:30. The landing spot was located where the gulch widened and the bottom flared out so that the men did not have to scramble across any sort of gully to begin the ascent of the north-facing slope. Nonetheless, the footing was rough, especially across the occasional scree-filled rock slides. The wind picked up and blew directly into their faces, with heavy gusts sometimes blinding them with dust. Robert marched in the middle of the line, behind Newton Thompson, a second-year jumper from Alhambra, California.

"Ain't it great?" Newt turned and said. "Being paid to hike around like this."

"Yeah, but I'd rather be back on the other side of the divide," Bennett answered. "It's too dry over here for me. Give me a nice spring to drink from and a crick to wash in. That would make a good camp. But you're right. We can't complain."

About 150 yards up the slope, a thick patch of saplings that had regenerated after a fire a few years before blocked their way. The perimeter of the fire burned about a quarter-mile above. From that direction they heard Wag Dodge shouting orders to stay where they were.

"Take a break," Hellman said.

CHAPTER NINETEEN

Wagner Dodge

Mann Gulch
August 5, 1949

As Wag Dodge picked his way up the steep north-facing slope toward the fire burning about 900 feet above, he noticed the bite to the hot dry air rising out of the gulch. At times he stumbled. He recognized that it was going to be a messy mop-up in the rocky soil. And there would be burning trees to knock down. And smoking logs on the ground to kick apart. He also noted the extended pockets of shoulder-high Douglas fir and ponderosa pine that had regenerated in open areas after a previous fire. Their boughs entwined so that at times he had to part the branches with his forearms before slipping through. In other places, overgrown leafy brush reached to his shoulders.

Ground flames could easily climb up the undergrowth to deliver the blaze into the canopy of the larger trees. Once a fire crowned in this manner, a stiff breeze could push the heat to cook the gases out of the trees ahead. When the gases reached the combustible point, the flames would explode through the air, engulfing other trees. The crown fire would move so quickly that it would outpace the flames on the ground.

The fire could also surge ahead even when the fuel supply
thinned. Gusts of wind, generated by the fire itself, often blew
burning embers hundreds of yards ahead of the main fire.
These spot fires often burned into each other, eventually es-
tablishing another flame front. When Wag felt a strong breeze
blow up canyon from the river, he realized that he and the
crew had landed in a very dangerous situation.

If anything, Wag was a man for details. After eight seasons
with the smoke jumpers, he knew as much about fire as anyone. He first jumped a fire in 1941, then resigned the following year to serve in the U.S. Coast Guard. After eight months'
service he was discharged for medical reasons and returned
to Missoula to help train the conscientious objector smoke
jumpers. He held no grudge against them, finding the deeply
religious men both decent and honorable. He hadn't fraternized with them much, but Wag, a thoughtful, pensive person, usually kept to himself anyway. As a foreman he didn't
participate as much in the spring training sessions as the squad
leaders. Wag had jumped forty-one times and had been pro-
moted to foreman in 1945. For three seasons he had been in
charge of aerial attack on fires along the Continental Divide,
so he was familiar with the conditions in Mann Gulch.

Besides the familiar features of Hellman, Thol, and McVey,
Wag couldn't put names to any of the other faces in the crew.
More and more he had been pulled off of training and jumping duties to build things or repair whatever required fixing
around the base. The previous spring, he'd missed all of training to oversee the reconstruction of an old CCC barracks that
conscientious objectors had dismantled at Camp Rimini into
the fire loft at Hale Airfield. Dodge had carefully coded each
plank and two-by-four as the crew had ripped them off. He had
installed new hardwood floors and designed the high tower
where the men could hang the chutes full length. Later, he built

the long triangular tables where the men folded and packed the chutes. He had also overseen many construction projects at the Camp Menard training facilities. When no construction projects demanded his attention, Wag worked in the woodworking shop in the basement of the old army barracks at Fort Missoula, engraving the names of trailheads and roads into wooden signs.

At home, when he wasn't hiking or taking photographs with his wife, Patsy, Wag made things in his own shop. One day he surprised Fred Brauer and seven other jumpers with small tin badges to commemorate their work with a film company. The men had stood in for actor Fred McMurray for parachute jumps in the movie *Forest Ranger*. Each badge, about an inch long and wide, depicted a parachute in full bloom with a jumper dangling below.

Because he was married and more than a decade older than many of the new jumpers, Wag seldom fraternized with the men. And as a foreman he only jumped with sixteen-man crews. When working at Hale Airfield, he and Fred Brauer usually patronized a small joint just outside the airfield for lunch, while the jumpers ate at the cookhouse at the fairgrounds. And during training at Camp Menard, when he taught fire control, Wag seldom went down to Ninemile House after work with the other jumpers. In truth, many of the jumpers probably didn't know who the fastidiously dressed man was when they were first detailed to Hale Field.

Not too many people were able to get into Wag Dodge's head, not even Patsy. "I love him very much, but I don't know him very well," Patsy once confided. "If he said my red drapes were black, I would say, trying to keep myself intact, 'Yes, Wag, my red drapes are black.'" After they had been married a while, Wag had explained to Patsy his simple formula for a successful marriage: "You do your job and I'll do mine, and we'll get along just fine."

That afternoon at the base, as Wag climbed aboard the Doug, he had noticed more than a few surprised looks from the boys.

He was determined to remember all the crew members' names before this day was over.

As Wag ascended the steep flank, another strong gust of wind blasted into his face. He stopped, cocked his head, and listened, like a night watchman who had just heard a windowpane shatter. As the gust subsided Wag heard a "whoosh" as flames exploded through the crown of a pine tree. The sound chilled him to the bone. This was not a place to get caught if the fire blew downhill, he knew. The only escape zone was the open grassy area where he had left his crew, but even that wouldn't be safe for long if a wind carried the fire down the slope and across the gulch. The funnel-shaped gulch would act like a chimney if the wind continued from the south and got some fire before it. It would bring flames right to their feet.

And no fire line could stop a blowup. Best thing to do was to pull out to the river and anchor the line at the mouth of the gulch. Plus, they could always jump into the water if things got too hairy. But Wag found himself caught in a quandary. He wanted to go back and warn his men, but he also needed to get the hand crew, which he believed was working above, off of the ridge as well. At that moment, Wag spotted Jim Harrison practically skipping down the steep incline toward him, his Forest Service shirt stained with sweat and blackened with soot.

"Hey, I never thought parachutes could look so beautiful once I saw you guys start floating down," Jim said.

Wag nodded. "How many men you got with you?" he asked.

"Just what you brought along with you," Jim answered. "My name's Jim Harrison, by the way. I was a jumper last year. I remember you from Hale Field."

"Yeah. You look a little familiar too," Wag said, shaking Jim's hand. "You say you've been fighting this fire all by yourself?"

"I guess they thought a former jumper could handle it," Jim laughed. "Actually, I'm the recreation guard over in Meriwether campground. It's just down over the other side of the ridge. I came up to look for smokes earlier today. I tried radioing the station around noon, but I couldn't get through. But I see someone finally reported the smoke."

"Well, Jim, I think we'd better get the hell out of here," said Wag. "I don't like the way that wind's picking up. And I don't like this thick reproduction around here. We'll tie back in with the others and then head down to the river."

With Harrison falling in behind, Wag quickly retraced his steps. In a few minutes he spotted the rest of the crew below him. They had progressed about 150 yards up from the bottom of the gulch. Wag hollered for the men to wait where they were. When he came up to the jumpers, Harrison recognized a few faces and warmly greeted them.

"I thought we had gotten rid of you," Eldon Diettert said, shaking Harrison's hand.

"I tried my best, but there's no escaping you guys," Jim said.

"How come you didn't try for another hitch this summer?"

"Ah, you know. I'm just getting too old for that type of stuff. Besides, they're keeping me busy chasing bears away from all the cute high school girls down at the campground."

"You guys can save your hugs and kisses for after we get the fire out," Dodge interrupted. "Right now let's get the hell away from this thick reproduction. It's a death trap. It'll be safer to work the lower side of the fire. Me and Harrison here are going back to the gear to get some grub. The rest of you cross to the other side of the gulch and start heading down to the river so you can work the fire from behind the wind. But don't go straight down the gully. Angle up a bit and follow the contour of the slope high enough so you can keep an eye on the flames."

Although a few of the men picked up that Dodge was shaken and wanted them out of there, they weren't too concerned.

CHAPTER TWENTY

Silas Thompson

Mann Gulch
August 5, 1949

Silas Raymond Thompson Jr., nineteen years old, pulled out his shirttails and fell into the middle of the line of jumpers. The slovenly look was a small trick he had learned at training camp. With shirttails out, burning embers or twigs that happened to fall through the collar of the shirt could more easily roll out at the waist. He also tugged on the red felt hat that all smoke jumpers wore. Fred Brauer had come up with the idea. Not only did they protect the head from radiant heat and flying embers, but the bright color made it easier for spotters in a plane to see them. As the line of men snaked down the south side of the gulch, Wag Dodge and Jim Harrison took off in the other direction toward the landing spot.

Each man walked a few paces behind the one in front, out of reach of back-swinging branches and the heads of shovels and pulaskis. This far down the gulch they had to skip down the steep bank of a gully and scramble back up the other side onto the base of the south-facing slope. Someone called out for the time and a voice shouted, "About 5:20." On this slope, the men entered a transition zone. Trees stood farther apart and bunch grass battled the cheatgrass in the open areas. Ahead, at the mouth of the gulch, waited a thick stand of trees, but behind and up the slope mostly grass grew.

"Don't make any sparks with your tools off the rocks in this stuff," Hellman hollered over his back. "This cheatgrass doesn't burn, it explodes."

Before long, half a dozen men diverted from the main group onto a game trail that seemed to follow a slighter incline. Ten minutes later, when Hellman realized he'd lost sight of some of his crew, he halted the main body of jumpers, waiting for the others to catch up.

"Hey, Rumsey. You need a break from that water can?" Navon asked.

"Any time," Rumsey said.

Navon turned over the two-man saw to Rumsey and placed the water can between his feet and sat down upon it. Rumsey took the saw to the end of the line, where his pal, Bob Sallee, shouldered the other saw.

"Can you see the others from back there?" Hellman asked.

"Nope," Sallee answered.

"I think they might have gotten in front of us," Rumsey said.

"Hey, where the hell are you guys?" Hellman shouted. A return shout situated the wayward crewmembers above and behind them, about 500 feet. A bulge in the hill blocked them from view.

"Damn if that fire isn't beginning to cook," Navon said, studying the opposite ridge.

The wind had picked up again and the men distinguished slender snake-tongues of flame flickering into the air at various spots. At one point a large tree torched. Still, the fire didn't seem to be in any hurry.

Silas Thompson was glad to be back in the "wilds of the West." Until last week, he'd been stuck at an army reserve training camp back east, then, like Stan Reba and Joe Sylvia, he'd rushed through two days of refresher training. Silas had grown up in Charlotte, North Carolina, where he graduated from Central High School in 1945. The next fall, he had enrolled at North Carolina State College in Raleigh to study forestry. For the summer vacation he had worked as a fire spotter atop Copper Butte Mountain in Washington State and the experience had changed his life. He swore he would never move back east.

In North Carolina, Silas had hunted and fished, trapped, and skied, but the West offered much more. Forget the raccoons, possums, and rangy deer of the Southeast. Out West roamed the majestic elk, mule and white-tailed deer, and moose, not to mention beavers, bobcats, lynxes, martens, wolverines, coyotes, and bears. Some said even a wolf or two, and a few grizzly bears still lingered in the high lonesome country around Glacier National Park and the Mission Mountains. With his nonconformist attitude and risk taking, Silas fit in well with the individualist-oriented society of the western states.

A profession in forestry would keep him in the woods, but the wages from the lookout job couldn't pay the college bills. In September 1946, Silas had enlisted in the army to qualify for the GI Bill. After training at Fort Bragg, he had ended up as a paratrooper with the 11th Airborne in Japan. Two years later, upon discharge, he had traveled to Missoula to enroll in forestry school. The jumpers had accepted his application for the summer of 1948.

"Hey, Silas. You got a new poem for us?" asked David Navon. In Navon, the world traveler and adventurer, Silas had found a kindred spirit. One night, over beers at Ninemile House, Silas had recited some of his poems to Navon. Navon had not only listened but had even offered some insightful criticism without offending the young bard. So if David Navon wanted a poem, Silas would give him one.

Let me breathe the clean pure air
That blows only in the wilder places
Send me far from the tainted cities
Packed tight with mongrel races.

Let me quench my thirst
In pure crystalline springs
That bubble from the living rock
Shadowed only by an eagle's wings.

Let me follow the untrod trail
Roaming freely till the end of my days
And watch the dusty red sun
Set the heavens and mountains ablaze

Let me, alone, eager and forever,
Follow and fight the naked wild
And when I die, mark me down
For what I am—Nature's Child.

"What do you call that one?" Navon asked.

"'A Woodsman's Prayer,'" Silas replied.

"I like it," Navon said. "All except the reference to the mongrel races. Sounds too much like something Hitler would have said."

"Yeah. I guess you're right." Silas blushed.

At that moment the rest of the crew straggled over the hump in the hill and fell in with the column.

"Where the hell did you guys go?" Hellman asked. "This isn't a god-damned sightseeing tour."

"We got on some game trail and it petered out after a while," Newton Thompson said. "That grass up there is slicker than snot."

"Well, pardon me, ladies," Hellman said, a bit frustrated. "I should have escorted you to the escalator for the easy way out."

The men's interest in the fire was already waning and they hadn't even unsheathed their pulaskis yet, Hellman thought. That's the trouble with the big fires that have already made their run. Too boring. After lining the fire, they'd spend a day or two digging out the smoldering roots, turning over logs, and eventually shedding their leather gloves to cold-trail their bare hands through the ash in search of hot spots. If the wind kept up, maybe it would liven things up, get these guys interested in fire again.

"Check it out, guys," Hellman said. "That thing's beginning to come to life. We'll have some fun yet today. Now let's hump it down to the river so we can get started."

Another fifty yards or so as they traversed the south-facing slope to keep out of the gully, Walt Rumsey, at the end of the column, heard noises from behind and turned to see Wag Dodge and Jim Harrison scurrying to catch up to them. Hellman wondered why they had cut their lunch break so short.

"Okay, guys, get the lead out," Dodge called out as he moved through them to the head of the line.

"What's up?" Silas Thompson asked Navon. Navon, who had just taken out his camera and hung it around his neck, shrugged his shoulders. With Dodge in the lead, Hellman dropped to the rear. Dodge led the crew at a brisker pace, angling upward at a steeper grade through the timber but still in the direction of the mouth of the gulch. A low lateral ridge directly ahead blocked the view of the Missouri River.

While the other men concentrated on their footing, Dodge continuously glanced at the fire across the gulch and sniffed the stiff breeze blowing in his face. The fire looked to be a safe distance away, but he didn't like the fact that wind now blew smoke across the mouth of the canyon directly ahead of them. Ten more minutes and he wouldn't have to worry. They'd be at the shore of the river and out of this natural chimney. This day wasn't turning out to be the cakewalk some of the boys had envisioned. If the fire ever spotted down from the ridge and got into the grass, the gulch would be history. Once beyond that low hogback ridge that blocked their view, the mystery of what the fire was doing at the mouth of the gulch would be solved. No more unknown factors to figure in. No more calculating with human lives. Dodge hadn't said anything to the men, not wanting to spread the panic that he felt in the pit of his stomach. The men followed him with anticipation but with an attitude that appeared as if they were strolling to a party rather outmaneuvering a fierce enemy.

About a quarter-mile farther down the gulch, Dodge glanced at his watch: 5:45. When he looked up again, past the lateral ridge, he stopped dead in his tracks. A heavy funnel of smoke now boiled up over the hogback ridge.

"We've got to head back up the hill, men," Wag said, promptly reversing direction himself. As he passed the men to take the lead once again, he avoided looking into their eyes. He had no time to stop and explain. He ordered Hellman to bring up the rear and told Sallee and Rumsey to "throw those damn saws away before you injure somebody." The two young men did so and then dropped in line directly behind Dodge.

Silas Thompson took one last look toward the mouth of the gulch and scratched his head.

"Let me roam the untrod trail," he said aloud.

CHAPTER TWENTY-ONE

Robert Jansson

Helena, Montana
August 5, 1949

By 2:20, Bob Jansson and his assistant, Hank Hersey, had recruited only ten men for a ground crew. Jansson thought the procedure would have gone more smoothly since earlier that spring the Helena National Forest had contracted with Canyon Constructors and the Bureau of Reclamation to send men to a fire when needed. But the bureau officials interpreted the agreement as binding only when its employees were off duty. When Jansson had called for support that afternoon, they had informed him that none of the shifts had been let off yet and men wouldn't be available until after 6:00. Jansson and Hersey had then started working the bars. Some of the men they had rounded up were still a bit tipsy.

Jansson had handed out bedrolls to the men and herded them into the back of a truck used to transport horses for the 20-mile drive to Hilger Landing, while Hersey remained in Helena to round up more bodies. When Jansson had called the landing from Helena, Harvey Jensen, the tour-boat captain, had promised to wait, but when the firefighters reached the landing, Jansson found an empty slip. A deck hand explained that a load of tourists had showed up at the dock with hard cash in hand, wanting to be ferried downriver to view the fire. Jansson was furious.

By 3:00, Hersey reported that he had rounded up twenty more men. Jansson, who hoped to find a boat and disembark before Hersey got to the landing, instructed the assistant ranger to follow him upriver and establish a base camp at the mouth of Mann Gulch, where he planned to land the first group. Then he told Hersey that he planned to scout the fire and contact the smoke jumpers.

About 3:55, Fred Padbury, a Helena druggist and state legislator, cruised up to the dock in his launch and offered to ferry Jansson's crew downriver. As they pulled out, they spotted Jensen's tour boat plying back to the landing. By the time Padbury's gleaming mahogany boat with its inboard motor reached the mouth of Meriwether Canyon, six miles down river, the faster tour boat had picked up Hersey's crew and caught up with them. It was about 4:30.

"I've changed my plans," Jansson yelled to Hersey over the idling motors. "The fire has slopped over the ridge from Mann Gulch into Meriwether Canyon. I want you to land here with your crew and begin cutting fire line on the ridge to keep the fire from creeping down into the canyon. Let the gulch go for now. If the fire gets down in here we'll lose all of it, plus part of Coulter Gulch and probably upper Willow Creek. That will give us a burn of fifteen to twenty thousand acres. If we lose Mann Gulch, it's only going to cost us three or four thousand acres, provided we can control it by tomorrow.

"Take my men with you. To hell with setting up camp. Someone coming down later can do that. You've got to jump on it. Tell your men to hold the upgulch side so that the jumpers can get through and join you. And radio Canyon Ferry and instruct Dave to get in touch with the jumpers by radio and tell them to hook up with you. We're also going to need two sector boss units, another fifty-man outfit as a starter, and a communications setup. And warn Moir this is no training fire. Make sure he doesn't send us any greenhorns. If I run into the jumpers at the mouth of Mann or Elkhorn, I'll ferry them back in this boat."

A few minutes later, as Padbury's launch approached Mann Gulch, heavy smoke from the southern ridge blew across the narrow mouth of the gulch. Jansson instructed Padbury to continue motoring a mile farther downriver to Elkhorn Creek so he could ascertain if the fire had spread in that direction. It was about 4:35. Although Jansson spotted no flames in the gulch, ashes floated in the air all about him. By the time the boat returned to Mann Gulch, Jansson could not see through the heavy smoke. He told Padbury to set him ashore so he could assess the fire. After leaping from the prow of the launch, the ranger noted the time: 5:02. He then walked into the wall of thick smoke.

About ten minutes later, Jansson had penetrated a little more than a quarter-mile into the gulch. Although he saw no flames, he sensed that things had picked up on the slope to his right. The 60-year-old trees in the bottom stood about forty feet tall with their crowns tightly interlaced. Although smoke continued blowing across the mouth of the gulch, Jansson felt the downriver winds being sucked into the mouth of the gulch, where they bounced off the canyon walls in all directions. The fire was getting ready to whirl but was not yet big enough to overcome the winds. The gusts bent the pole-sized tree trunks deeply, an indication of a wind speed of twenty to forty miles per hour. Jansson frequently stepped over broken branches that littered the forest floor. Glancing up the slope to his left, he saw some small spot fires smoldering above him where embers had flown across the gulch and landed in the grass.

Without warning, flames suddenly flashed from a clump of brush directly behind Jansson. At the same time, flaming debris rained down from the slope above. As the fire whirled, flames set in a little gulch that stood opposite the trail leading up and over to Meriwether Canyon. Farther up the gulch the ranger noticed spot fires burning on the northern flank, on the ridge in front of him, and all around him. Still he pushed on to where he could see the ridge below where the fire had started. There, he saw flames climb the tree trunks into the crowns, catch the gusty winds, and flash up the natural chimney formed by the gulch.

Jansson carefully picked the spots where he walked, sticking mostly to places with light fuels or already charred spots. Firebrands drifted through the air, landing and igniting fires a quarter-mile ahead of the main fire. Rocks, dislodged by the fire above, crashed down the steep slopes. A hundred yards ahead, dense black smoke bellowed into a convection column. At that point the ranger thought he heard a sound ahead, rising above the roar of the fire. Although his right ear was virtually deaf to consonant sounds, it was supersensitive to high-pitched tones, enabling him to hear sounds of certain pitch and resonance over long distances. He first thought he had heard someone shouting. But he immediately dismissed that notion. It could not be the jumpers. He hadn't received any report that they had even jumped the fire that afternoon. And any firefighter would surely have fled the heavy smoke that now choked him. If the jumpers had landed they would surely have headed up to the ridge above Meriwether Canyon if they had not pulled out altogether to the Ives Ranch, beyond the gulch and the national forest boundary. Now, Jansson realized, was time for his own retreat.

A high wall of flame had eaten through the timber clear to the bottom directly behind Jansson, cutting off his escape to the river. When a streamer of fire swept by him he ran, the acrid smoke burning his throat. He took shallow breaths, trying to protect his lungs from the heat. All about him the vortex gained power, whirling like a small tornado, but the superheated gases forced from the trees by the radiated heat had yet to burst into flame because of the lack of oxygen. In a matter of moments, when fuel, heat, and oxygen coincided, the fire would blow up, creating a veritable whirlwind that could rage as high as 100 feet into the air. Jansson skidded and slid down the gulch. As the vortex shrank in from all sides, he folded an arm before his face, held his breath, and ran through a wall of flames. Moments later, he fell senseless from the smoke, the exertion, and holding his breath. The ranger collapsed on his left elbow; his forearm immediately swelled down to the wrist, but his momentum carried him out of the flames and he rolled downhill out of the flames.

Ten, twenty seconds longer and the creeping ground fire might have ignited Jansson's clothing and charred his flesh. Searchers would have found the remnants of his body the next day. Or maybe they would have mistaken his corpse for a charred tree stump and passed it by, not smelling him out for another couple of days. But when Jansson regained consciousness the flames were still a few feet away, allowing him a chance to crawl out of the area. When he stopped to rest he retched violently and vomited. After regaining his breath he checked his watch: almost 5:30.

"Damn, we thought we'd lost you," yelled Fred Padbury from the launch as the ranger staggered into the river and splashed water on his face. "There's nothing we can do here," he said when he straightened up. "Let's go back to Meriwether."

As Fred Padbury chucked the engine into reverse, Jansson leaned close and asked, "Did you hear anyone calling out a few minutes ago?"

"No. Couldn't hear a thing except that fire," Padbury said. "Did you call out for help?"

"Nah. Just thought I heard something. That's all."

As Padbury idled the craft in the middle of the river, the boat party watched the fire blow up Mann Gulch. But after a few minutes, Jansson asked Padbury to head back upriver. On the ride back to Meriwether Canyon, he apologized to Mrs. Padbury for the vomit on his clothes and moved to the back of the launch. Life had never tasted so sweet as at that moment. He just wanted to hurry back to Canyon Ferry, kiss his wife, and hug his kids. He tried to brush the soot from his khaki pants and shirt.

Around the next river bend, they met a speedboat containing Helena National Forest supervisor Arthur Duncan Moir Jr. From 1926 to 1936, Moir had honed his firefighting skills on forests in Montana, Idaho, and Washington, working on fires ranging from 600 to 6,000 acres in size. But the supervisor had seen little action on the ground since. He had transferred to Helena in 1944. Dan Roose, a foreman from the Lincoln district in the Helena National Forest, was also aboard. As Padbury cut his engine, the boats drifted together.

"How's the fire at York?" Jansson asked.

"It's blown up too," Moir said. "Do you want John Eaton's help on this fire?"

"I can sure use him, but I think probably Slim Mayer needs him worse over by York, since it's his first big fire. They've got more to protect over there with the town and those ranches. If we can save Meriwether, our fuels are going to be easier for a while over in the next drainages—Willow Creek and lower Elkhorn. Barring bad breaks, we'll be OK here the rest of the way."

"Good," Moir said. "Slim keeps sobbing hysterically over the radio, 'Send us men, more men. Send us all the men you can get.' We can't get through to him, but I figure things are in bad shape at York and Slim is just reflecting the general panic. Why don't we scramble up to the ledge across the river and see what going on up this gulch?" (Later, the men would learn that the voice on the radio at York belonged to an overexcited laborer without any position of authority who had been sent back to camp to get him out of the way. He had inadvertently come across the radio and had broken the receiver in his excitement.)

Jansson transferred to the speedboat, and by 6:00 the two had scrambled up to an observation point on the bench land across from Beartooth Mountain. The spot offered a direct view into Mann Gulch. The head of the fire was no longer in sight; however, they could see that flames had slopped over the north ridge of Mann Gulch into an unnamed gulch.

"Looks like the blowup is over," Jansson said.

"Not much left up there, is there?" Moir added.

CHAPTER TWENTY-TWO

Joseph Sylvia

Mann Gulch
August 5, 1949

After Wag Dodge brushed by him to lead the crew back up gulch, Joe Sylvia looked to his buddy, Stan Reba.

"What the hell's going on, Stan?" he said. "This guy's going to make us hike twenty miles to get to a fire that's half a mile away. They should have just sent in some groundpounders, for crying out loud."

"Relax, Joe. It looks like the fire has spotted down in the mouth of the gulch," Stan said.

"Then let's go put it out," Joe said.

"I heard Wag's a good fire boss," Stan said.

"He sure is a cool cucumber. You never know what he's thinking," Joe said.

"But he always knows what he's doing," Stan said.

Working on instinct as well as experience, Wag, indeed, understood that he needed to lead the men to a safety zone. He checked his watch: almost 5:40. Half a mile behind him, near the mouth of the gulch, Ranger Bob Jansson sat in a boat in the middle of the Missouri River watching the fire begin to make its run. If Wag could have seen the fire at the mouth of the gulch through the hogback ridge where the gulch doglegged down to the river and blocked his view, he would have ordered the crew to hump it straight up to the ridge top as fast as they could move to escape from the flames headed their way. Instead, unaware of the imminent danger, he headed laterally up the gulch.

Few people beyond the distant lookout and the departing crew of the Doug had noticed an isolated thunderhead in the vicinity of Mann Gulch that day. Smoke and the steep slopes hampered the view of Ranger Jansson, Superintendent Moir, and the jumpers in the gulch. Days later, when Elmer Bloom developed the film he had taken from the Doug, he noticed that some of the footage showed rather intense downdrafts emanating from the thunderhead. These tumultuous winds that had rumpled the jumpers on their float down soon picked up over the fire, distributing burning embers in a helter-skelter fashion. Jansson was in the mouth of the gulch when burning debris began to hit the north slope. He also witnessed the strong wind blowing up the river canyon being deflected off the sheer rock walls to form a vortex that launched numerous firebrands into the air. At first, the firebrands ignited spot fires as big as camp fires. Quickly feeding off the pine needles, grass, and broken branches on the ground, the flames flickered up to five and a half feet high. At this point, the tree canopy acted as a buffer, slowing the wind to about five miles per hour at ground level. But the fire continually gathered strength as it moved up the 18 percent grade of the gulch at about twenty feet per minute. The flame front soon expanded to eleven feet in height. By 5:40, those hot flames were sending up the column of black smoke that startled the daylights out of Wag Dodge.

About ten minutes later, the surface flames hit a thick stand of seedlings and immature Douglas firs, snapping through them like firecrackers. Flames climbed into the crown of a mature pine. The breeze now directly fanned the flames and pushed the hot air ahead so that the bark and needles of a neighboring tree began to decompose and release combustible gases. Soon the fire jumped into that tree and then onto the next. Pushed directly upgulch by the turbulent wind, the fire swept through the treetops, covering up to 120 feet every minute, moving four to six times faster than the fire on the ground. The crew ahead began their retreat up the gulch with a 400-yard head start, a distance the fire could cover in six minutes.

Once again at the head of the line, Wag led the men at a steeper angle back in the general direction of the jump spot, about half a mile away. Soon the trees thinned out, giving the crew a startling view of the fire burning through the heavy timber on the south slope, about half a mile across the gulch. Tongues of whirling flame periodically flickered into the air, solitary trees torched like birthday candles, and ashes and embers swooshed into the air with ever-stronger gusts of wind. David Navon stepped to the side and calmly focused his camera lens directly into the fire.

"What a sight," he said as Sylvia pushed on by.

"Hey, get a shot of me so I can send it to my mom," Joe said.

"Later, when you're humped over the fire line and your butt is smiling at the lens, my friend," Navon replied.

But within a few moments, Joe Sylvia's mood shifted from excitement and anticipation to dread. Behind him in the trees he noticed a steadily increasing crescendo of sound. Loud popping and crunching noises reminded him of the sound a tank made rolling through a forest, knocking over trees, crushing fallen limbs, and splitting rocks beneath its tracks. When he gasped for breath, he tasted the flavor of stringent smoke for the first time. Increasing his pace, Joe stumbled on a loose rock.

Up ahead, Wag Dodge shouted: "Throw away everything that's heavy." Squad leader Bill Hellman, a few places behind

Dodge, stepped to the side and encouraged the men to drop their packs as they ran by. Some men didn't follow the order. Jim Harrison, who had already hiked up and down the steep slopes twice that day and dug fire line by himself for hours, slumped against a tree in exhaustion. Someone stopped to get him back in line, but still he kept his pack.

Joe Sylvia shed his fire pack like a snakeskin and carefully leaned his shovel and pulaski against a tree where he could easily find them. But even without his pack he found himself falling farther behind the older foreman who trotted through the trees. He looked up at the ridge to his left, thinking safety might lie there, but he couldn't see the top. It could have been a mile and a half up or a hundred feet. He continued upgulch behind the others. He could see Dodge and a small cluster of jumpers more than a hundred feet ahead.

Behind Joe, the ground fire picked up speed once it burned out of the thick timber into the more open area carpeted with grass and brush. The steep uphill grade slowed the crew, but it propelled the fire. In the thinner timber, the ground wind accelerated to seven miles per hour. Flame lengths leaped twenty feet into the air and spread ahead up to 280 feet per minute. The fire energy surged to 4,000 BTUs per foot per second. Eventually the ground fire caught up to its cousin in the canopy and began to outdistance it, only sixty seconds behind the jumpers.

A hundred yards after he dropped his tools, Joe Sylvia passed under the last line of trees. Although he felt relieved to be out in the open, Joe didn't realize he'd just entered the most dangerous fire zone east of the Continental Divide—well-cured late summer grass. The danger increased as the flames in the gully below outflanked the men. Furthermore, the fire had already burned through the landing spot where they had stowed their gear. The men still had to run a good mile to reach the head of the gulch. The route directly up to the ridge top was

Joe Sylvia of Plymouth, Massachusetts, 1948 or 1949. Courtesy U.S. Forest Service.

shorter—about 700 feet—but steeper, a 76-degree slope. For every ten feet a man climbed in that direction, he would gain only seven feet in altitude. Plus, the ridge top was capped by rimrock that looked as impenetrable as a castle wall.

Ahead, Joe saw Wag Dodge stop, fumble in his pocket, and then stoop down. About half the crew stood near him in two bunches. For a few moments the wind relented as the convection column overhead began pulling the local indrafts upward. Joe saw smoke suddenly sprout from the grass at the feet of Wag Dodge. With no wind to push Wag's fire laterally, it crisply burned up toward the ridge, blocking the path of the oncoming fire. Joe saw Wag say something to the handful of men nearest him. The other group, a little farther off, began running straight up the steep slope, to the right side of Wag's fire. Then Wag walked around the north rim of his quickly expanding fire. But the rest of the jumpers took off, most running laterally up the gulch. As Joe approached Wag's fire, he heard the foreman shout: "Up this way. Up this way." Joe couldn't tell what he meant. Did he mean straight up to the ridge? It looked too steep, and the main fire was only 100 yards behind. The route up to the head of the gulch, at an 18 percent grade, looked much easier to traverse. When his buddy Stan Reba swept past him, Joe fell in behind. The other stragglers—Leonard Piper and Jim Harrison, still wearing his backpack —also ignored the foreman's entreaties, as if he were a drunken panhandler.

At Joe's heels, 30-foot flames swooped through the grass at rates up to 600 feet per minute. Back in the trees, flames lofted seventy feet into the air. In the two minutes since Wag had ordered the men to drop their packs, the crew had covered about 240 yards. The fire covered the same distance in about half the time.

The wind picked up again, now hugging the ground, and gusting to forty miles per hour. The fanned flames chewed through the carpet of cheatgrass and fescue like a swather, reaching heights from ten to forty feet and still moving about 600 feet every minute. The competing rising heat and blowing wind rolled and sucked at the pulsing flames, which burned red hot in some areas and cooler in others. Flames skipped across the lighter fuels, leaving small pockets of bunch grass or the heavier stems of forbs standing but smoldering. At the wind's slightest suggestion, the fire changed direction. Temperatures within the flames reached 1,800 degrees Fahrenheit—lethal with one inhalation. The fire's progress accelerated to 100 yards per minute.

Joe frantically churned his short legs, trying to keep up with the taller Reba, the former football lineman. The smooth soles of his boots slid from under him on the slick knee-high grass. His ankles wobbled as he dislodged grapefruit-sized rocks.

Both men sank farther toward the gully as they lost elevation along the contour. At one point, Stan turned around to shout encouragement. Joe couldn't hear him but he could read his lips: "C'mon, Joe. C'mon." In the thick smoke, Joe lost sight of the others farther ahead. Then he noticed the flames charging up from the gully below. Stan must have seen it too, because he changed tactics and sharply veered uphill toward the rimrock. Joe followed, falling even farther behind.

Joe's lungs, which already felt as if they were on fire, barely sucked in any oxygen amid the hot gases. Ahead, Stan disappeared into the smoke. A few moments later, something rolled out of the smoke from above and swept past Joe. Something big and colorful. Something making a sound Joe could not distinguish. In a terrifying instant, Joe thought it was the tumbling body of Stanley Reba. He looked down into the gulch, but the object had already disappeared into thick smoke again. A half second later, an upright figure emerged from the dark haze, hopped to the side, and then quickly sprinted past Joe. This time Joe recognized the form of a deer. The buck seemed to have just stepped out of a steam bath, vapor rising from its hairless hide.

Only twenty-five yards behind and below him, ten-foot-high flames lashed out at Joe. Now he couldn't breathe at all; the hot gases seared his throat. Joe wiped something that ran from his nose, then saw the blood on the back of his hand. The skin on his body felt pricked by a billion needles. Near a flat rock as large as a conference table, Joe Sylvia stumbled and fell.

CHAPTER TWENTY-THREE

Wagner Dodge

Mann Gulch
August 5, 1949

As Wag Dodge broke out of the trees, he assessed the situation. Below, deep at the bottom of the gulch, a wall of flame was beginning to outflank his crew. And 100 yards behind, flames crested through the treetops. The smoke belched so thickly from the burning pine needles and grass that he caught only momentary glimpses of the imposing wall of rock that loomed directly above on the ridge top. Far up the gulch, fire had already overrun their landing spot and formed a crescent surrounding them on three sides.

Wag felt beat up and instinctively cupped his free hand around his injured elbow. His side, which he had also banged upon landing, also felt sore. No way could he outrun the fire. He estimated he had thirty seconds to do something. The attitude of his men perplexed him. The eight men who had stopped near him stood nonchalantly watching him as the others, strung out about 100 feet behind, hustled to catch up. They obviously didn't understand the extreme danger they faced. How could he communicate that to them? He thought that ordering them to drop their fire packs and other heavy equipment would have been enough to grab their attention. But some had not even shed their packs. Instead, they had dropped their tools, which they could have used to scrape away fuels from the ground if their last resort was to lie down in the path of the fire and hope the hot gases quickly swept over them. Wag banged the head of his shovel into the ground.

The approaching fire sounded like what—a train? A jet engine? A flooded river? An avalanche? The rising crescendo of the fire outdid them all. Wag knew that once the fire exited the trees, the flame lengths might decrease but they would move even more quickly through the grasses. Maybe some of the crew could outrun the fire, but Wag was sure he didn't have a chance. And he considered it a toss-up as to whether anyone could reach the ridge before the flames knocked them down. And going back into the burn, which would have been the safest escape route, was out of the question. The advancing fire presented a flame front 300 feet thick.

Those men standing by at first stood and stared at him, waiting for orders like good soldiers. Those who were coming out of the timber about 300 feet below looked like they were right in the fire. In desperation, Wag reached into the pockets of his tan canvas pants and took out a book of paper gopher matches—the men called them that because when you tried to light a fire with one you had to immediately "go fer" another. Striking a match head against the black scrape strip on the folded book, Wag bent over and set the keyhole-sized flame to the base of a clump of grass. He then struck another match, but the wind blew it out. As he looked up again, he saw his fire quickly spreading uphill through the grass.

"We'll wait a few seconds to give it a chance to burn out inside the flame ring," he hollered. "And then we'll get into the black where we can make a good stand." The men stared at him, at his fire, then at each other. Wag began circling his fire, hollering and motioning to them to follow, but no one did. Instead, Wag heard someone say, "To hell with this, I'm getting out of here," and the group began to scatter. Bill Hellman turned and began running straight uphill toward the ridgeline. He chose a route that took him up the left side, or downgulch of Wag's fire. Others, who started off walking up the gulch along the more gradual slope, did not seem panicked. The flames were about 100 yards behind them.

Wag couldn't believe his eyes. He crossed his arms before his face and waded through the waist-high ring of flame, then slid about thirty feet down the slope, all the while desperately yelling at the stragglers to join him in the burn area, but they either ignored his pleas or couldn't understand him. If only he'd had a gun he could have intimidated them into the safe zone, just as Ed Pulaski, the hero of the 1910 fires, had done to prevent his crew from retreating from the shelter of a mine adit. But Pulaski had had no trouble getting his men to enter the haven of the cozy tunnel in the first place. It was a different story to get men to lie down on an open hillside when they could see a wall of flame coming right at them. Within moments after Wag dropped to the ground, the main fire swept up to the perimeter of his burned area. As the hot gases enveloped him, Wag turned on his side, poured water from his canteen onto a handkerchief, and held the cotton cloth over his nose and mouth. Where the main fire met the escape fire, huge tongues of flame wagged around the circle of black. Dodge pressed his mouth to the scorched earth to suck in the scant oxygen.

Finding no fuel to sustain their fury, the huge flames quickly subsided where they hit the charred ring. Wag suddenly felt buoyant, as if he were in a big vacuum, and the extreme gusts of hot air lifted him from the ground three separate times. With each onslaught, the foreman flattened his body as shoulder-high flames raced around his sanctuary in pursuit of his crew.

Five minutes passed. Wag sat up but could see little through the smoke. Fifteen minutes after he had started his fire, Wag stood up and brushed himself off. His clothing, covered with soot, showed no scorch marks. He tenderly ran his hand along the skin of his face and through his hair. He felt no burns, and better yet, his sense of touch tingled everywhere, a good sign that his skin had escaped undamaged. He could see little through the thick smoke that choked the gulch. He felt sick to his stomach. He looked at his watch: 6:10.

Moments later Wag's heart stopped when he heard the sound of a shouting voice from a short distance to the east. They must have made it, he thought as he walked toward the voice. About 100 feet below his position and 200 feet farther up the gulch, Wag found Joe Sylvia. But when he approached the kid, Wag felt like dying. Flames had burned away most of Joe's clothes and the flesh of his face had rolled away in places, like crumpled onion paper. Joe's hands were charred to stumps.

"What's your name, son?" Wag gently asked.

"I'm Joe Sylvia. From Plymouth, Massachusetts," he said. Wag found Joe's burns so unsettling that later he would only remember that the kid's last name started with an "S."

"I should have stayed with you," Joe said. "I would have made it. I just couldn't tell what you wanted. I just didn't know."

"You did make it," Wag consoled him. "We'll get you to a hospital. You'll be all right."

Wag helped Joe sit atop the rock that had saved his life by deflecting enough of the heat and burning gases to allow him to continue breathing. Still, as he cut the lacings off Joe's boots, Wag was disturbed by the sandpaper sound of Joe's breathing. After carefully pulling the boots off Joe's swollen feet, Wag placed his canteen on the rock next to Joe.

"I'll go find the other guys and we'll come right back and help you out of here," Wag said. "They should have found shelter on the other side of the ridge." Wag then headed up the scorched hillside into the fog of smoke.

When Joe reached for the canteen he discovered he couldn't pick it up with the blackened stubs that were once his hands, but he didn't call Wag back to help him.

CHAPTER TWENTY-FOUR

Walter Rumsey and Bob Sallee

Mann Gulch
August 5, 1949

Walt Rumsey, Bob Sallee, and Eldon Diettert stopped a little beyond their foreman when he called a halt. Another clump of about five men grouped nearer to Dodge.

Both Rumsey and Sallee had originally been hiking at the back of the line. When Dodge abruptly reversed direction away from the river, they had found themselves at the front of the line. As Dodge passed them to take the lead he had told them to toss down their saws. Unencumbered, the two followed the foreman. When Dodge suddenly stopped again, they drifted by him a little, then pulled up to await further instructions. When Rumsey noticed that Diettert still carried his shovel, he wrestled it from him and threw it down the slope.

Meanwhile, the foreman stooped down and threw a lit match into the grass at his feet. As he fumbled with another match, Wag's fire spread uphill more than 100 square feet in a matter of seconds. Dodge turned and said something to the group of men standing closest by him, but Sallee, Rumsey and

Diettert could not hear. At first Sallee thought the foreman had lost his senses. They had never heard anything about escape fires, not even in training. As Wag's fire took off, the foreman waved to them, yelling, "Up this way." The group of men farthest away could see his mouth move, but they couldn't hear anything over the roar of the fire.

"He wants us to follow alongside his fire," Sallee said. "He's lit it to cut off the main fire."

Rumsey had been eyeballing the ridge for some time, but couldn't see the top through the smoke. But now, as the smoke cleared, he saw that it loomed only about 100 yards above. He took off running on the right side of Wag's fire. Diettert followed close behind him. Sallee hesitated only a moment before chasing after them.

All three anticipated that the main fire would slow down as it broke over the top of the ridge. They had learned that theory of fire behavior in training camp. Wag's fire might add to their chances.

Twenty-one-year-old Walter Bliss Rumsey was no mountain man. He was the second of three children. His parents had worked a patch of land half a mile from the confluence of Pawnee Creek and the Arkansas River near Larned, Kansas. Growing up, Walt had spent many a day with his older sister, Mary Lou, and younger brother, Reed, fishing and hunting ducks. Their parents welcomed the additional protein to the Dust Bowl supper table. Sometimes the children floated the waterways on homemade rafts, pulling ashore to explore long-forgotten Indian campsites.

In high school, the lanky youth had earned an Eagle Scout badge. A short time later, while working in a greenhouse, Walt had decided that he wanted to be either a forester or a farmer. But he had also taken flying lessons and earned a pilot's license by the time he left school to join the navy at seventeen.

Walt told friends he had dropped out of school because he didn't want to depend financially on his mother, who was single by that time. After his discharge, Walt had hooked up with the Forest Service as a lookout, and in 1948 he had worked on the Superior Ranger District in northwest Montana. Now he was on his first fire as a smoke jumper.

It was the alphabet that had initially connected Walt Rumsey and Bob Sallee; whenever foreman Al Stimson barked out assignments for four-man squads, he called: "Rude, Rumsey, Sallee, Sampsel." Walt had been glad to find his close friend from Camp Menard already at Hale Airfield when he had arrived the previous Thursday. Walt was the only smoke jumper in camp who knew Bob's secret—that he was only seventeen years old, a year too young for smoke jumping, according to the regulations.

But despite his youth, Robert Wayne Sallee from Sandpoint, Idaho, presented an imposing figure. At the time of his physical, he had weighed 200 pounds—ten pounds over the official weight limit—but Bob had conned the doctor into noting on his medical record that he would quickly shed the extra weight during training sessions. Bob had also told Earl Cooley, the personnel director, that he was twenty years old even though he had actually been born in 1932.

In 1947, at age fifteen, Bob had begun seasonal work for the Forest Service at a blister-rust camp that was part of the futile multimillion dollar effort to save the western white pine and its cathedral-like forests. The exotic disease had arrived on Vancouver Island from imported white pine seedlings grown in France. The seedlings carried a fungus that colonized the ubiquitous currant and gooseberry shrubs and then spread to the white pines. Blister rust quickly spread to the mainland, where loggers often harvested as much as 50,000 board-feet of white pine per acre, enough to build five medium-sized homes. The timber industry was desperate to protect the valuable resource.

The camps, spread all over the Idaho Panhandle, western Montana, and eastern Washington, employed many high school and college youth during the summer. Every day the men strung lines fifty feet apart through the forests and then worked back and forth between the lines, uprooting all the currant and gooseberry bushes they found. The government would finally give up the battle in the 1960s. Bob escaped the boring work only when he was dispatched to a forest fire.

The next year, in 1948, Bob could not find a better job so he had returned to the blister rust program. When his boss had asked for volunteers to stalk the disease in the Kaniksu Forest, Bob was one of the few who had stepped forward. The new position was a solo job, and most of the other young men preferred the camaraderie of the blister-rust camps. During that wet summer, Bob had charted the spread of blister rust through rugged lonely country. Near the end of the season, a couple of smoke jumpers had joined him. As they described their firefighting adventures, Bob had become enchanted with the idea of parachuting out of an airplane. That winter he had added three years to his age, applied for a position with the jumpers, and had been accepted.

Like most jumpers, Bob especially enjoyed the parachuting. One specific practice jump he would never forget. He liked to tell it this way: "I think there were some politicians involved in it also. They had actually set them up in a little bleacher out beside the spot. It was kind of windy, and when they dropped us—most of the guys weighed about 140 pounds—it blew them completely off the spot. But I weighed 190 and I hit that spot right square in the middle. The only thing is I didn't roll. Cooley said: 'Goddamn you, Sallee. I spent all this time teaching you how to roll and you land like a sack of shit in front of all these people.'"

Walt and Bob had bonded like brothers while training at Camp Menard. When Bob had hesitated before taking his first jump off the tower, Walt had offered encouragement. When Walt had been about to give up on the obstacle course, Bob had urged him on.

Bob hadn't seen Walt since training camp had ended. He'd been working on the Clearwater National Forest at Canyon Ranger Station in Orofino, Idaho, helping out on a trail crew. He had chosen the detail because the Forest Service paid room and board on project work. If he had stayed at the smoke jumper base, he would have had to pay 5 dollars a day for his meals and $1.25 for lodging, even if he had chosen to sleep outside at the fairgrounds.

When he had landed at the ranger station, along with a dozen other jumpers, his boss had offered him the choice of pulling brush or doing trail work. Bob had chosen the trail crew; he had made many friends with district personnel on the trail. Although a packer delivered fresh groceries once a week, the trail boss didn't believe in using mules to transport equipment. Every day, with heavy packs strapped to their backs, the boys raced each other along the trail to the worksite. When they weren't cutting trail, they were scaling trees to repair backwoods telephone lines. After a month of climbing trees and steep mountain paths, Bob had shed the ten pounds plus a few more.

During their flight from the fire in Mann Gulch, Sallee soon took the lead, with Rumsey following and Diettert in the rear, a little to Walt's right. The trio kept to the edge of Wag Dodge's fire. The flames wavered from waist high to shoulder high and Bob felt the heat for the first time. He tried to maintain a course straight up to the rimrock, but the flames kept crowding him away. Walt at one point thought about vaulting the wall of flames and crashing into the black to find shelter there. But the radiant heat from the main fire, which bit through his shirt, kept spurring him on toward the ridge.

None of the trio sprinted outright. No man could on the steep grade. But they maintained a steady pace, lifting knees high with every step. The experience reminded Sallee of the races on the trail crew. Pacing was all important. Still, he struggled for breath and could no longer hear the roar of the fire above his own gasping. At one point he began to have doubts about their escape route. Maybe they should angle off upgulch with the others. On the more gradual slope they could cover more ground. Maybe if he stopped for just a moment to catch his breath he could make it. Even though he felt as if he were running up a vertical wall, he kept moving. His legs didn't feel tired, but he felt as if he couldn't get enough breath into his lungs with all the smoke.

In many ways smoke jumping had presented a series of steps that Bob considered a test of manhood, or at least a process to overcome fear. When he was a boy, he had felt afraid of everything. But one by one he had overcome his anxieties. Smoke jumping had allowed him to put the question of courage aside forever. When he had first joined the jumpers, he had lain awake nights thinking about falling through the sky. When it came to experiencing the big drop from the shock tower for the first time, he had looked down, gritted his teeth, stepped off the 40-foot-high platform—and survived. His next task had been overcoming the fear that he wouldn't be able to step out of the plane on his first practice jump. That would have led to mortification in front of his buddies. But when the spotter had thumped the back of his leg, Bob had taken that long first step. It had seemed to take forever for the 20-foot static line to pull open his chute, but the moment he felt the thump though his body he realized he had become one of an elite group. Outrunning fire seemed just one more test of courage.

"Please, God, please, let me see the top of the ridge," he prayed, something he'd never done before, since he'd never attended church. As if in answer, the wind lofted the blanket of smoke over the ridge at that very moment, exposing the perpendicular rimrock only ten yards ahead. Simultaneously Bob spotted a cleft in the 20-foot-high wall, wide enough for a man to crawl up and through. Without breaking stride Bob angled his shoulders and pushed through. As he stopped atop the rimrock Walt staggered past him, tripped, and collapsed onto a twisted dwarf alpine fir. Bob turned to look for Eldon Diettert but saw no sign of him. For some reason, Eldon had turned aside to run east along the base of the rock wall, searching for another avenue of escape.

As Walt struggled for breath, Bob skipped to the edge of the precipice and looked down upon Mann Gulch. He saw that Wag had entered the charred area ringed by the flames of his expanding fire. Wag still shouted and beckoned to the other jumpers, some of whom were just then passing below him. He couldn't see anyone else heading up toward the rimrock, but he caught a glimpse of David Navon cutting off up hill away from the crew. Then, before heavy smoke once again obscured the scene below, Bob saw Wag lie down in the smoldering ashes at the same time the main fire reached the bottom of his fire. Glancing upgulch, Bob couldn't spot any of the others. With one last look across the top of the rimrock, he looked for Diettert, but couldn't see him.

"So that's what Dodge wanted us to do," Bob thought, "get into the black with him."

Looking westward toward the mouth of the gulch, Bob saw the flame wall from the main fire already breaching the rimrock about a quarter-mile away. He didn't even have to warn Walt. His friend could see by the look on his face that it was time to move again. After crossing the top of the ridge they looked down into a short bowl-shaped gulch that rolled down to the Missouri River. The sight of the water instantly reinvigorated them. The sun, beginning its descent behind the Rocky Mountain Front, appeared as a rosy shadow through the smoke.

Rescue Gulch. Author's collection.

Their initial inclination was to run directly downhill to the water, but the fire that was spilling into the bowl cut off that route. Instead, the two turned and sprinted about 100 yards across the top of the ridge before angling downhill to a rock slide several hundred feet long and seventy-five feet wide. Black lichen covered the rocks.

"We'd better stay here," Walt said. "I don't think the flames will reach us if we stick to the center."

Five minutes passed. They sat facing uphill, waiting. Finally, the fire burst over the ridge directly above them. Buffeted by opposing winds, the flames flapped like flags, sometimes turning downhill toward them, sometimes running sideways along the ridge top. At one point the fire jumped a small gully to establish another front and then jumped back.

Once below the rimrock, it burned straight toward the two jumpers with such intensity that it created an updraft. Minutes later, the fire flanked both sides of the rock slide, forcing Walt and Bob to scurry from side to side to dodge eight- to ten-foot flame lengths. Then it was suddenly over. The fire flowed downhill toward the river. The smoke cleared. They could breathe. The two young men stood up, feeling optimistic that the others had survived as well. The others were waiting around somewhere, just like they were.

"Looks like we dodged that bullet," Bob said.

CHAPTER TWENTY-FIVE

Bill Hellman

Mann Gulch
August 5, 1949

Bill Hellman cursed as the two fires began to pinch together. Wag Dodge's fire cut him off to the right while the wild fire advanced from his left and from below, surrounding him on three sides. Ahead lay the rock wall. The grade was so steep he often had to scramble on all fours. Bill knew that if he couldn't find an escape route through the rock above, he was a goner.

"Damned fool," he yelled, but could hardly hear his own voice above the sound of the inferno. The smoke burned his eyes. Tears streaked the soot on his cheeks. His legs felt heavy, his lungs hot as the fire. But he had not given up.

"Be a blackfoot man. Keep one foot in the black. That's where safety lies."

Although Fred Brauer's familiar training mantra echoed in his mind, Bill could not act. He'd never experienced a fire like this before. In 1947 he'd worked one Class C fire—one that was more than ten acres in size, less than ninety acres—and he'd seen two more in 1948. But they had been well-behaved pure-bred puppies compared to this rampaging back-alley mongrel.

To his right the flames of Dodge's fire flared shoulder high, but Bill couldn't see how thick the ring of fire burned. To his left the flames of the main fire swirled twenty to forty feet into the air and seemed to be hundreds of feet deep. If he couldn't make the top, his only chance was to hold his breath and run through the wall of Dodge's fire. He screamed in anger again as the heat bit at his back. The rock wall stood only twenty yards ahead, but when he reached its base Bill stopped dead in his tracks. He saw no passageway through. If he was going to turn and find shelter in the black of Dodge's fire, he had to do it now. Even as he hesitated, the wind blew the two fires together in a pincer movement. Flames from the main fire bulged out toward him, their tops billowing above his head. Where his shirt and pants fit his body snugly, the hot cloth burned his skin. He tugged the red felt cap lower on the back of his neck. Farther to the east, the main fire hit the rock wall, the flames sweeping over the impediment like a storm surge crashing over a seawall. He was trapped.

Out of the corner of his eye Hellman spotted the crack in the rock face. It wasn't much—a narrow passageway strewn with debris. There was no other shelter. He stumbled into the crevice and flopped onto his belly as the hot gases around him burst into flame. The heat seared his lungs. Bill passed out.

When he recovered consciousness, Bill gagged for breath. He hurt both inside and out. He was alive, but his throat felt as dry as parchment. Then he noticed that his boots were partially burned off. He reached down and beat out flames eating away at the bottom right leg of his pants. The flames burned the palms of his hands. Slowly he crawled ahead out of the narrow crevice. On the ridge top, the grass smoked like a spring pasture burn. Behind, black skeletons of charred trees stuck out above the acrid smoke engulfing Mann Gulch. Retching in a coughing spasm, Bill dropped to his knees. He couldn't seem to get air into his lungs. And he craved a drink of water.

Atop the ridge, the few stunted trees that had been able to take root and survive in the windswept environment still burned. Bushes that were sheltered in rock crevices had survived unscathed. On the other side of the ridge, the flame wall slowly rolled down through a gentle basin. Occasionally, a gust of wind hurried the fire, lofting smoke into the sky. At those times Bill caught glimpses of the welcome water of the Missouri River, just half a mile below. The sight made him even thirstier. A mile to the east, the fire had reached the head of Mann Gulch. Despite the heat still rising from the ground around him, Bill felt cold. It seemed so far to reach the water, but he felt so thirsty.

Bill took mincing steps as he picked his way down into the bowl. The ash-covered slopes proved to be even more slippery than the grass had been. After he descended about thirty yards, he heard footsteps running in long strides down to him. But when he turned, he saw a keg-sized boulder bouncing toward him. Bill lost his footing and fell on his back. His bones ached from the impact, but the sensation felt strange. After he pulled himself to his feet, he reached behind to feel his back. He felt no shirt. Plus the seat of his pants was gone. But worse, Bill felt no sensation on his skin where he touched with his fingers. He screamed, not from physical pain but from fear. In the next instant other voices yelled out to him from the east. Others had made it. The thought consoled him. He wouldn't die here alone. Maybe he would even be rescued. The guys had survived the fire. Now that was a story to tell Gerry. And his son, when he grew up.

Bill heard the men sidehilling toward him, dislodging rocks, cursing when they slipped. He didn't recognize the voices that called out. Maybe they weren't even from the crew. Eventually two figures emerged from the smoke, wearing the distinctive red felt caps. He watched them cross a little draw. He finally recognized Rumsey and Sallee.

"You boys bring any water?" Bill asked. The two stood staring at him.

"You feeling okay?" Walt asked.

"Thirsty as hell," Bill said. "And like a piece of toast in some places. I made it almost to the top when it got me." His face, arms, and legs were also severely burned, with loose flesh hanging in patches.

"Did you see another guy up there?" Bob asked. "There was someone right behind us, but he didn't follow us through the passage in the rock."

"No. I haven't seen anyone," Bill said. "Damn, boys. Give me a drink, will ya? It feels like my throat's full of sand."

Hellman took a canteen from Sallee, took a sip, and then coughed it back up.

"Better drink slowly," Rumsey urged. "There isn't much left in there anyway."

Hellman drank again, this time holding it down. Rumsey and Sallee helped him climb up on a large flat rock to keep his wounds out of the ashes. That's when they saw the burns on his back. They looked across at one another, fear in their eyes. The two young men encouraged Hellman to keep talking to get his mind off the pain, but the sight of the Missouri River in the waning light drove Bill crazy.

"Maybe I should go back over the ridge and get the first aid kit," offered Sallee, a bit unnerved.

"You think it wasn't burned up?" Rumsey asked.

Sallee shrugged.

"Can you lug back a water can too?" Bill asked. "I feel so goddamn thirsty I could drink that river down there."

"Yeah. Go ahead," Rumsey urged his friend. "Maybe you'll run into some of the other guys. Bill's going to need some help getting down from here."

Bob Sallee felt relieved to go on a quest. It had been hard for him to look at Hellman's burns, to smell the odor of charred flesh. He just wanted to keep moving, find the others, and go fight the fire. The world had changed into something he no longer understood, and he wanted things to get back to normal. Put out the fire, lug the jump packs down to the river, enjoy a nice boat ride, then fly back to the Clearwater Forest and go back to work on the trail crew. Except for Rumsey, Bob didn't know any of the guys who had scattered across the gulch. He didn't even know one personal fact about the kid who had followed them to safety only to turn away at the last moment. And Bill Hellman had made him promise to give a message to his wife—only now, Bob couldn't remember what he had said.

Things weren't supposed to happen this way. No one had prepared him to deal with such a tragedy. "During travel carefully choose best routes . . . study your map . . . identify country with map . . . follow instructions and trust your foreman." The trainers had talked as if there would always be a convenient place to run to for safety should a fire blow up. Like the forest was designed that way, just to protect firefighters. Or if worse came to worse, you ran into the black. Just like Fred Brauer always said. But what if you couldn't see the black? What if an intensely hot orange wall blocked the way? The whole afternoon had been like a test that was staged to see just how good the men were. When he and Walt had survived unharmed, his first thought had been that they had passed the test. So the others must have too. After all, they were smoke jumpers. They were the best. They could run faster, dig line longer, and outlast any groundpounder. But the sight of Bill Hellman had crushed that feeling of invincibility, and suddenly Bob lost his desire to pursue a full-time job with the Forest Service.

When Bob surmounted the ridge top, the youngster looked down into a black pit sprinkled with small fires that looked like tiers of candles in a darkened cathedral, their smoke rising like burning incense. In some places, blackened clumps of grass smoldered without flame. He took a couple of tentative steps over the edge toward the bottom but quickly stopped. He did not want to go back into the place from which he had escaped. And what was the point? He could see that the fire had pushed past the head of the gulch. All the equipment would have been reduced to cinders, including the first aid kits. Bob turned back. But just as he reached Hellman and Sallee, he heard a holler from above. When he turned, he saw a lone figure on the ridge top silhouetted against the smoke. Bob hollered back and began retracing his steps up the slope.

"What's your name, son?" Wag Dodge asked as the two met.

Bob studied Wag's face and clothes. The black smudges on his face did not have the crisp texture of burns. He could not detect a single singe on Wag's shirt or pants. He stopped himself from walking behind to inspect Wag from the rear. The foreman looked dumbfounded.

"You okay?" Bob asked.

"Yeah. Where are the others?"

"Hellman and Rumsey are down below a ways," Bob said. "Hellman doesn't look so good. He got caught by the fire."

"We'd better get down to them," Wag said. "I came across another fellow in pretty bad shape on the other side."

As Bob led the way, Wag thought about the cussing he'd give Hellman. He had even almost grabbed this kid, whose name he'd already forgotten, to shake him. Why the hell hadn't he come when he had called? All it would have taken was one other man to get behind his escape fire, and they all would have followed like mules after a bell mare. And now they would all be walking safely out of Mann Gulch, slapping each other on the back, and thanking the good Lord. Instead, he had two men injured, two safe, and eleven nowhere to be seen. They could still be running for their lives for all he knew. But hopefully they had stumbled upon some rock slide or had been able to angle back behind the fire. Or better yet, they had made it down to the river. Wag could still hear the fire as it roared north across another ridge. He then altered one option—no way could they still be running.

Wag saw his squad leader and the other jumper in the gloom, sitting near a big rock. Hellman should have known better than to try and outrun the fire. Stick to the black, that's basic training. Hellman himself must have repeated it to the recruits a hundred times every spring. And if there's no black, what do you do? You create your own safety zone. But that wasn't standard training. That idea had come to Wag in a flash the moment he emerged from the trees and spied the short flashy fuels spreading out before him like a dried-up lawn. It had been pure instinct—light the grass, get rid of the fuels, and you have a chance. Hellman should have seen it too. The damn fool should have known he couldn't outrun a fire like that. But when Wag got close enough to see Hellman's damaged skin and smell the burned flesh, his anger melted like ice in fire.

"How's it going, Bill?" Wag asked.

"Fine," Hellman answered. "Feels like I got burned up a little. I'm thirsty as hell. You got any water?"

"No, I left a canteen with another fellow over on the other side," Wag said. "I can't remember his name. Began with an 'S' . . . S something-or-other. Wait a second." Wag fumbled in a pocket of his jacket and pulled out a can of Irish white potatoes.

"I picked this up when me and that fire guard went back for dinner," Wag said.

"Damn, I feel all dried out inside," Bill hoarsely muttered.

"Don't worry," Wag said. Wag took off his coat and placed it on the rock near Hellman. He also set down the pulaski, but held onto his shovel. "We'll get you out of here as soon as we

can. One of you guys come with me. We've got to get to a telephone. The other stay here with Bill."

Bob Sallee stepped forward. "I'll go with you." He cast an
anxious glance toward Rumsey. Walt, still exhausted from his
race with the fire, didn't argue.

"Hurry back," Walt said.

As he watched the two jumpers descend the slope, Walt settled down on a flat rock opposite Hellman. When Hellman
complained of thirst again, Walt punctured the tin of Irish potatoes so Bill could drink the liquid from the can, but the salted
water only made him thirstier. At first Hellman expressed no
hope that he would survive, but as time passed he regained
some confidence. He talked of his wife and new child and how
his parents had often encouraged him to attend Catholic Mass
more often. "Now I wish I had," he told Rumsey. "Will you pray
with me for a while?" Rumsey agreed, but the two soon realized they did not know any prayers in common, so they prayed
quietly to themselves. Later on, all Bill Hellman could talk about
was how thirsty he felt.

As Dodge and Sallee picked their way down the slope, the
smoke occasionally lifted, allowing them a glimpse of the river.
When they caught up with the fire, they easily hopped over
the slow-creeping three-foot flames. A few minutes later, as dusk
fell, they stood on the shore of the Missouri River.

"I never got a map from that fireguard," Wag said. "I have
no idea which way to go. Do you have a compass?"

"No," Bob said.

Wag tied a red bandanna to his shovel handle, then stuck
the tool into the sand. Then the two headed north, downstream. Out on the dark river they heard motorboats passing
by, ferrying locals who had come to look at the fire. The two
jumpers hollered and shined their flashlights, but the motors

drowned out their voices. The boats turned and began heading back upstream.

"You know, I think the Meriwether guard station is the other way," Wag finally said. "That marina must be back up that way too. We'd better turn around." They retraced their steps, but another hundred yards brought them to a sheer rock cliff that abutted the river, blocking their passage.

"What now?" Bob asked.

"I guess we've got to climb the damn thing." At that moment they heard a dog barking from across the river.

"You think there's a house over there?" Bob asked.

"Not way out here," Wag said. "Probably campers. Or they could just be sitting out there in a boat. . . . Hey, anyone out there on the river?" he hollered.

The dog barked again. Then they heard a voice say: "Just us duckies."

"Could you please help us?" Wag hollered. "We've got some injured firefighters up on the ridge."

A moment later an outboard motor coughed to life and Gene Naegel of Helena guided his craft in to pick them up.

CHAPTER TWENTY-SIX

Rescue Party

Meriwether Campground
August 5, 1949

Forester Robert Jansson stared into the face of Wag Dodge and intently listened to every word the soot-covered man said. Still he could make neither heads nor tails of what he heard. Just minutes earlier, Jansson had finally gotten radio confirmation from the Helena dispatcher that the smoke jumpers had indeed parachuted into Mann Gulch. But no one could tell him what their present location was. The men had not contacted Hale Airfield in Missoula or Canyon Ferry by radio. Jansson assumed they had pulled out of the head of Mann Gulch and crossed over, either into Willow Creek or Elkhorn Creek.

Up to that point, Jansson had had enough to worry about concerning his own men. When he had returned to Meriwether Campground, he had radioed in the next day's order, then tried to calm the new arrivals. He heard no word from his assistant, Hank Hersey, who was still on the ridge with the first batch of recruits. The orange light from the raging inferno above spooked the men in the campground. Knowing he was dealing with a lot of greenhorns, some of whom were still drunk,

Jansson started organizing them. He assigned a camp boss, a foreman, a timekeeper, and a radio operator. He also ordered the cooks to prepare supper for the thirty tired and hungry men who would be coming off the fire line soon. Jansson was unaware that some of the men hanging around the fire camp were actually tourists wanting to get in on the action.

Earlier that evening Jansson had sent orders up to Hersey, via a water buck, to bring his men down before dark. Now the light had faded, and still there was no word from Hersey. The nervous strain was getting to the ranger; he had to keep busy. In the back of his mind, Jansson kept hearing the sound of a voice calling out through the fire whirl. At 8:50, just as he got on the radio to find out the exact location of the jumper landing spot, Wagner Dodge entered the cabin. A dozen men who had been hanging around the campfire followed him in. Bob Sallee, who had accepted a proffered sleeping bag, lay down outside near the fire pit.

"The fire blew up on us," Wag repeated. "We couldn't see it behind a finger ridge by the canyon mouth until it was too late. And we had to make a run for it. I've got two men injured, burned up pretty bad. And I'm missing eleven others."

With every word Dodge muttered, the men surrounding him relayed the information to those gathered outside the door. The buzz in the cabin affected Jansson's faulty hearing and he became even more confused.

"You were in Mann Gulch?" he asked. "How did the men get injured? What are you trying to tell me? Wait. Follow me."

Jansson led Wag out the cabin door and up the trail. When others began trailing them, Jansson turned on them. "Don't anyone come up here and bother us, or you'll never earn another penny from the Forest Service," he said. About fifty yards up the trail, Jansson stopped and told Dodge to repeat his story. This time the words sank in. Two men badly burned. Three men safe. Eleven men missing. Dodge believed they had outrun the fire.

Jansson led him back to the cabin, where he radioed Helena to send medical help. Dodge walked with a slight limp and clutched his ribcage. His punctured elbow also hurt.

"Do you want us to head up there?" one man asked.

"No," Jansson answered. "There's nothing we can offer those men until the doctors get here."

"We should do something right now," another said. "We just can't sit here."

"We'd better get the hell out of here ourselves before that fire burns down into the canyon," said another.

"What if Hersey and his crew are burned up too?" someone shouted.

"Maybe we should drag some hose up there and start wetting down the wall of the canyon," another voice offered.

"Dammit!" Jansson shouted. "I won't have my men panicking. If you guys are worried about getting burned up, go stand by the river. If the fire comes on down, just wade out into the water. Tell Fred Padbury to stand by in case we need to evacuate the camp by boat." Turning to an assistant ranger from the Lincoln Ranger District who had been assigned to the fire, he said, "In the meantime, Roos, you organize a rescue team."

About 10:10 a crowd of men once again squeezed through the doorway of the small cabin.

"Now what the hell's going on?" Jansson asked. Then he saw Hank Hersey, the foreman of the ground crew, in the doorway.

"Good to see you, Hank," Jansson said. "Everybody OK? Everyone make it down?"

"Yeah. Everyone's safe. But that damn fire has turned into a real hellhole."

"Any sign of Harrison?" Jansson asked.

"We found the line he started digging. But no sign of the kid. He dug a hell of a long way, but the fire eventually jumped his line. He must have been burned up for sure."

"We met a fireguard up there," Wag Dodge offered.

"Jim Harrison?" asked Jansson.

"I don't remember his name," Wag said. "He was wearing glasses. I think he might have jumped with us last year."

"That's Jimmie," Jansson said. "And you think he's all right?"

"I'm hoping so. We didn't hear anyone else in that neighboring gulch answering our calls after the fire. Most of the other guys took off sidehilling upgulch rather than straight up and over the ridge. I'm thinking they made it into the next drainage."

With Jim Harrison involved, it became a personal matter for Robert Jansson. He had taken a shine to Jim the moment he'd met him. A bright, responsible college kid who always worried about getting into town on Sunday to go to church. Early on, Jansson had realized that someday Harrison would join the agency permanently and likely become a ranger himself. Suddenly the fire didn't seem to matter. Let the trees burn, let the flames char the beautiful wilderness. All that mattered was rescuing the injured men and locating the missing. Wag Dodge accepted a sleeping bag and joined Sallee outside, but he could not sleep. After a few minutes he got up and limped back into the cabin.

At about 10:30, a young man burst into the cabin. "Ranger Jansson," he said, "a boat just passed by, they said they'd spotted a bunch of men huddled by the river up near Elkhorn Creek."

"Did they talk to them?" Jansson asked.

"No."

"Are they still here?"

"Who?"

"The people who reported the sighting."

"No. They just shouted as they motored by, heading toward Hilger Landing."

Jansson looked at Dodge. The foreman's face flushed to life.

"You had better stay here, Dodge," Jansson said. "You look pretty done in. We'll take that other fellow you brought out to lead us back to the injured fellows when the doctors get here. I'm going to head down river now to find the others. Roos, you get enough men to carry two stretchers and wait until the doctors get there. After I pick up the other men, I'll tie in with you at Mann Gulch."

But the mystery of the missing men remained unsolved and the report of them huddled at the mouth of Elkhorn Creek proved to be false. Jansson shouted repeatedly from the bow of the boat but aroused no replies. He later discovered that the reports had been based on sightings of Sallee and Dodge. Much discouraged, he returned upriver to Mann Gulch, where half a dozen boats and about twenty men had assembled, including Doctor T. L. Hawkins and Doctor R. S. Haines of Helena. But there were two problems. Bob Sallee pointed out that the wounded Hellman waited in a little gulch farther downstream from Mann Gulch, where it would be easier to reach him. Plus, the doctors, in their haste, had forgotten to bring litters to carry out the wounded.

Jansson sent the fastest speedboat back to Hilger Landing for the stretchers, then winnowed out his troop of volunteers, telling the tourists, or kibitzers, as he called them, to go home. "I appreciate your concern and the fact that you want to help out these boys," Jansson said, "but we don't want too many people climbing up there. We're going to be walking through a fire area and there will be danger from rolling rocks and snags. We can't afford to take chances, so I want only the following men to come with me: Granville Edgmond, James Taylor, Frank Holland, Marvin Simmons, Jack Diamond, Martin Wolstein, Stanley Grudisher, and Don Roos. Harvey Jensen, if you can hang around with your boat, we'll use you to run messages over to Mann Gulch and to ferry out the injured."

Five minutes later, the rescue crew landed at the mouth of the unnamed bowl north of Mann Gulch on Elkhorn Bay that in the coming days would be called Rescue Gulch. Some men

fidgeted while others silently stared up at the scattered fires still
burning on the slope and atop the ridge. Bob Sallee, tired and
ragged, kept to himself. He wasn't the type of person who could
describe how it felt to look death in the face. When one of the
rescuers asked him what it had been like, he had no answer.

Finally, at about 11:30, the drone of a speedboat bounced
off the canyon walls. As soon as the craft landed, the rescuers
took up the litters and plasma and gathered around Jansson.

"Be cautious, men," Jansson told them. "Stay together in single file. And keep your eyes open."

The small fires scattered across the slope created an illu-
sion that an army of men with their cook fires was bivouack-
ing on the hillside. But nothing stirred in the quiet night as
the rescue team angled up the slope, with Bob Sallee leading
the way. At one point, the trunk of a dead tree blew to pieces
when its resin became so hot it passed the point of ignition.
Overhead, where the smoke thinned, bright stars shined in
the tranquil sky. A slight aura of orange glowed over the ridge
to the east, where the head of the fire had slowed for the night.
The men continuously flashed their headlamps to the slope
above, searching for burned-out snags or dislodged boulders
and logs. As he emerged from behind a line of big rocks two-
thirds of the way up the hill, Bob Sallee heard a shout. Soon
his friend, Walt Rumsey, was standing in the light of his headlamp.

"What are you doing down here, Walt?" Bob asked. "Is
Hellman all right?"

"Yes, I guess," Walt said. "He just drove me nuts asking for
water all the time. He threatened to walk down to the river
himself if I didn't come down and get him something to drink.
I'm sure glad you guys showed up."

Jansson recognized Rumsey from a former work detail and
fell in behind him as they continued up the hillside. "Any sign
of Jim Harrison up there?" he asked.

"No," Rumsey said. "I don't think he got through. He looked pretty beat last time I saw him, having done all that hiking and digging all day. But you know, we all could have made it if we'd only followed Wag. The only reason I made it was that the Lord was good to me—he put wings on my feet, and I ran like hell."

Rumsey, Sallee, and Jansson pushed ahead of the main party with a water canteen. They heard Hellman hollering about half a mile away. They reached him about 12:35 on the morning of August 6th. The district ranger bit his tongue as the beam of his flashlight brushed across the firefighter's face. Flesh had sloughed off Hellman's hands and face. Even though the smell of burned flesh almost overwhelmed him, Jansson moved to Hellman's side and steadied a canteen at his mouth. But rather than feeling refreshed, Bill Hellman clutched his stomach after taking a sip and bent over in pain.

"Are you a doctor?" Bill gasped.

"No, they're right behind us," Jansson told him.

"I think I need a doctor," Bill said. "I think I'm in pretty bad shape."

When the doctors arrived about fifteen minutes later they administered a shot of morphine to Hellman and set the intravenous tubes to administer plasma. They decided to leave his charred clothing where it stuck to his skin and spread a thick salve over the exposed areas. Through it all, Bill Hellman never complained. Some of the men standing in the shadows began to weep.

At 1:20, Jansson instructed Sallee and Don Roos to accompany him over the ridge into Mann Gulch to locate the other injured man. They hoped to find Joe Sylvia by the time the doctors finished with Hellman to avoid any further delay in his treatment.

CHAPTER TWENTY-SEVEN

Joseph Sylvia

Mann Gulch
August 6, 1949

Joe Sylvia didn't feel much pain. In fact, he felt euphoric. The flames had burned deep enough to kill the nerve endings in his skin. Every once in a while he put his charred fingers to his face and felt nothing. At one point, he noticed that a patch of what seemed to be limp tissue paper stuck to his finger. Skin, he thought.

After Wag Dodge left him, Joe stood on the tabletop surface of the large rock, watching dusk turn to darkness. In spots, the fire still burned rich in the gully below and in clumps of trees on the opposite slope. In the grass, the flames had for the most part subsided. As the smoke lessened, Joe watched the stars appear. For each star, a memory of childhood entered his mind, and Joe often fell into surreal dreams through the long night.

Joe dreamed he was back home in Plymouth, plying his homemade kayak through the placid waters of Massachusetts Bay. The outdoors had always attracted him more than schoolbooks, and when he wasn't working odd jobs to supplement the family income he had spent his time hunting, fishing, and swimming. Joe dreamed of digging for quahogs on the beach and looking for horseshoe crabs and conches as he raced his four brothers through the knee-deep shallows at low tide.

"Shark," his sister, Thelma, shouted, sending all but Joe wildly splashing out of the water to the security of the beach. Joe knew better. One evening, he had watched a fisherman reel in a six-foot-long shark.

"What's that?" he asked.

"A sand shark," answered the young man, who wore the brimless cap of a grease monkey. Joe recognized him from the garage at the end of the block.

"Can those eat you?" Joe asked, staring at the tightly closed mouth of the fish.

"Nah. Teeth too small." As the man pried open its mouth and jerked out the hook, Joe stared down the shark's throat. When the man looked up again, Joe saw the face of his friend, Stanley Reba.

"Hey, Joe."

Sylvia snapped his head up. Had someone called? He couldn't tell if he had dreamed the sound or actually heard it.

"Stan?" Joe whispered. He cleared his aching throat, then in a louder voice he called out, "Anyone down there?"

A small fire that slowly ate at a log crackled. Joe Sylvia hunkered down, hugging his knees, trying to keep from sliding off the slanted rock. He shivered. When this was all over, the first thing he planned to do was head back to Minnesota with Stan. They were a good team. Joe kept Stan laughing with his wise-cracks and antics, Stan led Joe back to safety whenever he pushed things too far. Stan called him Whitefish, never Little Joe. He'd be damned if he let anybody call him by that nickname again. Some wise-guy jumper—a navy bum, no less—had called him Little Joe when he was working on the Clearwater National Forest in Idaho a couple of years ago. Joe had punched the guy in the nose. How dare a sailor get smart with a marine?

Another time, he and the same sailor had gotten into a shoving match while waiting in line for chow. Stan had pulled them apart, saying: "You guys have already burned up too much energy today." But Joe had been more careful around the smoke jumper camp. Fred Brauer did not allow any fighting. "You guys don't have to love each other, you just have to respect one another," Fred had said once. "You'll never know when you'll have to depend on the next guy to save your life."

Joe now realized the wisdom of those words. He pressed the canteen between his burned stubs and gave it a shake, just to hear the water slosh around. Why hadn't he asked Wag Dodge to loosen the cap for him? And where had Dodge put his boots? Them puppies had cost him a fortune. He and Stan had driven all the way to Spokane to the White factory so the cobbler could measure their feet. Stan had taught him the smoke jumper technique of tying the laces. Rather than lace the boots straight up, you skipped every other hole when you got to the ankle area, then laced back down and continued back up. That way the tongue of the boot didn't crinkle at the ankle. Joe had never gotten a blister or a callous wearing those boots. The canteen slipped out of his hands, teetered on its side, and rolled off the rock.

"Stanley?" Joe yelled this time. "Anyone? Hey guys? Where'd you all go?"

"Over here," a voice from the ridge yelled. "Shout again so we can find you."

Joe wasn't asleep this time. That was no dream or ghost.

"Is that you, Stan?" he yelled. "Come on. Let's get the hell out of here."

Minutes later Joe saw the columns of light from the headlamps of District Ranger Robert Jansson and Assistant Ranger Don Roos. He also spotted Bob Sallee's beam heading back to the top of the ridge. "Geez, it didn't take you long to get here," Joe Sylvia amiably said as the men reached him.

"I thought we were pretty slow," Jansson said.

"What time is it? About five o'clock?" Sylvia asked.

"Nah, it's only two," Jansson said. The ranger's headlamp momentarily lit up Joe's face.

"Please don't look at my face," Joe said, as he jerked his head to the side. "It's too awful."

"Hell, I wish I looked that handsome," Jansson said, taking off his headlamp.

"I don't think I'll be able to walk down out of here," Joe said.

"Your walking for this night is through," Jansson said. "You're going to get a free ride out. The doctors will be here in a little while to take care of you. Then we'll carry you out on a stretcher. You're going to be all right."

"Where's Stan? Is he with you?" Joe asked.

"I don't know," Jansson said. "So far we've rounded up Wag Dodge, Bill Hellman, Sallee, and Rumsey."

"Stan Reba. That's the guy I want to see. He's a big Polack and a hell of a guy."

"The rest of the men must have made it over the head of the gulch," Jansson said. "They're probably holed up in some other drainage tonight. I'm sure we'll find them in the morning."

"Yeah. I'm sure Stan's all right," Joe said.

Jansson climbed up on the rock and knelt next to Sylvia and offered him a drink from the canteen. Joe had sat alone for seven hours with no water.

"Why don't you sit down, son? I'll steady the canteen for you," Jansson said. He noticed that the flames had reduced Joe's hands to charred stubs. When Joe finished drinking, Jansson peeled an orange and fed it to Joe section by section.

"My boots?" Joe said. "My foreman cut the laces and slipped them off my feet for some reason. I've got to find them. I think he put them under the rock."

Dan Roos flashed his light beneath the lip of the rock and found the boots. When he placed them at Joe's feet, the injured man seemed to calm down. "Thanks," Joe said. "Say, you guys didn't bring a blanket with you by any chance? It's gotten real cold. Don't you think?"

The two men, dressed only in thin cotton shirts, looked helplessly at each other. Roos had given his jacket to Rumsey. Jansson hadn't felt the need for a jacket on this warm night, especially with the strenuous climbing and the fires burning all about. Both men pulled off their shirts and slipped them over Joe's shoulders. Then they cuddled up to Sylvia on either side and put their arms around him, hoping their body heat would give him some comfort. Both rescuers breathed shallowly through their mouths, turning their heads away from the man sandwiched between them, trying to avoid the overwhelming odor of Joe's burned flesh. Even before they had reached Sylvia, they had smelled the scent rising from the hillside.

About 2:20, Sallee led the doctors and the litter crew to the site. Six other men had stayed with Hellman, waiting until dawn to carry him down to the river. Sallee went to the far side of the rock, sat down, leaned his back against it, and tried to sleep.

"Are we jeopardizing these men by waiting for daylight?" Jansson asked.

"No," said Doc Hawkins, in a voice loud enough so that the injured jumper could hear. "Joe's going to be all right. The wait won't endanger him. It would hurt him more if we drop him on this steep slope. Right, Joe?"

Since the doctors had left the only blanket with Hellman, the rest of the men removed their jackets and shirts, some even their undershirts, and piled them atop the shivering Joe Sylvia. As the painkillers took effect, Joe became quite calm. At dawn, Jansson called four stretcher carriers away from the rock. "The kid said he might have heard voices from below," he said. "But he wasn't sure. Let's string out here a few yards apart and sidehill for a

hundred feet or so and see what we come up with. If this guy
made it only this far, there may be others nearby who are un-
conscious. Move slowly, and try not to line up right above the
next guy. You don't want to get hit by any loose rocks."

Jansson took the top position and headed out first. He had
taken only a few steps before he spotted a body. The other men
quickly huddled around the corpse. The body pointed uphill.
One of the dead man's legs was cocked at the knee, the other
outstretched. Death had come instantaneously, the smoke and
poison gases smothering him in midstride. All the clothing but
the shoes had burned off the body. Flames had charred the flesh
over 100 percent of the exposed skin. No hair clung to the skull.

"Poor bugger," someone said.

"It looks like he was shot through the heart in midstride,"
another said. "I saw that during the war."

Robert Jansson knelt down, inspecting the area around the
body. "There must have been a terrific draft of superheated
air that knocked him down," he said. "I saw that wall of flame
early last evening about when I was scouting the mouth of the
gulch. It must have been 600 feet high to roll over the ridge
and down the other side like it did. It must have covered 3,000
acres in ten minutes or less. What's this here?"

Jansson picked a small tin box out of the ash. He flicked
back the sliding lid and two tabs of Vaporole ammonia cap-
sules tumbled out onto his palm.

"Looks like a snakebite kit," one man offered.

"Look around, men," Jansson said. "See if you can find anything else."

The men bent down to inspect the area at their feet. "Here,"
one man said, "a compass box."

"Here's a pocketknife and a comb," another said.

One man found two Indian-head pennies.

Jansson looked more closely at the head of the dead man
and could see the wires of eyeglasses still in place behind the

ears. A gold medallion with a Catholic emblem hung around the neck of the body. Another man handed a key to Jansson. "It's a Forest Service key," he said.

"Sweet Jesus," said Jansson as he flashed his headlamp on the key. "It's got number 18 engraved in it. This is the key to the Meriwether guard station. That's Jim Harrison. And that snakebite kit. I gave that to him just last week. Just before he started mowing the lawn at the station. I can't believe it."

Robert Jansson felt crushed. He had never lost a man on the job before or had any seriously hurt. He took out his note-book and wrote: "James Harrison—found by Robert Jansson." He tore out the page and placed it under a rock near Harrison's right hand. Then he picked Jim's pocket watch out of the ash.

"There's more men to find, I'm sure," Jansson said, getting to his feet.

Artifacts found near body of James Harrison. Courtesy U.S. Forest Service.

Jansson studied the watch face. The hands of the clock were frozen at 5:56. Below the regular clock face, the small second hand, with its separate circle of sixty hash marks, had stopped at forty-five seconds.

Remembering that Rumsey had reported that Harrison had seemed exhausted when the men began their final sprint from the fire, Jansson assumed the other men had made it farther up the gulch or over the ridge into Rescue Gulch. So he guided the searchers farther up the slope. But they found no more bodies. From the ridge top he hollered down to Hellman's crew to begin carrying the wounded man back into Mann Gulch. As he headed back down to Sylvia's rock, a number of searchers simultaneously spotted another body. They called Bob Sallee to join them.

"I think it's Bennett," Sallee said. "Robert Bennett."

Jansson again wrote the man's name on a sheet of paper stating that Sallee had identified him, signed his name, and then placed the sheet under a rock by the hand of the body. He looked at his watch—4:35.

When Hellman's crew reached the others, four men hefted Sylvia's stretcher while Jansson and the doctor led the way. They picked their way slowly down the hillside. Ash puffed from the ground with every footstep. Lying on the stretcher, Joe Sylvia stared into the sky. Every once in a while, a stretcher-bearer asked, "How you doing, champ?" Sometimes Joe smiled and murmured a reply, other times he didn't seem to hear them. Soon the group entered the forest of blackened trunks. Without needles, the tree branches seemed like contorted wire sculptures. The forest floor was completely clear of brush. An occasional flame still flowered from a log or fallen trunk. Something below caught Jansson's eye—another badly burned body.

"You guys wait here," Jansson told his men. "And don't put down that stretcher." The doctors walked with him to the body.

"Poor son of a bitch," Doc Haines said. "See that bone. Looks like he broke his leg and rolled downhill directly into the fire. Landed on his back. Looks like he was in agony."

"Not much left of him," Jansson said. "I wonder who it is?" He didn't bother leaving a note with the body.

At the bottom of the gulch, Jack Diamond, one of the stretcher-bearers for Bill Hellman, glanced back up toward the area where they had found the three bodies and saw three small fires burning in a pattern that formed a perfect cross.

CHAPTER TWENTY-EIGHT

Lois Jansson

Canyon Ferry Ranger Station
August 7, 1949

Lois Jansson clipped out the articles about the Mann Gulch fire from the daily newspapers and stuffed them into a large envelope. With the ranger station converted into a dispatch center, she had no time to read them now. The phone continually rang. Voices squawked out of the radio. Outside the building, drivers waited by their vehicles to run errands into town or to pick up tired firefighters waiting at backcountry trailheads. When she wasn't needed in the office, Lois hurried over to her kitchen to cook for hungry sooty firefighters.

On Friday evening, Lois had gotten an inkling of what was going on at Mann Gulch when her husband, Bob, hadn't shown up for a picnic dinner with their old college friends, Bob and Helen Casebeer. After dinner Lois had taken the party over to the office to listen to the chatter from several fires over the short-wave radio. As the night had worn on, the messages had become more and more urgent. After the Casebeers departed, Forest Service worker Bill Fry had reported for duty to help his colleague Dave Schmitt. At about 10:00, Lois had put the children to bed and then headed back to the office, carrying a tray of sandwiches. As she passed an open window, she had heard Dave say to Bill: "My God. Bob is going up there into the fire. They haven't found Hank yet and Jim Harrison is still missing. Whatever you do, don't let Lois know. We've got enough trouble without a couple of hysterical wives on our hands."

Without a peep, Lois had turned and retraced her steps back to the house, picked up the phone, and dialed the number of the office. Dave had answered.

"You guys hungry?" she asked. "Do you want some ham sandwiches and coffee?"

"Yes, we sure do," Dave said. "But neither of us can leave to come over and get it."

"Don't worry. I'll be right over."

After delivering the food, Lois bid the men good night. That night she laid down on her bed without undressing, trying to pray for her husband, Jim Harrison, and Hank Hersey, but her mind kept wandering. She imagined the jagged cliffs of the Gates of the Mountains trapping fleeing firefighters like a cage. She had hiked that country and knew how rugged it was. She couldn't imagine what it would be like to be walking about in the darkness or in the dim light of shadowy fires. At about 5:00 Lois got up, made breakfast, and carried it over to the weary fire dispatchers. She found Bill asleep on a cot. Dave, exhausted and looking quite haggard, sat near the main desk in the lobby. He was very agitated.

"Hank's crew came into Meriwether last night, and they're safe," he said. "But Bob headed back out to the fire. Rescuers are on the way with two litters for the wounded smoke jumpers. And some guys have died. Maybe even Jim. But me and Schmitty, we told each other we won't believe it until it's verified. Jesus, Lois. The whole world's falling apart. I don't know if I can take this."

Lois looked out the office window at the lawn Jim Harrison had mowed just a few days before.

"They'll find him somewhere on the fire line," she said. "I'm sure he's all right. Don't worry, Dave." But even as she pronounced the words of hope, she felt sick inside.

That had been two days ago.

Lois folded the papers, set down the pair of scissors, and picked up a paring knife. At the sink she washed a cauldron full of carrots and potatoes—the fixings for a beef stew for hungry dispatchers and stray firefighters. Through the sheer curtain over the half-window above the sink she saw the silhouette of her seven-year-old daughter, Ruth. "Finally, outside," Lois sighed.

For hours on end during the preceding two days, Ruth had sat before the cabinet radio in the living room, tuning from station to station, only stopping when the newscaster reported more lurid details of the fire in Mann Gulch. "Thirteen firefighters perish, thirteen firefighters perish, including a dozen smoke jumpers." Ruth would turn up the volume whenever she heard the phrase, as if no one in the house knew about the tragedy yet. Finally Lois had pulled the radio plug and ordered the girl outside.

Now something about Ruth's posture caught Lois's attention. The girl was dallying where the grass had turned brown; no one had moved the sprinklers for the last few days. She was staring down at something in her hand. When Lois parted the curtains to get a clearer look, she saw tears streaming down her daughter's cheek. Lois turned off the faucet and ran out the back door, grasshoppers zapping out of the grass before her.

"Ruth, honey, what's the matter? Ruth? Did a bee sting you?"

Lois knelt before the seven-year-old. Ruth held out her right hand. In her palm rested a limp piece of chewing gum.

"What is it, honey?"

"Jimmie gave me this," Ruth said.

"What do you mean?" Lois asked.

"Jimmie gave me this. It's Juicy Fruit. I'm going to keep this forever because Jim gave it to me the last day he was here."

"Oh, my poor baby."

As Lois cradled her daughter in her arms, she fought back her own tears. Jim Harrison had always shown an interest in the children, often wrestling with them. When he had been constrained by an official task, he would play hide-and-seek with them by telling them to go and hide. But he would always come back to find them later on. Lois wished her husband was there to help comfort and soothe the children, but she hadn't seen him since the day before the tragedy. She needed him too.

After Ruth went to look for her brother, the sacred piece of gum in her pocket, Lois turned to a gruesome task she had been avoiding. That afternoon, Bob had sent in the Forest Service key he had found near Jim's body. He wanted Lois to clean it off with salt and soda. Gary Nelson, who was going to represent the district at Harrison's funeral in Missoula later that week, planned to present it to Harrison's mother. Bob also had sent word to have his wife write a letter to the Harrisons. Lois sat down at the desk and tried to compose herself.

"My husband, Ranger Robert Jansson, and all the boys who worked with Jim this summer deeply regret that they could not attend Jim's services, but the fire was still in such a critical stage that it was impossible for them to leave, so Gary Nelson represents us all," she typed.

Lois almost yanked the letter from the machine but hesitated as she grabbed a corner. Whatever could she say to these people to alleviate their grief? What could she say or do to alleviate her own grief, for that matter? She had thought of Jimmie often since Saturday when the dispatchers had confirmed they had received word that his body had been identified. As the local radio stations broadcast the news, some members of the Gates of the Mountains Boat Club had visited the ranger station to talk about Jim. He had been very popular with the visitors at the campground and they had found him very courteous and helpful, and such good company. They recalled how Jim had often helped haul bedrolls, groceries, and personal belongings from their boats. How he offered his living quarters to backcountry riders who had lost their horses. How he made coffee for them and shared his lunches. Some of the visitors had wept as they told their tales. Lois began crying again, just thinking about it. Jim had been such a handsome young man. So full of life and joy. It was impossible. She just couldn't do it. She'd leave that to Bob. He had a way with words. Plus, he had known Jimmie better than she. She continued typing:

> Bob will write to you when he is able, but it may be weeks before this emergency is over and I did not want to wait to tell you that, in attempting to rescue Jim, he knows that the end for him came—mercifully—very quickly. If there is anything you wish to know about it, please write him, or come over and visit us if you would care to.
>
> You also may not know that Jim attended church each time he had an opportunity, including the last trip he made to Helena, when he told me he went to confession at the cathedral. He endeared himself to all who worked with him here.
>
> May God be with you in your sorrow.
>
> Very sincerely, Mrs. J. R. Jansson

Around 9:00 that evening, Lois heard Bob's truck pull into the driveway, but she did not recognize the man who struggled out from behind the wheel. In the past, whenever Bob spent a day performing hot sweaty manual labor in the backcountry, he always maintained a neat and clean appearance. Now, even though he'd washed his face, streaks of soot ringed the edge of his scalp, behind his ears, and down the neck of his shirt. The cuffs of his shirt were totally black. His boots were caked with dusty grime. Bob stood stoop-shouldered and lifted his head only for a second to look at her before dropping his chin to his chest again. He flinched as Lois hugged him, so she pulled away. Bob turned his face so she could not look into his eyes.

"I'm dog tired," he said. "I've just walked through hell and back."

When the children came running across the lawn, Bob whispered to Lois to keep them away. But Ruth and Paul stopped in their tracks on their own accord, waiting for the strange-looking man to give them some sign of recognition.

"I'll talk to you two later," Bob said. "I've got to get away from this smell."

Ruth ordered the kids to stay outside as she followed Bob into the house and began drawing a bath. "Damn these boots!" Bob cursed. "They've been too frigging big on me and now I can't get the damn things off." Lois jumped to help, hoping her gestures of care would dispel his anger and disassociation. As she tried to pull off his socks, Bob yelped in pain. Then Lois noticed the stiff dark stains in the socks, the remnants of discharge from running sores and blisters on his feet.

"Let's soak these off," she whispered.

As Jansson eased into the tub, the warm water instantly turned black, as if someone had spooned in instant coffee. Lois rolled the saturated socks off his feet, softly soaped his body, and then helped him to sit on the side of the tub as she let the dirty water drain. She refilled the tub.

"Take my shirt and undershirt and burn them," Bob said. "But honey, I can wash . . ."

"Dammit! Just burn them!" he shouted. "They smell of death." Then in a hushed voice, he tenderly asked, "Please wash my hair. I'm too weak to do it." Although Lois soaped and lathered his scalp twice, Bob insisted that the stench of death persisted. Lois thought he imagined the smell until she picked up his watch from the washbasin. Bob's leather watchband had pressed against Joe Sylvia's skin as he had sat with his arm around the injured man. Lois almost retched as she smelled the watchband. She immediately went outside, put some sticks in the burn barrel at the end of the driveway, and poured on some kerosene. When she dropped a lit piece of newspaper into the barrel, the whoosh of flame startled her. She tried to block the image of James Harrison's charred body from her mind. Fire suddenly seemed a thing to fear. The children ran up to her. She dropped the watchband and the clothes into the flaming barrel.

"What's happened to Daddy?" Ruth asked. "Why is he being so mean to us?"

"Daddy's very, very tired," Lois said. "He's been through a lot working at the fire and he hasn't slept in three days."

"Did Daddy see Jimmie up there?"

"No, Ruthie. You know Jimmie died in the fire."

"I mean his body. Was it all burned up?"

"I don't know, Ruthie," Lois hugged the two children to her apron. "It's going to be all right. Jimmie's in heaven now anyway."

But the children would not settle down and go to bed until after Lois spanked them. Eventually they cried themselves to sleep.

When she returned to the bedroom, Lois found Bob sitting on the edge of the bed, his pajamas in hand. "I don't seem to have enough energy to get these on," he said, without turning to her.

"Let me help you, darling," she said.

Bob lifted his arms and legs to accept the clothes like a man recovering from paralysis or a stroke. Lois yearned to hold him through the night, to nurture him back to health, to reclaim her husband from the fiery demons that seemed to possess him. The horror he had seen the last two days would fade. He would once again take pleasure in their children's laughter. He would not cringe from her touch. Let sleep do its work and dissolve the hurt in his heart, she thought, all the time trying to reassure herself that everything would be all right. Then Bob curtly said, "I don't want you to sleep with me." He lay down and faced the wall.

Even the family dog, Lassie, a Scotch collie, sensed that something was wrong and paced around the outside of the house, moaning. Fearing the dog might awaken her husband, Lois let her inside, where she settled to sleep at the foot of the bed.

At first, Lois snuggled into a sleeping bag on the davenport in the living room, but time and time again Bob called out for water like a small child afraid of the dark. The man drank glassful after glassful with great, gulping swallows. After he called out the third time, Lois arranged some scatter rugs at the foot of the bed and lay down next to the dog. Throughout the night, she listened as Bob tossed and turned, often moaning out loud. At one point he screamed out "Go away, go away" and kicked and writhed about the bed in agony.

Toward morning, as the station began to stir with life, Bob fell into a deeper sleep. Lois placed a pillow over the phone in case someone called and pasted paper over the doorbells. She begged the children to play outside away from the house or to be quiet if they stayed indoors. Finally, around mid-morning, Bob awoke. When he tentatively smiled at her, Lois knew that her husband had finally come home.

CHAPTER TWENTY-NINE

Julie Reba

Pierz, Minnesota
1959

Julie Reba put down Stanley's letter before she had finished reading the first line. Sometimes the letters momentarily made her happy. She had loved to receive them and had anxiously awaited the postman's delivery every day, even long after the official confirmation of Stanley's death, even long after the day she had visited the spot where the fire had overtaken her husband. Maybe, just maybe, he had had a chance to post one final letter before he left for Mann Gulch. Apparently it had gotten lost somewhere, but it would show up someday. She yearned for one last moment of contact with him.

"My dearest wife . . ." That was all she allowed herself. If she read on, his words might once again divert her from her course. In the past his wonderfully hopeful and self-confident vision of love and life, preserved on paper, had successfully turned her away from the only path Julie believed would lead her back to him. She returned the letter to the suitcase, which she pushed back beneath the bed.

At her night table, Julie shuffled through a stack of records and flipped one onto the turntable. The soft tones of violins and violas played one of Stanley's favorite Viennese waltzes. Also a lover of music and quite a good piano player at one time, Julie appreciated her husband's eclectic musical tastes, although she did not necessarily approve of all his choices. Stanley had quickly evaluated Julie's likes and dislikes and often teased her by turning the volume up whenever he played Tex Ritter's "Rye Whiskey" or Hank Williams's "Lost Highway." About the only other fault Julie found in him during their short courtship and ten-month marriage had been that he danced like a football player.

Julie understood that if Stanley were to walk into that room at that moment, he would not recognize her. The young woman he had married had been full of life and walked with a spring in her long stride. Her green eyes, sparkling with enthusiasm and excitement, had mesmerized him. She had always been the life of the party and quick to laugh at his corny jokes. But now Julie felt helpless to change back to that young girl. The woman who stared back at her from the bureau mirror moved listlessly; her eyes projected no inner spirit. Nowadays, Julie slept little and was afraid of the dark. Even with the lights on, the image of the young men running from the fire could ambush her at any moment. She spent most nights listening to a radio program of poetry readings. Within her own volume of poems, she had underlined these verses by nineteenth-century poet Francis William Bourdillon:

> The night has a thousand eyes
> And the day but one;
> Yet the light of the bright world dies
> With the dying sun.
>
> The mind has a thousand eyes,
> And the heart but one;
> Yet the light of a whole life dies
> When love is done.

A couple of years after Stan perished, Julie had returned to Minneapolis to work as a secretary. But the city had brought back haunting memories of warm nights in each other's arms in the cramped trailer near the campus. After less than a year, she had returned home to stay for good. But even surrounded by loved ones, Julie could not speak about the dark visions that haunted her. Soon her parents and younger sister, André, learned to step carefully around her. At first they shared her grief, but as it extended through the years, they came to suspect that she had gone mad. The expressions in their eyes shifted from sympathy to fear and finally to shame. Her parents feared that they might eventually have to commit her to a mental institution, a most unimaginable shame for the entire family. Julie didn't care. Without Stanley, nothing in life mattered.

Although ten years have passed since the fire, Julie can vividly recall the moment when her world began to fall apart. On August 6, 1949, an extremely hot and humid Saturday, her sister-in-law dropped by to tell Julie's mother, Maude, about a report she'd heard on the noontime radio news broadcast. A large fire was burning in western Montana, the area where Stanley Reba was working as a smoke jumper for the Forest Service. The out-of-control blaze, covering 5,000 acres, was burning at a place called Mann Gulch. The radio broadcaster had calmly reported that some men had burned to death after their parachutes had gotten hung in the trees directly before the advancing flames that towered 600 feet high. The fire, moving faster than a jet plane, had burned them to a crisp before they had even had a chance to lower themselves to the ground and make a run for it. Maude Nagel recalled how Stanley had often described just such remote, inaccessible areas in the mountains.

Since their son-in-law had left for Montana only a week before, Maude and Frank Nagel reasoned that he would still be in training and would not have been dispatched so quickly to a fire. Still, they decided not to mention the news to Julie. They didn't want to see her go into a funk of worry. But that evening as Julie stepped into the living room, the evening newscaster identified one of the men who had died in the Montana fire as a University of Minnesota student named Joseph B. Sylvia. At that moment, life drastically changed for all the Nagels as they collectively fell into grief and shock.

As soon as the radio broadcast ended, Julie rushed into the kitchen to telephone the smoke jumper base in Missoula, Montana. If Joe Sylvia had been on that fire, then most likely Stan, his best friend, would also have been. After one short ring a man answered, his voice sounding expectant, hopeful. But after he listened to Julie's questions, his voice became flat and hollow.

"Stan's on call," he said. When Julie pressed to know what "on call" meant, the man said that Stanley had been sent out on a fire. "Sorry, miss, I don't have any more information right now," he added. Then for a fleeting moment, he seemed to regain some of his initial energy and added: "There's a lot of fires burning in the mountains and we're trying to get it all straightened out about who's on which fire."

About 2:00 AM on Sunday, a different voice from the jumper base phoned back to confirm Julie's suspicions. Stanley was a member of the sixteen-man crew that had been dispatched to the Mann Gulch fire. This man, sounding very businesslike, told her that one man hadn't jumped, three survivors had walked out, and two men, including Joe Sylvia, had died at a hospital. But eleven men were still missing and were presumed to have outrun the fire and were probably hiking back to civilization at that very moment. But the cold tone lurking at the corners of his voice didn't sound convincing. Curiously, Julie was only able to focus on the fact that the man's math had been off. He had accounted for seventeen instead of sixteen men. But she didn't bother pointing this out to him.

Unable to sleep, Julie went down to the kitchen, surprised to find the rest of the family, even young André, gathered round the table. At Frank Nagel's suggestion, the family dressed and walked through the quiet streets of the town of 1,000 souls to the nearby parish church. They found the tall wooden doors unlocked, even at that early hour. Inside, they knelt together before the altar to pray. That afternoon the phone rang again. Frank Nagel answered it, listened a moment, and then suddenly broke into uncontrollable sobbing. Although Julie had been anticipating the dreadful news, her father's emotional outburst unnerved her. It was the first time she had ever seen him cry.

Julie picked up the gun from the bed and hefted it in her hands. "Tonight, my love, tonight," she whispered.

Julie often wondered if she could have survived Stanley's death if she hadn't insisted on visiting Mann Gulch. She remembered meeting Lois Jansson in the house trailer near the construction site of the new ranger station. Lois had searched through a closet for a pair of walking boots that might fit her. Robert Jansson had agreed to lead Julie and her father into Mann Gulch.

The ranger's wife had picked up a pair of ankle-high laced boots and clacked them together by the heels to dislodge some caked mud from the soles. The dirtballs exploded into fine white dust when they hit the carpet.

"A thick pair of socks might help," she said.

Julie could tell the woman was nervous, probably fearful that she'd get stuck with a hysterical woman on her hands. The soft-spoken girl commented on the beautiful scenery of the area.

"Oh, you should have seen the old ranger station before they tore it down," Lois said. "We finally had to move last month. Wait until you get on the river. It's God's country up there, even with everything burned up the way it is." Lois hesitated. Now why on earth had she said something as stupid as that? But Julie had seemed to think nothing of it.

The Nagels. From left:
Cornelia ("Maude"),
Marne, Julie, André, and
Frank, ca. 1943. Courtesy
Mrs. André Anderson.

"I'll be excited to see it," she replied.

In the days leading up to Julie's visit, Lois Jansson had worried about how her husband would react upon returning to Mann Gulch, especially with a widow of one of the victims. Bob still woke her at night sometimes, tossing and turning, moaning, sometimes screaming out in his sleep. She'd already spoken to Helena National Forest supervisor Arthur Moir about possibly transferring him to another district. Other parents, brothers, and sisters of the dead had called to ask Bob to guide them into the gulch come springtime. Who knew when his heart condition would finally flare up and claim him as another victim of the fire? Or when he would lose his mental health? Moir had informed Lois that he had already found Bob a new position at Priest Lake in Idaho and was only waiting for the ranger to personally request the transfer.

The night before Julie's visit, Jansson had confided to his wife that he would be okay as long as Reba's widow did not ask him the particulars about how he had found Stan's body. So far, Julie Reba hadn't even mentioned her husband's name.

The slanting fall sun reflected gloriously off the east wall of the river canyon as the motorboat plied downstream. With no wind, the waters stood as placid as a birdbath. At Hilger Landing, Julie's father sensed some tension in the ranger and the car dealer began to make small talk, asking Jansson how the Forest Service purchased their trucks, what makes and models they preferred. When the pinging of the outboard motor drowned out all conversation, Julie's dad sat back, relieved that he could abandon the conversation.

Although strangers may have gotten the impression that Julie was handling the situation well, her father grew more worried with each passing day. At home, his once-vibrant daughter hardly ever came down from her bedroom. And she never mentioned Stanley's name. When he would make some reference to his beloved son-in-law, Julie would either ignore him or quickly change the subject. He wondered how long she would grieve in solitude. When would she come back into the family fold? During the river trip, Julie sat in the prow of the open wooden boat, her hair blowing behind her, her sallow cheeks momentarily displaying a rosy hue. As the boat kissed the shore, Ranger Jansson jumped over the side into the knee-deep water to help Julie out.

"How do the boots fit?" Jansson asked as they began hiking.

"A little loose, but I'll be fine," Julie said. "Is this really the way?" she asked, glancing up at the tall green trees congested in the mouth of the gulch.

"Yes," Bob said. "The fire spotted from the ridge up there to the south, down to a spot not too far from here. These trees were the few that survived."

At the burn area, the charred surface resembled the black soil of groomed midwestern farm fields where the plow had kicked up grapefruit- and potato-sized rocks to the surface. Jansson led the two through the grove of charred snags. At least, he thought, they wouldn't have to climb very far. Stanley Reba's marker was the lowest of all. If Mrs. Reba asked why he had remained so far behind the others, Jansson was prepared to lie. He couldn't tell her about the broken leg, the agonizing roll downhill into the flames. He would just say he didn't know. Of all the men who died at Mann Gulch, Stanley Reba had haunted his dreams the most.

As they skirted the finger ridge that blocked the head of the canyon from view, Julie was the first to point out a white wooden cross. "There," she said, as she stood behind her father so he could follow the direction her finger pointed.

"I just don't see it," he said.

"There are others," she continued. "Straight across the top. And farther below."

When her father still couldn't pick out the crosses, Julie forged ahead of the two men, intent on verifying reality. She stopped at the lowermost cross.

"Whose cross is this?" she asked.

"It's Stanley's," Jansson confirmed.

The ranger then noticed something on the ground, half hidden in the ash. The tip of a thin gray object lay near a charred bit of wood. When Jansson recognized it for a bone fragment, he gingerly stepped around to the other side of Julie and nonchalantly stepped on the object. For the longest time Julie stood silently staring down at the ground near Jansson's boot. Then she asked, without looking up, "Who found Stanley?"

"I did," Jansson said.

"What position was he lying in?" she asked.

"On his back," he said.

"Oh," Julie muttered. She continued staring at the ground as Jansson pointed out the other crosses to Julie's father, explaining that the jumpers seemed to have run in three waves.

They had found Joe Sylvia almost directly above Stanley. Eldon Diettert had almost made it to the top of the ridge, straight above. He didn't tell them that Eldon had eventually fallen amid some logs and died with one arm sticking up toward the sky. Search party members who combed the area first mistook the charred bone of his arm for a branch; consequently, Diettert's had been the last body found. Silas Thompson had fallen on the slope between Stanley and Joe.

The next wave of four crosses strung out another twenty-five to one hundred yards up toward the head of the gulch, at various heights along the contour of the hill. No one knew why they hadn't headed straight up to the ridge. "Probably because of better footing or something," Jansson said. Of that second wave, Robert Bennett's cross was the closest to where they stood, then Newton Thompson, Leonard Piper, and the fireguard, James Harrison.

Four more crosses depicted the last wave, about 100 yards farther up the gulch. The fire had knocked Marvin Sherman down low on the slope, about parallel with Joe Sylvia. David Navon had fallen about ten yards above him, then Philip McVey.

"Henry Thol Jr. got so close to the ridge top that it makes me feel like crying every time I think how close the kid came to escaping," Jansson said. "His dad, you know, took it real hard. He's probably contacted you about the lawsuit against the Forest Service."

Frank Nagel just shook his head as he looked at Stan's cross. "How could anyone have . . ." He let his sentence trail off as Julie abruptly turned and began walking back to the river.

Ten years later, Julie understood that it wasn't the gulch that had finally broken her spirit. At first she had felt invigorated by her trip to western Montana. The landscape had been everything Stanley promised it would be—snow-capped mountains, rushing clear creeks, softly hued lakes encircled by towering trees. She had enjoyed the boat ride down the Missouri River and had even found the stark desolate beauty of the burned gulches and hills appealing. Standing above Stanley's cross, she had felt a deep affinity with the land and her dead husband. Then, that thing on the ground had caught her eye.

At first she hadn't been sure what it was. A stone? A bleached bit of wood? It had drawn her eye like a magnet, and she had been about to bend over and pick it up when the kind ranger had stepped around her and put his foot over it. That was when she had realized that it was part of Stanley. For what seemed an eternity, she had waited, almost without breathing, for the ranger to move away. Finally, she realized he was not going to let her pick up that lingering part of her husband. As they walked back to the boat, she wanted to make up some excuse to go back, but her spirit seemed to lift out of her and float back down the gulch. She had never felt the same about life after that.

Julie picks up the gun, unaware that the needle of the record player is repeatedly scratching in the last groove encircling the RCA Victor label. She waits for the fire to return. She knows it will. It always does.

Just as she is about to doze off, the first man rushing up the hill startles her. Unlike in her previous dreams, this time Julie recognizes his face and knows his name.

"William Hellman," she says.

And for the first time, the man speaks to her. "Yes, ma'am. Sorry, I don't have time to stop and chat now. I've got to get home to see my little boy. I hear he's about ready to begin walking and I sure don't want to miss that first step."

As always, the others follow single file, close on Hellman's heels.

"Henry Thol," Julie teases. "You have such wonderful ears."

"Thank you, ma'am," he says. "The guys sometimes call me Jumbo, you know, after the elephant." He laughs.

"Yes, I know," she says. "I'm sure it's because they like you so much."

The boy blushes as he passes.

"Phil McVey," Julie greets the next figure. "You're wearing your baseball glove. Are you late for a game?"

"You bet, sweetheart. We'll start up a game as soon as we mount this ridge. Say, do you know how the Cleveland Indians are doing? I haven't been able to get at the box scores the last couple of days."

"David Navon," Julie says to the next figure. "You are such a romantic fellow, and handsome to boot."

"With all due respect, ma'am, I don't like to flirt with married women," Navon says. "Especially when they're married to a friend of mine."

"Of course not," Julie says. "Forgive me. It's just that I feel like I know you so well."

After he passes, Navon looks back over his shoulder and smiles. "Someone should paint a portrait of you," he says. "You'd look wonderful hanging in the Louvre."

Marvin Sherman comes next.

"Looks like you're late for a date," Julie greets him.

"Sure thing, miss," Marvin says. "Mary Ellen is waiting. We'll be getting married as soon as I graduate, you know."

"Yes, I know. And what a wonderful life you'll share," Julie calls after him.

As Eldon Diettert approaches, Julie asks, "Will you stop and identify the wildflowers for me?"

"Can't right this moment, ma'am," the tall lanky kid says. "But it's like a rainbow over on the other side of the ridge. You'll be able to pick a bouquet full of yellow arrowleaf balsamroot, pink shooting stars, vermilion Indian paintbrush, and blue larkspur. I'm going to paint them all someday." He does not break stride.

"Leonard Piper," Julie salutes the next young man. "Your folks are expecting you to visit them in Pennsylvania this fall. Don't let them down."

"Oh, I won't, ma'am," Leonard answers, huffing a little from his run.

"And Newton Thompson," Julie mockingly scolds. "You must stop and tell me something about yourself when you have the time."

The handsome man demurely grins but says nothing as he passes by.

Robert Bennett stumbles a bit as he gains Julie's level, then stops and asks if there is anything he can do for her.

"Oh no, but thank you," Julie says. "My husband, Stan, is coming up behind you. Do you know him?"

"Sure I do," Robert smiles. "Everyone knows Stan. He's a swell guy." And he once again proceeds up the hill.

Next Julie greets James Harrison, asking, "Will we see you in church Sunday, Jim?"

"Come hell or high water," he answers. "If you'll pardon the expression."

As Joe Sylvia approaches, Julie calls him Little Joe. The tough cookie from Massachusetts grins from ear to ear. "I'll only let beautiful women call me that," Joe says. "By the way, how's that cute sister of yours? Tell her I'll be back when she graduates from high school."

"And Silas Thompson. Have you a new poem for us?" Julie asks the next man.

"A wonderful sonnet awaits," he theatrically proclaims. "Just over yonder ridge."

Far below the others Julie sees the top of a large head bobbing up the trail. It is Stanley, as usual bringing up the rear.

Behind him, Julie sees the fire, swirling and licking at her husband's heels. This time Julie steps directly into the trail to make Stanley stop.

"Stanley, you're running in the wrong direction," she says.

"I just don't know which way to go, Julie," he says. "Could you help me, my love?"

"We need to go back into the fire," Julie says, pointing downhill. "See Wag Dodge over there? He knows how to save us. All we have to do is walk back through the fire into the black and we'll be safe. Weren't you paying attention at training camp this year?" she gently teases.

When Stanley turns and looks down the ridge, he sees a dim figure waving to them from the far side of the fire. He slips his arm around Julie's waist and the two lovers begin walking down the hill.

"I love you, Stanley. I always will," Julie Reba whispers as she touches the tip of the gun's barrel to her temple.

This time the fire consumes her.

CHAPTER THIRTY

Aftermath

A total of 450 men fought Mann Gulch fire before it was controlled on August 10. By that time it had covered 5,000 acres. The continuing conflagration didn't stop the smoke jumpers from retrieving the bodies of their lost brethren. Around noon on August 6, 1949, a Bell 47-D helicopter flew the last of the bodies out of Mann Gulch. The Forest Service had leased the light craft as part of an experimental project to see if it could ferry smoke jumper gear out of the back-country.

Later that day Henry Thol Sr. received the official notification that his son was dead. He immediately got into his car and drove from his home in Kalispell to Helena. Thol felt that he could not accept the tragedy until he looked at the body of the boy upon whom he had bestowed his own name. He arrived in Helena late in the evening. At the morgue, Robert Jansson informed Thol that his son's body lay at the Opp-Conrad Funeral Parlor.

"Are you certain of the identification?" Thol asked. "I don't want to bury some other father's boy." Jansson assured the distraught man that they had properly identified the body, describing the features of the boy. When Thol arrived at the funeral parlor, he ran into Earl Cooley, who had driven over from Missoula earlier that day to help identify the remains. Cooley reported that some of the bodies had been so badly burned that he had had to identify them from telltale characteristics or from personal possessions retrieved at the site. For instance, he had identified Philip McVey by the way his shirttails were knotted around his stomach and Stanley Reba by a car key that was a duplicate of the one Joe Sylvia carried in his pocket. Cooley told the elder Thol that the body of his son had already been sealed in a metal tube for transport to Kalispell. Thol insisted that the coffin be opened, saying: "My wife will never be satisfied unless she knows it is him that's in there." When the undertaker refused Thol's request, the old man threatened to get a court order.

"I strongly urge you not to follow this course," Mr. Retz, the undertaker, said.

But Thol demanded to see his son one last time, and Retz reluctantly led them into a back room, where the casket lay on a high metal table. Bolts were set at three-quarter-inch intervals around the lid. The undertaker handed tools to Thol and Cooley, removed a few bolts himself, and then excused himself and left the room. When Cooley took out the last bolt, he stepped back and let the father lift the lid. Henry Jr.'s head and hair had not been scorched, but fire had burned out his stomach. Undeterred by the grisly scene, Henry Thol Sr. reached into the casket and brushed his hand over his son's head. Cooley later described the scene as "the most emotional thing I ever saw."

Later that night Mr. Retz called the home of Favre Eaton, assistant supervisor of Helena National Forest, concerned about Thol's bizarre behavior after he left the funeral parlor. Eaton was not at home, but Retz talked to Mrs. Eaton, who immediately drove down to the neighborhood to search for Thol. When she asked a couple of pedestrians if they had seen the ranger, they said he was walking down the street sobbing and yelling at the top of his lungs. Mrs. Eaton never located the distressed father.

Henry Thol Sr. never forgave the Forest Service for the death of his son. He was convinced that the agency had needlessly put the men in a dangerous position from which they could not possibly escape, and he harshly criticized Wag Dodge's judgment. Thol eventually convinced other parents to join him in suing the agency.

On the last day of the Board of Review hearings in Helena—September 28, 1949—Thol presented his accusations and points of view. He first argued that the men never should have jumped into the gulch so near the fire. He disputed the agency's contention that the fire was not active at the time the Douglas C-47 first flew over the scene. Thol argued that the fire was most likely burning well down the slope of the north ridge, and he pointed out that smoke often will "trail along the bottom through the heavy green timber until finally it shows up." If the fire had in fact burned lower on the slope, it would have been that much easier for hot rocks or tumbling pine cones to ignite spot fires downhill. "There was no assurance that there was no . . . fire down to the bottom of the gulch . . . ready at any moment to take up on . . . a whiff of wind," he said. Thol also pointed out that the men had arrived at the peak time of the day for fire danger, after an afternoon of relentless hot sunshine had dried and primed the fuels to peak flammability. He insisted that the men should not have jumped at that time of the day under the current conditions and in such a place.

Thol argued that once the jumpers hit the ground, Wag Dodge should have realized that digging line on that fire under those conditions would have been a waste of time, that an eighteen-inch trench was not going to contain that type of fire. Thol insisted that Dodge's first course of action should have

Wag Dodge leading the rescue team, August 6, 1949. Courtesy Dick Wilson.

been to get the men out of harm's way by leading them up to the ridge on the south slope, half a mile away from the landing spot. From that vantage point, they could have clearly witnessed the progress of the fire. Otherwise, Dodge should have "looked around and found" a clear escape route that would have led the men to a safety zone, such as the scree slope that Sallee and Rumsey stumbled upon in Rescue Gulch. According to Thol, Dodge should have told the men that "if something goes wrong . . . here's the place we go."

In summary, Thol contended that Dodge was more concerned with putting out the fire than evaluating the safety of his crew. "The value of human life didn't mean much" to Dodge, Thol testified. "He took that big, big risk. . . . The canyon was running east and west with the prevailing wind. He should make doubly sure—try to look for an avenue of escape and protect the human life first." Instead, Thol argued, Dodge had led the men "into a trap."

Even if the men had sensed their danger, they had no recourse but to follow their foreman, Thol continued. It was either obey orders or get fired. And by the time Dodge set his escape fire, Thol speculated, the men had given up on him as a leader. The fact that they would not follow him into the black of his safety burn indicated that they had thought he didn't know what he was doing. When "there is life or death involved," Thol asked, "should I still obey him?" As for Dodge's fire itself, Thol stated that although it might have saved the foreman, it ended up killing most of his men. Thol said the escape fire "caught up with some of the boys up there above him" and "prevented those below him from going to the top. The poor boys were caught; they had no escape."

In its final assessment of the tragedy, the Joint Boards of Review report refuted all of Thol's arguments. The Forest Service supported the decision to drop the jumpers as well as the one to land them at the chosen spot. They supported Dodge's strategy to fight the fire and described his decision to lead the crew to the river as being "logical." The sudden explosive runs of the fire from the upper slope of the ridge between Mann Gulch and Meriwether Canyon across the lower end of Mann Gulch "could not reasonably have been expected," the findings stated. The report also described Dodge's "coolness and good judgment" in setting the escape fire and said that "all evidence available to the Board indicated that the escape fire in no way impeded the progress of the men seeking to attain the ridge, or was otherwise instrumental in causing or contributing to any of the deaths." Thol was not the only person to call the findings a whitewash. When an administrator handed Robert Jansson his copy of the report, he commented: "Well, Bob, they have decided to whitewash us all."

Henry Thol Sr. pressed the issue in court, encouraging other families of the victims to do the same. Within two years, four suits were brought in federal court against the Forest

Service in connection with the deaths of the firefighters. But the cases eventually bogged down in the legal system and were dropped after exceeding the statute of limitations.

Whether Thol was right or not in questioning the judgment of Cooley for delivering the jumpers that day or the judgment of Dodge for his leadership on the ground, he made some good points, the most important being that "the value of lives of men should be given first consideration." To its credit, the Forest Service took Thol's top commandment to heart.

In the years following the Mann Gulch fire, the U.S. Forest Service created technical and research centers in Montana and California dedicated to developing equipment to help protect firefighters from a multitude of dangers on the fire line. Probably the most dramatic invention was the aluminum foil–coated pup tent–like fire shelter that reflects radiant heat and gives a firefighter a better chance at surviving an entrapment. Today the centers also study a myriad of health and safety issues, from the long-term effects of smoke inhalation on firefighters to driver safety in and around large fire camps. The agency has also constructed a fire laboratory in Missoula, Montana, where scientists study and analyze fire behavior. The research has led to educational videos, pamphlets, and other training methods that give wildland firefighters a clearer picture about how local weather conditions, topography, and fuels interact with fire. This knowledge enables firefighters to better predict how volatile fuels, temperature, humidity, wind speed, and slope can quickly alter the characteristics of a fire and pose a threat to workers. In addition, the agency issues maps and hand-held radios as standard equipment to firefighting crews.

But probably the most important change is the emphasis the agency puts on individual safety training, from the incident commander who coordinates a fire camp of hundreds of workers to the individual groundpounder. All firefighters receive this training while qualifying for what is called a red card. Without the card, they cannot work the fire line.

The most recent development in safety training for wildland firefighters is called Lookouts, Communication, Escape Routes, and Safety Zones, or LCES. The message of LCES saves lives on the fire line because it is so simple. The idea was born on June 26, 1990, when Paul Gleason, superintendent of the Zigzag Interagency Hotshot Crew of elite firefighters at the time, watched a wall of flames in the Dude fire in Arizona rush through continuous vegetation and overtake the Perryville inmate fire crew, killing six men. The crew had posted no lookouts and they hadn't designated any escape routes. Gleason reasoned that by covering the four points of LCES, firefighters accomplish all of the Ten Standard Firefighting Orders and observe the proper caution for the Eighteen Situations That Shout Watch Out, two training protocols developed by the Forest Service in the decades after the Mann Gulch fire. Gleason thus laid the foundation for new training methods for wildland firefighters, but more hard work was needed to get the information to the fire line.

After the South Canyon Fire killed fourteen firefighters in Colorado in 1994, Ted Putnam, a former smoke jumper and a researcher with the Missoula Technology and Development Center, also began looking for answers to safety problems. In his studies with airplane pilots, Putnam found that even the sharpest individuals can normally process only a handful of elements at one time. And when a situation becomes intense, individuals can focus on only one or two things at a time. Consequently, Putnam organized the Human Factors Workshop. Paul Chamberlin, a 30-year veteran smoke jumper, used Putnam's and Gleason's studies as the basis for a new training method for firefighters. Gleason's goal was to simplify the "complicated and inaccessible nature of the amassed Orders, Situations, Guidelines, and Denominators."

Chamberlin, who personally decided to follow LCES every time he went on a fire, got his chance to test Gleason's theory on the ground during the 1995 fire season. As deputy incident commander on the 6,000-acre Sprite fire in the wilderness of New Mexico's Gila National Forest, Chamberlin followed LCES to the letter. He ordered crews to spruce up hiking trails to act as fire lines within the wilderness. He stationed seasoned veterans to watch the fire from clear vantage points and frequently check radio transmissions to ensure good communication. If for any reason communications went down, Chamberlin suspended operations. Firefighters also identified safety zones and escape routes at every briefing, and they continually updated the information. Sometimes Chamberlin personally walked people over to the safety zones. "We elevated and integrated LCES into everything we did," he said. "Everyone got involved in the safety process—hotshots, type II crewmembers, the overhead team, and crew bosses." The interaction generated a dialogue among the firefighters themselves, and Chamberlin walked away from the Sprite fire convinced that LCES was the best possible way to train workers to avoid dangerous situations while fighting fires. "When you get away with an unsafe act once in a while, you reinforce your comfort level," he said. "There's too many times we approach a fire and think we'll get away without a lookout this time. And we think that if we worry about safety, production will go down. But actually, it goes up."

Lookouts are essential, according to Chamberlin. Although the Standard Orders call for posting a lookout only "when necessary," Chamberlin believes that "we can have a lookout at all times." Mann Gulch, Storm King Mountain, and other killer fires have proven that small incremental changes in the nature of the fire environment can lead to an unacceptable situation. The wind picks up a little, the vegetation gets thicker, and the humidity drops a notch, some of the things that Wag

Dodge may have picked up on when he decided to retreat to the river. "You notice these things on the fire line," Chamberlin said, "and you get a little nervous, but the line's holding and you keep moving. Lookouts are often better situated to notice the cumulative changes of fire behavior. Most fires seem to posture to make a run before moving. Depending on the fuel types, you might have twenty minutes during this time to pull out before it blows up." Instinctively Dodge realized this, but he spent those twenty minutes heading in the wrong direction.

Chamberlin, along with the help of fellow smoke jumpers Ken Heare and Paul Fieldhouse and Nelda St. Claire Vorce, intelligence coordinator for the Bureau of Land Management in Montana, designed a new safety training method that not only emphasizes LCES but also gets firefighters more committed to the training process. LCES training is now standard fare for wildland firefighters across the country.

There is one other significant change in firefighter training that would have warmed Henry Thol Sr.'s heart. Today, fire management teams encourage their groundpounders to question their superiors. If an individual feels nervous about being sent into a certain situation or thinks that following orders will put him or her in jeopardy, he or she has the right to refuse to follow that specific order without fear of losing his or her job. In most cases, a threatened mutiny will force the overhead team to assess a situation more carefully, which is never a bad idea. Today's Forest Service stresses the notion that safety of firefighters comes first; trees and private property a distant second. That's the rule everybody follows, or else.

Of course, nature will continue to ambush wildland firefighters no matter how careful they are. No matter how many theories humans develop, nature will find ways to subvert them. The only way to ensure that no human being ever perishes again in a wildfire is to stop fighting these fires. No matter how much prescribed burning or mechanical thinning public agencies and private owners execute in the forests, wildfires will continue to blow up in the future under the right weather conditions. Humans may mitigate the potential for crown fires, but we will never completely control the situation. Until politicians decide that it is more prudent to let nature take its course, we will continue to read of new deaths on the fire lines.

CHAPTER THIRTY-ONE

Survivors

Bob Sallee, the only remaining survivor in 2007 of the tragedy, remains adamant that the smoke jumpers—and especially Wag Dodge—followed appropriate procedure that fatal day, up until the point when they ignored Dodge's pleas for them to get behind his escape fire.

"I really think that fire we saw when we flew over there was a typical smokejumper fire," Sallee said. "And if they didn't jump on that fire they wouldn't have jumped on half the fires they jumped on that year. So I don't think it was a mistake to jump. After we got on the ground I think it was a freak of nature that caused the wind to do what it did and to pick those coals up and drop them in the canyon below us. With hindsight it's pretty obvious if we'd had gone from the jump spot out over the top we'd have had no problem. But that's hindsight, and there wasn't any way, when all this was happening, for Wag to determine that. He thought he could take us down to the river and we'd be safe, and when we got almost down to the river there was the fire in front of us. So we couldn't get down. So no, I don't think it was a mistake. I don't think it was a mistake to jump, and I don't think he made any mistakes in what he did. If there are any mistakes in the whole thing, the

mistake was in not training people about [escape] fires. So the
people who had an opportunity to get into his fire didn't do
it—they didn't recognize it as an opportunity, so they didn't
do it. If they had, they'd have all been safe, the ones that had
the chance to get in there."

When Sallee took those few moments to gaze back into Mann
Gulch once he had topped the ridge, thick smoke prevented
him from seeing the progression of the men who had made
it farther up the gulch, but he remains adamant that Dodge's
fire could not have impeded them. "Some people have said
that they thought Wag's fire burned the people who got past
where he lit his fire," he said. "I don't believe that's possible
because Wag's fire was burning in those ebb currents that are
associated right in front of a large fire. The fire's drawing oxygen in from all directions and it was drawing air in from back
in front of it. Any fire will do that. . . . Wag lay down in his . . .
burned-over area and the main fire jumped across him. The
main fire jumped across Wag's fire, so there's no way, in my
mind, that Wag's fire burned anybody."

For years Sallee never thought or talked about the tragedy—
not with Rumsey or with his family. "I went thirty-five or forty
years without talking to anybody about Mann Gulch," he said.
He and Rumsey, he said, were able to turn it off so that at times
it seemed as if it hadn't happened.

"In the quiet times when we were alone with just ourselves
we were thanking the good Lord that he had chosen to let us
live longer," Sallee said. "I spent a lot of time for a few years
after that wondering why. But I finally decided there wasn't
any answer to that question and just went on with my life."

That all changed when Norman Maclean began research-
ing his book *Young Men and Fire* "and a lot of people started
talking about it." Sallee and Rumsey escorted Maclean and
smoke jumper Laird Robinson into Mann Gulch in the mid-
1970s. Each tried to recreate his escape route and mark the

place where Wag Dodge had started his fire. Sallee is sure they got it right. "I came at it one way and Rumsey came at it another and we were fifty feet apart and there's no question," Sallee said. Yet Maclean insisted that they were mistaken, saying the location did not fit into his analysis and re-creation of the events. Maclean also questioned the location of the escape route that the men retraced for him.

"In Rumsey and Sallee's memory," wrote Maclean, "the experience of their flight from death is not bound together by narrative or cartographic links—it would be hard to make a map from it and then expect to find ground to fit the map. It has the consistency more of a gigantic emotional cloud that closes things together with mist, either obliterating the rest of objective reality or moving the remaining details of reality around until, like furniture, they fit into the room of our nightmare in which only a few pieces appear where they are in reality."

Over the years Sallee grew resentful of Maclean's insistence that he and Rumsey couldn't exactly recall their actions that day. "I would never agree with Maclean [about his theory]," he said. "I never forgot that opening in the rocks. . . . I remember that crevice. . . . I don't know [exactly] where Wag started his fire, but I do know where the crevice was. . . . They [Maclean and Robinson] tried to tell us what we had had for breakfast that day. I just told him he was wrong." Sallee believes that if he had agreed with Maclean, the author would have pushed forward with his project and published his book. Instead, Maclean set the manuscript aside and it wasn't published until 1992, two years after his death.

Sallee's good luck seemed to have followed him throughout life. He continued to jump fires throughout the 1949 season and into 1950. In 1951, he abandoned his dreams of working full-time with the Forest Service to pursue a career in the paper industry. With a business degree in hand from

Eastern Washington University, Sallee first worked for Potlatch Forest, Inc. in Lewiston, Idaho, then moved on to Hoerner-Waldorf, based in Missoula. Later he worked for four years as a paper consultant with Sandwell International in Portland, Oregon, during which time he traveled extensively around the world. Bob ended his career as the director of special projects for the Inland Empire Paper Company in Spokane, where he still lives.

Walt Rumsey also led a productive life until fate finally caught up with him. After opting not to return to smoke jumping, Walt earned a double degree in range management and watershed science from Utah State University in Logan. In 1950, he married Mary Williford; they farmed for eighteen months outside of Larned, Kansas. Thinking they would never be able to buy a farm of their own, Walt went to work for the Soil Conservation Service and the couple moved to Utah. Walt's career in what became known as the Natural Resources Conservation Service lasted twenty-eight years and took the family, which eventually included three children, from Utah to Colorado, Idaho, and New Mexico. In 1980, the Rumseys ended up in Lincoln, Nebraska. On June 12 of that year Walt was flying home from a business trip in South Dakota on a commuter plane when a thunderstorm slammed the aircraft to the ground. Fifteen of the seventeen people aboard died, including Walter Rumsey. He was fifty-three years old.

When the third survivor, Wagner Dodge, returned home from Mann Gulch, he told his wife, Patsy, that "the Old Boy upstairs has been riding in my hind pocket." But the grace didn't last very long. Wag attended many of the funerals of the victims and spoke to all the parents. Although he boarded a plane for a fire jump a couple of times, he never could step out of the plane. In 1950, he left the smoke jumper program but continued to work for the Forest Service. Still, the tragedy seemed to haunt him. Just five years after the fire, at the age

Mann Gulch, 1999. Author's collection.

of thirty-eight, Wag died of Hodgkin's disease at Saint Patrick Hospital in Missoula. Many friends, like Fred Brauer, refer to Wag as the fourteenth victim of Mann Gulch.

Shortly after Wag's death, Fred Brauer and some other smoke jumper friends took his ashes aloft in a Ford Trimotor and scattered them over a little lake in Idaho that Wag loved. On the second pass they dropped a cross that they had fashioned from parts of an old airplane.

Despite the dangers inherent in wildland firefighting, the job continues to attract tens of thousands of adventurous souls every summer from across the United States, and the competition remains especially fierce for coveted smoke jumper positions. Since the 1960s, the characteristics of the typical smoke jumper have changed. Although many college-age men and women still look to jumping as a job that will pay their way through school, many others approach it as a full-time (seasonal) career. Many professional firefighters return to jump summer after summer, continuing well into their forties or early fifties, sometimes even jumping beyond the twenty years it takes to qualify for retirement. Today's smoke jumpers include many women and minorities. There's a good reason why people still flock to the assignment. Men like Stanley Reba, Joe Sylvia, Robert Bennett, Silas Thompson, David Navon, Marvin Sherman, Eldon Diettert, Henry Thol, James Harrison, Phil McVey, Newton Thompson, Bill Hellman, and Leonard Piper all understood. Perhaps Bob Sallee summed it up best for them all: "Smoke jumping is the best job in the world."

Note on Sources

I had the good fortune to read personal letters and memorials written by the smoke jumpers and their family members and friends. These works provided the bulk of the new biographical information included in this work. The writers included Clarence Ames, a friend of Philip McVey; André Anderson, sister-in-law of Stanley Reba; Peggy Bale, daughter of Walter Rumsey Jr.; Ray Belston, cousin of Marvin L. Sherman; Gary P. Bennett, nephew of Robert Bennett; Eldon Diettert; Gerald Diettert, older brother of Eldon Diettert; jumper Stanley E. Farnham; Thelma Flannigan, sister of Joseph B. Sylvia; James O. Harrison; District Ranger Robert Jansson; Starr Jenkins, former smoke jumper; Marie A. Liebel, sister of Leonard Piper; Jerry Linton, friend of Phil McVey; Lucille Long, sister-in-law of Robert Bennett; Tom Magee Sr., friend of Marvin L. Sherman; Jack Matthews, friend of Philip McVey and Bill Hellman; Myron McFarland; Gerry McHenry, widow of Bill Hellman; Francis Middlemist, friend of Marvin L. Sherman; Anita Navon, sister of David Navon; Gary Nelson, co-worker of James Harrison in the Helena District; Johan

Newcombe, sister of Silas Raymond Thompson Jr.; Bobbie Parker, neighbor of Robert Bennett; Chuck Pickard, former smoke jumper; Althea Piper, Leonard Piper's sister-in-law; Joyce Russell, sister of Robert Bennett; Barbara Bingham Simons, schoolmate of Robert Bennett; Jack Thompson, cousin of Silas Thompson; Patricia Wilson, widow of Wagner Dodge; and Jim Wissler, former smoke jumper.

Over the years I have found the works of the three Steves—Stephen Arno and Steven Allison-Bunnell (*Flames in Our Forest: Disaster or Renewal?*) and Stephen Pyne (*Fire in America: A Cultural History of Wildland and Rural Fire*)—invaluable for understanding the nature of fire ecology.

I found much insight into the personalities of the smoke jumpers in the memoirs of two former smoke jumpers—Earl Cooley's *Trimotor and Trail*; and Starr Jenkins's *Smokejumpers, '49: Brothers in the Sky* and *Some of the Men of Mann Gulch*. Lois Jansson's unpublished memoir, *Have You Ever Stopped to Wonder?* shed much light on how deeply the tragedy affected her family and the community in general.

For the technical aspects of the fire behavior in the gulch and the movements of the crew I gleaned invaluable information from Norman Maclean's book *Young Men and Fire*; the pamphlet *Mann Gulch Fire: A Race That Couldn't Be Won*, written by fire scientist Richard Rothermel; and the pamphlet *The Thirteenth Fire*, by former Forest Service employee David Turner. And of course, the testimony included in the official report of the Board of Review of Mann Gulch fire was full of interesting details.

As he has throughout most of his life in dealing with the media, Robert Sallee refused to talk with me about his experiences in Mann Gulch except during a brief press conference at the 50th anniversary commemoration in Helena, Montana, in 1999. However, videographer Stevan Smith graciously allowed me to read a transcript of a lengthy recorded interview with Sallee that Smith filmed as part of a documentary that he produced on the history of smoke jumping for the National Smoke Jumpers Association. University of Montana journalism student Carl Gidlund was also able to interview Sallee in 1966 and incorporated many quotes and insights into his unpublished article.

For piecing together the day-to-day life at the jumper base in Missoula and what happened during the flight to Mann Gulch, I relied on interviews with many former smoke jumpers who worked the summer of '49, including project manager Fred Brauer, spotter Earl Cooley, squad leader Al Hammond, Michael Hardy, Gene Hinkle, Jack A. Rose, Merle Stratton, Skip Stratton, and Jim Wissler. Dr. Amos Little, a para-doctor who trained with the smoke jumpers during World War II, and Skip Stratton filled me in on many of the details of the rescue operation.

And last of all, the collection of texts in *Mann Gulch Remembered*, published by the Helena High School Excel Program, was certainly a stimulus for writing this book, if not my most valuable resource.

Notes

PREFACE

The information about the early years of the U.S. Forest Service smoke jumper program comes from Earl Cooley, *Trimotor and Trail* (Missoula, Mont.: Mountain Press, 1984); and U.S. Forest Service, *History of Smoke Jumping* (Seattle, Wash.: Pacific Northwest National Parks and Forests Association, 1986).

CHAPTER ONE

This chapter is a reconstruction of the events of the last night of Julie Reba's life as well as her state of mind at the time. I am grateful to Julie's younger sister, André Anderson, for providing me with the details of her life and death.

   5   Although the Nagel family didn't know for sure how Julie procured the gun, they suspected that she had purchased it through a mail-order catalog company.

   5   Julie stored Stanley's letters, photographs, and other memorabilia in such a suitcase. The plaque commemorating Stanley's death was presented to the family by the U.S. Forest Service. The suitcase and its artifacts have been lost.

CHAPTER TWO

André Anderson told me that Stanley was a prolific writer of beautiful letters. Although Anderson never personally read Stanley's letters, her sister often read sections of them aloud to her.

7   The history of Camp Rimini appears in Gary Glynn, *Montana's Home Front during World War II* (Missoula, Mont.: Pictorial Histories Publishing, 1994), 52–54.

7   Starr Jenkins, a smoke jumper during the summer of 1949, described the fire activity in Region 1 earlier that summer in Starr Jenkins, *Smokejumpers, '49: Brothers in the Sky* (San Luis Obispo, Calif.: Merritt Starr Books, 1995).

8   Former smoke jumper Stanley Farnham provided the information about the income of smoke jumpers during this period in a letter to the X-CEL program at Helena High School. His letter was buried in a time capsule at the Smoke Jumper Center in Missoula, Montana.

8–10   The biographical information and other intimate knowledge about Stanley and Julie Reba came from several interviews I conducted with André Anderson. Anderson also wrote a profile about Stan and Julie in Starr Jenkins, *Some of the Men of Mann Gulch* (San Luis Obispo, Calif.: Merritt Star Books, 1993).

10   André Anderson showed me this locket during one of our visits.

10   André Anderson described Frank Nagel's job offer to Stanley Reba and Joe Sylvia in the profile in Jenkins, *Some of the Men of Mann Gulch*.

CHAPTER THREE

12   The description of Phil McVey and information about his baseball talent came from an interview with his friend and fellow smoke jumper Al Hammond and in a letter Chuck Pickard sent to Helena High School's X-CEL Program, January 23, 1999. His letter is buried in a time capsule at the Missoula Smoke Jumper Center in Montana.

13   Most of the buildings at the Ninemile Remount Depot were still in excellent condition when the facility celebrated its 75th anniversary in 2005. The history of the depot can be found in H. L.

"Lee" Hames, *The Mules' Last Bray, World War II and U.S. Forest Service Reminiscences* (Missoula, Mont.: Pictorial Histories Publishing Co., 1996), 1–16.

13   Firefighters stationed at the Ninemile Ranger Station continue to help hay the fields during down time.

14–16   The descriptions of Camp Menard and its training facilities came from a number of interviews with Civilian Public Service smoke jumpers and those who trained there after the war. The buildings at Camp Menard were removed after World War II. The Camp Menard Picnic Grounds now occupy the site.

16   Cooley wrote about the attitude and stamina of Mennonite conscientious objectors in his autobiography, Earl Cooley, *Trimotor and Trail* (Missoula, Mont.: Mountain Press, 1984), 52. He told me in an interview that he wished he could have hired a whole contingent made up of just Mennonite smoke jumpers.

16   The story of the Civilian Public Service smoke jumpers can be found in Mark Matthews, *Smoke Jumping on the Western Fireline: Conscientious Objectors during World War II* (Norman, Okla.: University of Oklahoma Press, 2005). During the Smoke Jumper Association's 50th reunion in 1995, the "official" smoke jumper history that was read to the audience during the Saturday night banquet did not even mention the existence of the Civilian Public Service smoke jumpers. Many younger smoke jumpers were embarrassed by the omission. Since then the Civilian Public Service pioneers have been acknowledged in videos and written histories produced by the Smoke Jumpers Association as well as by the U.S. Forest Service.

17   One of the contributors to a collection of memoirs by Civilian Public Service smoke jumpers told the story of the removal of the ponderosa pine tree from the baseball diamond; Roy Wenger, ed., *CPS Smoke Jumpers, 1943 to 1946: Life Stories*, vol. 1 (Missoula, Mont.: R. E. Wenger, 1990).

17–18   Biographical information about Philip McVey was gleaned from letters by his friends Clarence Ames and Jerry Linton, collected in X-CEL Productions, *Mann Gulch Remembered* (Helena, Mont.: Helena High School, 1999).

18   Starr Jenkins describes thunder as the sound of money in Starr Jenkins, *Smokejumpers, '49: Brothers in the Sky* (San Luis Obispo, Calif.: Merritt Starr Books, 1995), 95. Modern firefighters still use this phrase.

CHAPTER FOUR

The lookout, Vincent, is a fictional character.

20   Virginia Vincent, a lookout for thirty years on Stark Mountain, reported the number of window panes she had to wash every week in an interview with me.

21   Information on the color of smoke came from Virginia Vincent and later appeared in a story in Mark Matthews, "Eyes in the Skies," *Wildland Firefighter* 1, no. 6 (October 1997): 44–47.

21–26   The information about lightning and weather came from C. Donald Ahrens, *Meteorology Today: An Introduction to Weather, Climate, and the Environment*, 5th ed. (St. Paul, Minn.: West Publishing Co., 1994), 406–412.

26   About one stroke out of twenty-five in the Northern Rockies packs enough punch to start a fire; Stephen J. Pyne, *Fire in America: A Cultural History of Wildland and Rural Fire* (Seattle: University of Washington Press, 1999), 9.

26   The description of the rain in Mann Gulch the day before the fire is in U.S. Forest Service, "Transcript of Board of Review of Mann Gulch Fire," Missoula, Mont.: September 26–28, 1949, 9.

CHAPTER FIVE

29   The statistic about the number of visitors to Meriwether Campground and Canyon in the summer of 1948 is in U.S. Forest Service, "Transcript of Board of Review of Mann Gulch Fire," Missoula, Montana, September 26–28, 1949, 172.

29   Harrison described his daily routine to his folks in a letter dated July 9, 1949, that was included in X-CEL Productions, *Mann Gulch Remembered* (Helena, Mont.: Helena High School, 1999).

29   Harrison's family contributed the items that were found with Jim to the Helena High School project.

29–31   Co-worker Garry Nelson described Jim's duties in an article titled "One Young Man and Fire," collected by the X-CEL Program and buried in the time capsule at the Smoke Jumper Center in Missoula, Montana.

31   Jim's accomplishments are listed in X-CEL Productions, *Mann Gulch Remembered*.

31   The statistics about fatalities of firefighters east of the Continental Divide versus those west of the Divide were recorded in U.S. Forest Service, "Transcript of Board of Review of Mann Gulch Fire," 172.

31   Jim described the back and forth about his job with Ranger Jansson in one of his letters home; published in X-CEL Productions, *Mann Gulch Remembered.*

31–32   Nelson described Jim's character and the extracurricular activities in "One Young Man and Fire."

32   Jim noted some of the differences in foliage on the eastern and western sides of the Continental Divide in one of his letters in X-CEL, *Mann Gulch Remembered*; I added others.

33   Jim included details about his interactions with visitors to Meriwether Canyon in his letters home; published in X-CEL Productions, *Mann Gulch Remembered.*

33   Robert Jansson described his radio transmission in his testimony: U.S. Forest Service, "Transcript of Board of Review of Mann Gulch Fire," 10.

CHAPTER SIX

Fred Brauer related to me his background, his service record, his daily routine, and specific details about August 5, 1949, in a series of interviews from 1999 to 2005.

38   Skip Stratton related the more intimate details of Fred Brauer's nature to me in an interview in 2005.

39   The headlines and the story of the fatality near Seeley Lake are in *Daily Missoulian*, August 5, 1949, 1.

39–40   The availability of planes on August 5 was noted in U.S. Forest Service, "Transcript of Board of Review of Mann Gulch Fire," Missoula, Montana, September 26–28, 1949, 30.

40–41   For the history of the Johnson Brothers Flying Service, see Steven Smith, *Fly the Biggest Piece Home* (Missoula, Mont.: Mountain Press, 1979).

CHAPTER SEVEN

43–44   The information about the effects of lightning is from C. Donald Ahrens, *Meteorology Today: An Introduction to Weather, Climate, and the Environment,* 5th ed. (St. Paul, Minn.: West Publishing Co., 1994).

43–44   The effects of a lightning strike on a tree and the process of pyrolysis is eloquently described in Stephen J. Pyne, *Fire in America: A Cultural History of Wildland and Rural Fire* (Seattle: University of Washington Press, 1999), 10–22.

44   Dave Turner describes the state of the vegetation in Mann Gulch on August 5, 1949, in Dave Turner, *The Thirteenth Fire* (Helena, Mont.: Helena Forest Foundation, 1999).

45   Fire ecologist Stephen Arno provided me with information about the ponderosa pine and its ecosystem during many interviews for various newspaper and magazine articles. Arno, along with coauthor Steven Allison-Bunnell, thoroughly describes the various fire regimes that exist across North America in Stephen F. Arno and Steven Allison-Bunnell, *Flames in Our Forest: Disaster or Renewal?* (Missoula, Mont.: Island Press, 2002).

46–48   The 1910 fire in Montana and Idaho and the congressional response to it are described in Pyne, *Fire in America,* 71–83. Pyne also provides a more succinct account in Steven Pyne, "The Big Blow Up," *High Country News* 33, no. 8 (April 23, 2001). Many Forest Service personnel who were on the fire lines in 1910 later recorded their recollections of the incident. I found most of the descriptions and statistics in Elers Koch, "History of the 1910 Forest Fires in Idaho and Western Montana," undated report written for the Forest Service. Koch also wrote an entertaining and informative memoir: Elers Koch, *Forty Years a Forester, 1903–1943* (Missoula, Mont.: Mountain Press, 1998).

49–50   The descriptions of the fire activity in Mann Gulch for August 4 and August 5, 1949, came from testimony, most notably that of Earl Cooley and Robert Jansson, in U.S. Forest Service, "Transcript of Board of Review of Mann Gulch Fire," Missoula, Montana, September 26–28, 1949.

50   Arthur Moir made the statement that most veteran firefighters "had a feel for that sort of thing" in his testimony to the Forest Service Board of Review; U.S. Forest Service, "Transcript of Board of Review of Mann Gulch Fire," 24.

CHAPTER EIGHT

Chuck Pickard described Bill Hellman and his activities at Hale Airfield that day in a January 23, 1999, letter collected by the X-CEL Program and buried in a time capsule at the Smoke Jumper Center in Missoula, Montana. The switch of squad leaders is also noted in Starr Jenkins, *Smokejumpers, '49: Brothers in the Sky* (San Luis Obispo, Calif.: Merritt Starr Books, 1995). The squad leaders usually split weekend shifts, working schedules from Sunday through Thursday and Tuesday through Saturday. Al Hammond and Skip Stratton told me that it wasn't uncommon for men to hang around the base on their days off if their names were near the top of the jump list.

52–55   Skip Stratton provided all the details of the flight to Washington D.C. and the promotional jump in an interview with me.

55–57   The biographical information about Bill Hellman came from documents written by Hellman's widow, Mrs. Gerry McHenry. These reminiscences were included in Starr Jenkins, *Some of the Men of Mann Gulch* (San Luis Obispo, Calif.: Merritt Star Books, 1993).

56   Gareth Moon talked about the financial straits of the young families in an interview with the author.

56   Hellman's frustrating trip to Yellowstone is documented in Jenkins, *Smokejumpers, '49.*

57–58   Skip Stratton filled in some of the details of Bill's last day at the base during an interview with me.

CHAPTER NINE

59   Jansson listed his firefighting credentials in U.S. Forest Service, "Transcript of Board of Review of Mann Gulch Fire," Missoula, Montana, September 26–28, 1949, 9.

59–61   The biographical information on the Janssons was gleaned from Lois Jansson, *Have You Ever Stopped to Wonder?* (n.p., 1965). Lois also described the elaborate celebrations in Helena that summer. She mentioned that the Forest Service workers dressed as Indians but that no real Indians were present despite the fact that there are seven Indian reservations in the state.

61   Jansson's claim that he had inspected every inch of his district is found in Norman Maclean, *Young Men and Fire* (Chicago: University of Chicago Press, 1992), 78.

61   Turner discusses the formation of the wild area in *The Thirteenth Fire* (Helena, Mont.: Helena Forest Foundation, 1999), 10.

61–62   Jansson's personal habits, religion, and management style are described in Maclean, *Young Men and Fire,* 78.

64–65   The description of the Gates of the Mountains Wilderness comes from my own experience of backpacking through the area.

65–67   Jansson's detailed account of his movements that day as well as his descriptions of the fire are recorded in U.S. Forest Service, "Transcript of Board of Review of Mann Gulch Fire," 9–15.

CHAPTER TEN

I reconstructed the birthday-party scene based on the recollections of Diettert's brother Gerald, a retired doctor in Missoula, Montana. Gerald Diettert saw his brother for the last time at the birthday party. He also provided many of the biographical details about his brother and the rest of the Diettert clan during an interview and in writings that appear in Starr Jenkins, *Some of the Men of Mann Gulch* (San Luis Obispo, Calif.: Merritt Star Books, 1993); and in X-CEL Productions, *Mann Gulch Remembered* (Helena, Mont.: Helena High School, 1999). Mrs. Diettert did make specially decorated birthday cakes for her children, but not necessarily the one described here.

68–69   Earl Cooley mentions the birthday party and his special relationship with Eldon in Earl Cooley, *Trimotor and Trail* (Missoula, Mont.: Mountain Press, 1984), 84.

72–75   I copied Eldon's letters before they were buried in a time capsule at the Smoke Jumper Center in Missoula, Montana. Parts of them are published in X-CEL Productions, *Mann Gulch Remembered.*

CHAPTER ELEVEN

Former smoke jumpers Al Hammond, Fred Brauer, and Earl Cooley provided me with most of the information about the jumper gear, how it was packed and delivered, and the activities that occurred at the fire loft that day.

79–81   The biographical information about Leonard Piper came from a testimonial written by his sister, Marie A. Liebel, for X-CEL Productions, *Mann Gulch Remembered* (Helena, Mont.: Helena High School, 1999) and from a newspaper article by Mike Sajna in the *Greenburg Tribune Review*, April 25, 1993.

CHAPTER TWELVE

The events in this chapter were recreated with information provided by Merle Stratton.

83   The order of the men as they entered the plane is documented in Carl A. Gidlund, "They Jumped to Death: The Mann Gulch Disaster," 1966, 2, unpublished manuscript, Missoula Smoke Jumper Center archives, Missoula, Montana.

85   Bill Hellman's interactions with Henry Thol to keep the rookie calm are documented in Gidlund, "They Jumped to Death," 3.

85–86   During the interview, Merle provided me with the biographical details of his life. Fred Brauer also spoke with me about this incident.

86   The description of the flight as "the roughest I ever took" is from Bob Sallee, quoted in Gidlund, "They Jumped to Death," 4.

CHAPTER THIRTEEN

91–92   Earl Cooley told me about Henry's role as a bull cook in 1948. Henry's experiences in smoke jumper training were related by his father in U.S. Forest Service, "Transcript of Board of Review of Mann Gulch Fire," Missoula, Montana, September 26–28, 1949, 192.

92   Henry Thol Sr.'s account of his conversation with his son about the qualifications of his instructors appears in U.S. Forest Service, "Transcript of Board of Review of Mann Gulch Fire," 191.

93   When relatives of miners living in Ireland wrote to their kin, they simply addressed the envelopes "Butte America."

93–94   A description of the flight to Yellowstone National Park appears in Starr Jenkins, *Smokejumpers, '49: Brothers in the Sky* (San Luis Obispo, Calif.: Merritt Starr Books, 1995), 9–12.

CHAPTER FOURTEEN

96   Earl Cooley told me about the infrequency with which he was called upon to be a spotter in an interview.

96   Fred Stillings said during his testimony that he had asked Cooley for a report of conditions at the fire; U.S. Forest Service, "Transcript of Board of Review of Mann Gulch Fire," Missoula, Montana, September 26–28, 1949, 113.

97–101   Earl Cooley wrote about his background and the details of his first fire jump in *Trimotor and Trail* (Missoula, Mont.: Mountain Press, 1984), 1–30.

97   "Adventurers, wanderers, Montanans, strangers, we get 'em all": Gidlund, "They Jumped to Death," 4.

98–99   The details of the cost savings of the early smoke jumper program are discussed in U.S. Forest Service, *History of Smoke Jumping* (Seattle, Wash.: Pacific Northwest National Parks and Forests Association, 1986), 4–5.

100   Fred Brauer discussed the attitude of the returning war veterans toward Cooley and the Civilian Public Service smoke jumpers in an interview with me.

101–103   Earl Cooley's experiences as a spotter are documented in U.S. Forest Service, "Transcript of Board of Review of Mann Gulch Fire."

101   Silas Thompson's spotting of the fire is documented in Gidlund, "They Jumped to Death," 5.

102–103   Cooley, Wag Dodge, and others described what they saw from the air that day in U.S. Forest Service, "Transcript of Board of Review of Mann Gulch Fire."

CHAPTER FIFTEEN

This chapter is a reconstruction of what Jim Harrison might have done on the ridge top on August 5th. Ranger Jansson recapped the details of Jim's movements that day in U.S. Forest Service,

"Transcript of Board of Review of Mann Gulch Fire," Missoula, Montana, September 26–28, 1949, 35. Jansson explained to the board why Jim could not get through by radio on pages 15–17.

106–107   The anecdote about the fire lookout and the Civilian Public Service jumpers came from Roy Wenger, ed., *CPS Smoke Jumpers, 1943–1946: Life Stories*, vol. 1 (Missoula, Mont.: privately published, 1990).

108   Norman Maclean describes the geological makeup of Gates of the Mountains in Norman Maclean, *Young Men and Fire* (Chicago: University of Chicago Press, 1992), 45.

CHAPTER SIXTEEN

112   Francis Middlemist, wife of the Lolo District Ranger, mentioned Marvin's fear in a letter included in X-CEL Productions, *Mann Gulch Remembered* (Helena, Mont.: Helena High School, 1999).

112   Francis Middlemist's letter in X-CEL Productions, *Mann Gulch Remembered*, quotes Marvin as saying he couldn't quit smoke jumping because he needed the money to get married.

113   The description of the photos of Marvin and Mary Ellen is based on photographs in X-CEL Productions, *Mann Gulch Remembered*.

115   Tom Magee Sr. described the escapades of the two boys in a letter published in Starr Jenkins, *Some of the Men of Mann Gulch* (San Luis Obispo, Calif.: Merritt Star Books, 1993).

115–116   Ray Belston described his adventures with Marvin on the ranch in a letter partially published in X-CEL Productions, *Mann Gulch Remembered*.

CHAPTER SEVENTEEN

117   Walt Rumsey's feeling of illness on the plane is documented in Carl A. Gidlund, "They Jumped to Death: The Mann Gulch Disaster," 1966, unpublished manuscript, Missoula Smoke Jumper Center archives, Missoula, Montana, 4.

118–121   Anita Navon described her brother David's family background and his activities and attitudes after the war in Starr

Jenkins, *Some of the Men of Mann Gulch* (San Luis Obispo, Calif.: Merritt Star Books, 1993).

120   Navon's college friend, Myron McFarland, wrote about their experiences in school and the vehicle they shared in Myron McFarland to Leonard "Nardo" Goodman, December 18, 1992. From the collection of Starr Jenkins.

120   Starr Jenkins wrote about David Navon a number of times; in Jenkins, *Some of the Men of Mann Gulch*; and Starr Jenkins, *Smokejumpers, '49: Brothers in the Sky* (San Luis Obispo, Calif.: Merritt Starr Books, 1995). In a letter to me dated December 30, 1999, Jenkins provided a physical as well as psychological description of Navon.

122–123   Starr Jenkins described the slip maneuver in *Smoke-jumpers, '49*, 45.

CHAPTER EIGHTEEN

126–127   Bennett's finding of the damaged radio is docu-mented in Dave Turner, *The Thirteenth Fire* (Helena, Mont.: Helena Forest Foundation, 1999), 20.

126–127   Earl Cooley explained the accident with the radio in U.S. Forest Service, "Transcript of Board of Review of Mann Gulch Fire," Missoula, Montana, September 26–28, 1949, 63.

127   Fred Stillings explained the shortage of maps in U.S. Forest Service, "Transcript of Board of Review of Mann Gulch Fire," 113.

128–130   Biographical background on Robert Bennett came from testimonials written by Joyce B. Russell, Gary P. Bennett, Barbara Bigham Simons, Mrs. Bobbie Parker, and Mrs. Lucille Long, all collected in Starr Jenkins, *Some of the Men of Mann Gulch* (San Luis Obispo, Calif.: Merritt Star Books, 1993); and, from Bennett's high school yearbook: E. W. Grove High School, *The Tower* (Paris, Tennessee, 1945).

130–131   Starr Jenkins wrote about the detail at Sullivan Lake in Starr Jenkins, *Smokejumpers, '49: Brothers in the Sky* (San Luis Obispo, Calif.: Merritt Starr Books, 1995), 126–135.

CHAPTER NINETEEN

134   Earl Cooley, Skip Stratton, and Fred Brauer discussed Wag Dodge's background and personality during interviews with me. Cooley also provided some background information on Dodge in Earl Cooley, *Trimotor and Trail* (Missoula, Mont.: Mountain Press, 1984), 95–96.

134   Wag Dodge admitted that he knew only three of the men in his crew in U.S. Forest Service, "Transcript of Board of Review of Mann Gulch Fire," Missoula, Montana, September 26–28, 1949, 126.

134–135   Fred Brauer, Skip Stratton, and Al Hammond provided details about Wag Dodge's woodworking during interviews with me.

135   Fred Brauer showed me one of the tin badges Wag had made.

135   Skip Stratton discussed Wag Dodge's independent nature in an interview with me. Norman Maclean described Dodge's relationship with his wife in *Young Men and Fire* (Chicago: University of Chicago Press, 1992), 40.

136   Robert Sallee reported Wag Dodge as saying that the crew's location was a death trap in a filmed interview with Stevan Smith for *Fire Fighters from the Sky: The History of Smoke Jumping* (Missoula, Mont: Smoke Jumpers Association, 2000), 12:17:36.

136–137   The survivors—Dodge, Sallee, and Rumsey—described the actions in the gulch that day in U.S. Forest Service, "Transcript of Board of Review of Mann Gulch Fire," Missoula, Montana, September 26–28, 1949.

137   The failure of the crew to sense Dodge's extreme concern about the danger they were in is documented in Carl A. Gidlund, "They Jumped to Death: The Mann Gulch Disaster," 1966, 6, unpublished manuscript, Smoke Jumper Archives, Missoula, Montana.

CHAPTER TWENTY

139–140   Johan Newcombe provided biographical details of her brother Silas Thompson's life in X-CEL Productions, *Mann Gulch Remembered* (Helena, Mont.: Helena High School, 1999). Jack Thompson, a cousin, also wrote about Silas in a letter.

140–141   Silas's poem "A Woodsman's Prayer" is published in X-CEL Productions, *Mann Gulch Remembered.*

142   When asked if the fire appeared dangerous, Walt Rumsey told the Board of Review: "The thought never entered my head. I remember thinking it would be an awful fire to mop up because it was rocky and steep, but it didn't occur to me that it was dangerous." U.S. Forest Service, "Transcript of Board of Review of Mann Gulch Fire," Missoula, Montana, September 26–28, 1949, 99.

143   Bob Sallee described Dodge's instructions to get rid of the saws in his video interview with Stevan Smith for *Fire Fighters from the Sky: The History of Smoke Jumping* (Missoula, Mont: Smoke Jumpers Association, 2000), 12:17:36.

CHAPTER TWENTY-ONE

Robert Jansson, Arthur Moir, and Hank Hersey described their activities on the afternoon of August 5th in U.S. Forest Service, "Transcript of Board of Review of Mann Gulch Fire," Missoula, Montana, September 26–28, 1949. In her memoir, Lois Jansson also included an report written by her husband soon after the fire that she pilfered from Forest Service files; Lois Jansson, *Have You Ever Stopped to Wonder?* (n.p., 1965). Richard C. Rothermel, a Forest Service researcher, reconstructed the movement and behavior of the fire in *Mann Gulch Fire: A Race That Couldn't Be Won*, Intermountain Research Station, USDA Forest Service, General Technical Report INT-299 (Ogden, Utah: Intermountain Research Station, 1993).

146–148   Jansson's experience within the fire is described in Carl A. Gidlund, "They Jumped to Death: The Mann Gulch Disaster," 1966, 6, unpublished manuscript, Missoula Smoke Jumper Center archives, Missoula, Montana.

CHAPTER TWENTY-TWO

151   Walter Rumsey said that Wag Dodge "always knew what he was doing" in U.S. Forest Service, "Transcript of Board of Review of Mann Gulch Fire," Missoula, Montana, September 26–28, 1949, 105.

152   The film Bloom shot that day has been lost; Richard C. Rothermel, *Mann Gulch Fire: A Race That Couldn't Be Won*, Intermountain Research Station, USDA Forest Service, General Technical Report INT-299 (Ogden, Utah: Intermountain Research Station, 1993), 5.

152–153   Forest Service researcher Rothermel reconstructed the movement and behavior of the fire based on certain points of time remembered by the survivors and on the physical location of the fire observed at those particular moments; *Mann Gulch Fire: A Race That Couldn't Be Won.*

153–154   Robert Sallee noted Dodge's command that the men drop their packs in U.S. Forest Service, "Transcript of Board of Review of Mann Gulch Fire," 75.

154   Joe Sylvia's inability to keep up with his colleagues is documented in Carl A. Gidlund, "They Jumped to Death: The Mann Gulch Disaster," 1966, 6, unpublished manuscript, Missoula Smoke Jumper Center archives, Missoula, Montana.

154   It was Rumsey who actually noted that he couldn't see the ridge top in U.S. Forest Service, "Transcript of Board of Review of Mann Gulch Fire," 108.

154   Walt Rumsey calculated that the stragglers were one hundred feet behind in U.S. Forest Service, "Transcript of Board of Review of Mann Gulch Fire," 103.

154   Robert Sallee noted the change in vegetation in U.S. Forest Service, "Transcript of Board of Review of Mann Gulch Fire," 74.

154   Wag Dodge noted that the fire burned through the spot where the smoke jumpers landed in his statement to the Board of Review; U.S. Forest Service, "Transcript of Board of Review of Mann Gulch Fire," 124.

156   Dodge described how the remaining men ignored his entreaties in his statement to the Board of Review; U.S. Forest Service, "Transcript of Board of Review of Mann Gulch Fire," 117.

157   *Life* magazine published a photo of an eight-point buck that died in the gulch in its August 22, 1949, issue on page 21. In an interview with me, Skip Stratton mentioned the rescue team passing the carcass every time they carried out a body.

157   Wag Dodge mentioned the large flat rock near the location where Joe Sylvia fell in U.S. Forest Service, "Transcript of Board of Review of Mann Gulch Fire," 117.

CHAPTER TWENTY-THREE

158   Robert Sallee said: "I'm not sure that is true, but you can check, but [the chief of fire control for the Forest Service in Region 1] asked Wag, 'Why did you stop?' And Wag said, 'I was bunged up so bad from the jump that I couldn't go any further'"; video interview with Stevan Smith for *Fire Fighters from the Sky: The History of Smoke Jumping* (Missoula, Mont: Smoke Jumpers Association, 2000), 13:21:35.

159   Wag Dodge estimated the chances that his crew could outrun the fire in U.S. Forest Service, "Transcript of Board of Review of Mann Gulch Fire," Missoula, Montana, September 26–28, 1949, 123.

159   Wag described how he started his fire in U.S. Forest Service, "Transcript of Board of Review of Mann Gulch Fire," 122.

159   Those who were coming out of the timber about 300 feet below looked like they were right in the fire: Bob Sallee is quoted as saying this in Carl A. Gidlund, "They Jumped to Death: The Mann Gulch Disaster," 1966, 7, unpublished manuscript, Missoula Smoke Jumper Center archives, Missoula, Montana.

160   Nobody knows for sure which route Hellman took, but Sallee told the Board of Review that he suspected Hellman ran to the left of Dodge's fire. U.S. Forest Service, "Transcript of Board of Review of Mann Gulch Fire," 117. Norman Maclean also portrayed Hellman taking that route in *Young Men and Fire* (Chicago: University of Chicago Press, 1992), 109.

160   Wag Dodge recounted the absence of panic in a report he wrote two years after the Board of Review that is published in Earl Cooley, *Trimotor and Trail* (Missoula, Mont.: Mountain Press, 1984), 98. Skip Stratton told me that a day or two after the fire, Robert Sallee told him that Bill Hellman was the man who had shouted, "The hell with that." Later Sallee testified that he did not know who had shouted the remark.

160   Robert Sallee reported Wag's movements during the fire in U.S. Forest Service, "Transcript of Board of Review of Mann Gulch Fire," 72–89.

160   Wag's attempt to convince his crew to join him in the burned area is chronicled in Carl A. Gidlund, "They Jumped to Death: The Mann Gulch Disaster," 1966, 7, unpublished manuscript, Missoula Smoke Jumper Center archives, Missoula, Montana.

160   Wag Dodge wrote about being lifted off the ground by the fire's updraft in the statement published in Cooley, *Trimotor and Trail*, 98. Gidlund also describes it in "They Jumped to Death: The Mann Gulch Disaster," 8.

161   Wag Dodge reported how he found Joe Sylvia in U.S. Forest Service, "Transcript of Board of Review of Mann Gulch Fire," 118.

161   Ranger Jansson told the Board of Review that by the time Wag Dodge reached Meriwether Canyon he could only remember the first initial of Sylvia's name. U.S. Forest Service, "Transcript of Board of Review of Mann Gulch Fire," 126.

161   Joe Sylvia told Robert Jansson that he hadn't known what Dodge wanted him to do when he lit the safety fire. Jansson recorded this in his unofficial report that appears in Lois Jansson, *Have You Ever Stopped to Wonder?* (n.p., 1965), 38.

CHAPTER TWENTY-FOUR

162–163   Walt Rumsey described the positions and actions of himself, Robert Sallee, and Eldon Diettert as Wag Dodge was lighting his safety fire in U.S. Forest Service, "Transcript of Board of Review of Mann Gulch Fire," Missoula, Montana, September 26–28, 1949, 103.

163   Robert Sallee mentioned thinking that Dodge had lost his senses in a video interview with Stevan Smith for *Fire Fighters from the Sky: The History of Smoke Jumping* (Missoula, Mont: Smoke Jumpers Association, 2000).

163   Robert Sallee testified to the Board of Review that he had never heard of an escape fire before; U.S. Forest Service, "Transcript of Board of Review of Mann Gulch Fire," Missoula, Montana, September 26–28, 1949, 86.

163   Robert Sallee said that Wag Dodge had told them to move alongside his fire at the Board of Review (U.S. Forest Service, "Transcript of Board of Review of Mann Gulch Fire," 77), and he reiterated this statement in the video interview for *Fire Fighters from the Sky*, 12:17:36.

163   Sallee estimated that the top of the ridge was 100 yards above Rumsey's position in *Fire Fighters from the Sky*, 13:28:30. He had originally told the Board of Review that he thought the distance was

200 yards; U.S. Forest Service, "Transcript of Board of Review of Mann Gulch Fire," 76.

163   Sallee talked of his momentary hesitation in U.S. Forest Service, "Transcript of Board of Review of Mann Gulch Fire," 103.

163   Both Rumsey and Sallee noted that they and Diettert expected the fire to slow down based on what they had learned in training in U.S. Forest Service, "Transcript of Board of Review of Mann Gulch Fire," 86, 103.

163–164   Walter Rumsey's daughter Peggy Bale provided biographical information about him for X-CEL Productions, *Mann Gulch Remembered* (Helena, Mont.: Helena High School, 1999).

164   Rumsey's description of the scene appears in Carl A. Gidlund, "They Jumped to Death: The Mann Gulch Disaster," 1966, 8, unpublished manuscript, Missoula Smoke Jumper Center archives, Missoula, Montana.

164   Bob Sallee reminisced about how he got into the smoke jumper program and became friends with Rumsey in *Fire Fighters from the Sky*, 12:14:12.

164   Information on blister rust and the white pine is in Mark Matthews, "The Return of the King," *High Country News* 35, no. 19, December 13, 2003, 4.

164–166   Most of the biographical information about Bob Sallee was gleaned from Stevan Smith's video interview with him for *Fire Fighters from the Sky*.

166   Bob Sallee described the behavior of the escape fire in the video interview for *Fire Fighters from the Sky*, 13:14.

166   Walt Rumsey described how he, Bob Sallee, and Eldon Diettert initially followed the edge of Wag Dodge's fire in U.S. Forest Service, "Transcript of Board of Review of Mann Gulch Fire," 103.

166–168   Bob Sallee described his flight up the hill in the video interview for *Fire Fighters from the Sky*, 13:28:30, 13:14.

167   Bob Sallee described his battle with fear in a speech he gave on May 8, 1991, at the dedication of the Mann Gulch memorial at the Missoula Smoke Jumper Center. Starr Jenkins included a transcript of the speech in Starr Jenkins, *Smokejumpers, '49: Brothers in the Sky* (San Luis Obispo, Calif.: Merritt Starr Books, 1995), 215–219.

167   Bob Sallee described his emotional state as he prayed for help in *Fire Fighters from the Sky*, 13:12:55.

168   Bob Sallee told the Board of Review that Diettert did not follow them through the crack. U.S. Forest Service, "Transcript of Board of Review of Mann Gulch Fire," 32.

168   Bob Sallee spoke about seeing David Navon moving away from the rest of the crew in an official statement taken two years after the Board of Review testimony that is published in Earl Cooley, *Trimotor and Trail* (Missoula, Mont.: Mountain Press, 1984), 102. The information on the actions of Dodge and Diettert appears in U.S. Forest Service, "Transcript of Board of Review of Mann Gulch Fire," 84.

168   "So that's what Dodge wanted us to do": U.S. Forest Service, "Transcript of Board of Review of Mann Gulch Fire," 84.

168   Bob Sallee described his view of the fire as he looked toward the mouth of the gulch in *Fire Fighters from the Sky*, 12:21:23.

169   Bob Sallee described the first impulse of his group to run directly to the river in U.S. Forest Service, "Transcript of Board of Review of Mann Gulch Fire," 79.

169–170   Walt Rumsey described the behavior of the fire as they waited at the top of the ridge in U.S. Forest Service, "Transcript of Board of Review of Mann Gulch Fire," 104.

170   Walt Rumsey described his and Bob Sallee's hope that others had survived as well in U.S. Forest Service, "Transcript of Board of Review of Mann Gulch Fire," 105.

170   Bob Sallee talked about how had he felt certain that others had survived in the video interview for *Fire Fighters from the Sky*, 13:08:27.

170   "Looks like we dodged that bullet": Bob Sallee quoted what he said in 1949 at a press conference I attended in 1999 at the 50 year commemoration of Mann Gulch in Helena, Montana.

CHAPTER TWENTY-FIVE

No one actually knows the route that Hellman took or when the fire hit him. Descriptions of the fire in this chapter are provided by Bob Sallee in U.S. Forest Service, "Transcript of Board of Review of Mann Gulch Fire," Missoula, Montana, September 26–28, 1949, 86.

172   Bob Sallee described the pincer movement of the fires in U.S. Forest Service, "Transcript of Board of Review of Mann Gulch Fire," 85.

172   Bill Hellman told Walt Rumsey that the flames had hit him just as he got to the ridge top. Rumsey noted the conversation in an statement written two years after the Board of Review convened that is published in Earl Cooley, *Trimotor and Trail* (Missoula, Mont.: Mountain Press, 1984), 109.

172–174   Walt Rumsey mentioned that Hellman's shoes had burned off and described his thirst and the other physical effects of the fire on the smoke jumper's body in U.S. Forest Service, "Transcript of Board of Review of Mann Gulch Fire," 106.

174   Bob Sallee talked about going back for the first aid kit in his video interview with Stevan Smith for *Fire Fighters from the Sky: The History of Smoke Jumping* (Missoula, Mont: Smoke Jumpers Association, 2000), 12:23:24. Gidlund mentioned his state of mind in Carl A. Gidlund, "They Jumped to Death: The Mann Gulch Disaster," 1966, 9, unpublished manuscript, Missoula Smoke Jumper Center archives, Missoula, Montana.

175   Bob Sallee stated that he didn't know any of the other firefighters in the gulch except for Walt Rumsey in the video interview for *Fire Fighters from the Sky*, 12:24:32.

175   Bob Sallee reported Bill Hellman's request that he take a message to his wife and the fact that he couldn't remember the content of the message in U.S. Forest Service, "Transcript of Board of Review of Mann Gulch Fire," 81.

175   "During travel carefully choose best routes. . . . Follow instructions and trust your foreman": smoke jumper training book, quoted in U.S. Forest Service, "Transcript of Board of Review of Mann Gulch Fire," 110.

175   Bob Sallee described how seeing the injured Bill Hellman changed his mind about his future career plans in *Fire Fighters from the Sky*, 13:07:15.

176   Bob Sallee described his decision not to go back into the burned gulch for the first aid kit in *Fire Fighters from the Sky*, 12:23:24.

177   Bob Sallee described his meeting with Wag Dodge in the midst of the fire in U.S. Forest Service, "Transcript of Board of Review of Mann Gulch Fire," 80, 85.

177   Wag Dodge's explanation of why he started his fire is in U.S. Forest Service, "Transcript of Board of Review of Mann Gulch Fire," 122.

177   Walt Rumsey mentioned the can of Irish potatoes in his statement that is published in Earl Cooley, *Trimotor and Trail* (Missoula, Mont.: Mountain Press, 1984), 109.

177   Wag Dodge described his conversation with and care of Bill Hellman in Rescue Gulch in U.S. Forest Service, "Transcript of Board of Review of Mann Gulch Fire," 118.

178   Walt Rumsey told how Wag Dodge left his pulaski with Bill Hellman in his statement in Cooley, *Trimotor and Trail*, 108.

178   Walt Rumsey briefly described what passed that evening with Hellman in the statement published in Cooley, *Trimotor and Trail*, 109.

178–179   Bob Sallee and Wag Dodge described their descent from the ridge and attempts to attract a boat in U.S. Forest Service, "Transcript of Board of Review of Mann Gulch Fire," 81, 118. Sallee also described the events in the video interview for *Fire Fighters from the Sky*, 13:02:45.

179   Gene Naegel was identified in a newspaper article a few days later; *Daily Missoulian*, August 8, 1949, 1.

CHAPTER TWENTY-SIX

The information in this chapter is from Jansson's report, which his wife "borrowed" from the U.S. Forest Service, copied, and incorporated into her own manuscript: Lois Jansson, *Have You Ever Stopped to Wonder?* (n.p., 1965), 35.

180–181   Jansson described his actions at the Meriwether fire camp in Jansson, *Have You Ever Stopped to Wonder?* 34.

181   Bob Sallee talked of trying to get some rest in his video interview with Stevan Smith for *Fire Fighters from the Sky: The History of Smoke Jumping* (Missoula, Mont: Smoke Jumpers Association, 2000), 13:04:23.

181   Bob Jansson described Wag Dodge's report to him when he reached Meriwether Campground in Jansson, *Have You Ever Stopped to Wonder?* 34–37.

183   Bob Sallee mentioned Wag Dodge's futile attempt to sleep in *Fire Fighters from the Sky*, 13:04:23.

183   The young man's erroneous report of stranded men near Elkhorn Creek is described in Jansson, *Have You Ever Stopped to Wonder?* 37.

183–184   Bob Jansson's recommendation to Wag Dodge that he stay behind and get some sleep is in U.S. Forest Service, "Transcript of Board of Review of Mann Gulch Fire," 127.

184   Jansson's futile search for the stranded men and the doctors' arrival without stretchers is described in Jansson, *Have You Ever Stopped to Wonder?* 37.

184   Jansson described his direction of the volunteer assistance in U.S. Forest Service, "Transcript of Board of Review of Mann Gulch Fire," 127.

184   Jansson's orders to the Forest Service rescue party is described in Jansson, *Have You Ever Stopped to Wonder?* 42, 36.

185   Bob Sallee later spoke of his inability to describe his experience in the fire to other Forest Service personnel in the video interview for *Fire Fighters from the Sky*, 13:07:15.

185   The arrival of the stretchers is described in Jansson, *Have You Ever Stopped to Wonder?* 37.

185   Bob Sallee described his reunion with Walt Rumsey in the video interview for *Fire Fighters from the Sky*, 13:04:23.

185–186   Robert Jansson told the Board of Review that Rumsey hadn't thought that Harrison had made it, then quoted what Rumsey had said about his winged feet in U.S. Forest Service, "Transcript of Board of Review of Mann Gulch Fire," 127.

186   Robert Jansson described how the rescue party found Bill Hellman in Jansson, *Have You Ever Stopped to Wonder?* 38; and in U.S. Forest Service, "Transcript of Board of Review of Mann Gulch Fire," 128.

CHAPTER TWENTY-SEVEN

187   I have creatively constructed Joe Sylvia's mental state on his last night. Doctor Amos Little told me during an interview that severely burned patients frequently experience euphoria. Dr. T. L. Hawkins described Sylvia's medical condition in a statement he wrote two years after the Board of Review hearings, published in Earl Cooley, *Trimotor and Trail* (Missoula, Mont.: Mountain Press, 1984), 116–118.

187–188   The biographical information about Joe was provided in a letter by his sister, Thelma Flanagan, written for X-CEL Productions, *Mann Gulch Remembered* (Helena, Mont.: Helena High School, 1999).

188   Robert Jansson informed the Board of Review that Sylvia had thought he heard voices after Wag Dodge had left him; U.S. Forest Service, "Transcript of Board of Review of Mann Gulch Fire," Missoula, Montana, September 26–28, 1949, 129.

188   Fred Brauer commented on the relationship of Stan Reba and Joe Sylvia in an interview. Jim Wisler recounted his run-ins with Joe Sylvia in an interview with me. Wisler admitted that he also could have been considered a cocky "wise guy" at that period of his life.

189   "You guys don't have to love each other. You'll never know when you'll have to depend on the next guy to save your life": Fred Brauer, quoted from an interview with me.

189   Robert Jansson discusses the sequence of events in the rescue of Joe Sylvia in Lois Jansson, *Have You Ever Stopped to Wonder?* (n.p., 1965), 38; and in U.S. Forest Service, "Transcript of Board of Review of Mann Gulch Fire," Missoula, Montana, September 26–28, 1949, 129.

190–191   Robert Jansson described finding Joe Sylvia and his conversation with him while they waited for the medical team in U.S. Forest Service, "Transcript of Board of Review of Mann Gulch Fire," 128–129; and Jansson, *Have You Ever Stopped to Wonder?* 28–29.

191   Bob Sallee described leading the medical team to Joe Sylvia and his attempt to catch some sleep in his video interview with Stevan Smith for *Fire Fighters from the Sky: The History of Smoke Jumping* (Missoula, Mont: Smoke Jumpers Association, 2000), 13:05:50.

191   Robert Jansson described the doctor's verbal assessment of Joe Sylvia's condition and the experience of finding the first burned body that night in Jansson, *Have You Ever Stopped to Wonder?* 39; and in U.S. Forest Service, "Transcript of Board of Review of Mann Gulch Fire," 129.

192   "'It looks like he was shot through the heart in midstride,' another said. 'I saw that during the war.'" Doctor Amos Little offered this description to me during an interview.

192–193   Robert Jansson's discovery of Jim Harrison's body is described in Jansson, *Have You Ever Stopped to Wonder?* 39.

193   Robert Jansson wrote about the loss in a letter to Harrison's family that is published in X-CEL Productions, *Mann Gulch Remembered*.

194   I recorded the time from Jim Harrison's recovered watch before it was placed in a time capsule to be buried at the Missoula Smoke Jumper Base.

194   Robert Jansson described finding the body they couldn't identify in the early morning of August 6th in Jansson, *Have You Ever Stopped to Wonder?* 40; and in U.S. Forest Service, "Transcript of Board of Review of Mann Gulch Fire," 130.

195   The image of the three fires burning in the shape of a cross is from *Daily Missoulian*, August 9, 1949, front page article.

CHAPTER TWENTY-EIGHT

All the details about the Jansson family and the activity around the ranger station were gleaned from Lois Jansson, *Have You Ever Stopped to Wonder?* (n.p., 1965).

200   Robert Jansson detailed Jim Harrison's popularity at the campground in a letter to Harrison's parents that is published in X-CEL Productions, *Mann Gulch Remembered* (Helena, Mont.: Helena High School, 1999).

CHAPTER TWENTY-NINE

205   André Anderson commented on Stan Reba's musical taste and dancing ability in an interview with me.

205   André Anderson identified Francis William Bourdillon's poem as one of her sister Julie's favorites.

206   André Anderson told the details of Julie's mental state in an interview with me.

208   André Anderson described her father's dramatic reaction to the news of Stanley's death in her interview with me.

208   Erroneous news reports that smoke jumpers were caught in the trees were discussed at the Board of Review with a regional personnel officer named McLaughlin. U.S. Forest Service, "Transcript of Board of Review of Mann Gulch Fire," Missoula, Montana, September 26–28, 1949, 158–159.

208   André Anderson provided details of the activities at the Nagel house on the day they learned of Stanley Reba's death.

208–210   Lois Jansson provided some details of Julie Reba's visit in Lois Jansson, *Have You Ever Stopped to Wonder?* (n.p., 1965), 48.

209–210   Robert Jansson told his wife that he was most haunted by Stanley Reba's death; Jansson, *Have You Ever Stopped to Wonder?* 48.

211   The story of the Robert Jansson seeing a bone fragment at Stanley Reba's gravesite on the day Julie visited it may be apocryphal; it was related to me by an old smoke jumper in Mann Gulch during the 50th-anniversary commemoration of the tragedy. I did not record the storyteller's name.

211   Robert Jansson recorded Julie Reba's asking who found her husband in an official report published in Jansson, *Have You Ever Stopped to Wonder?* 48.

CHAPTER THIRTY

217   Squad leader Al Hammond provided the information about Forest Service use of the Bell 47-D helicopter to remove the bodies from Mann Gulch in an interview with me.

217–218   Lois Jansson described Henry Thol Sr.'s determination to see the body of his son in *Have You Ever Stopped to Wonder?* (n.p., 1965), 38.

218   Earl Cooley described the methods he used to identify the bodies of the fallen smoke jumpers in *Trimotor and Trail* (Missoula, Mont.: Mountain Press, 1984), 88.

218   Cooley described his exchange with Henry Thol Sr. about opening the casket of his son in an interview with me.

218   Henry Thol Sr.'s threat to get a court order and the undertaker's reluctant acquiescence to his demand to see his son's body is recorded in Jansson, *Have You Ever Stopped to Wonder?* 49.

218   Early Cooley described the process of opening the metal casket in *Trimotor and Trail,* 89.

218   Earl Cooley described the moving moment when Henry Sr. caressed his son's head in an interview with me.

218–219   Henry Thol Sr.'s public display of grief after he had seen his son's body is described in Jansson, *Have You Ever Stopped to Wonder?* 50.

219   Henry Thol Sr.'s appearance at the Board of Review is recorded in U.S. Forest Service, "Transcript of Board of Review of Mann Gulch Fire," Missoula, Montana, September 26–28, 1949, 186–197.

219–220   Henry Thol's opinion of the strategy Wag Dodge should have used once his team had landed at the fire site is in U.S. Forest Service, "Transcript of Board of Review of Mann Gulch Fire," 197.

219–220   Henry Thol's description of the kind of safety plan he felt Wag Dodge should have used is in U.S. Forest Service, "Transcript of Board of Review of Mann Gulch Fire," 189–190.

220   Henry Thol's contention that Wag Dodge led his men into a trap because he was more concerned about putting out the fire than he was about protecting human life is in U.S. Forest Service, "Transcript of Board of Review of Mann Gulch Fire," 187.

221   Henry Thol's assessment of the weakness of the Forest Service's military-style chain of command in a situation when men have lost confidence in their leader is in U.S. Forest Service, "Transcript of Board of Review of Mann Gulch Fire," 192, 197.

221   Henry Thol's contention that Wag Dodge's safety fire ended up killing some of his men is in U.S. Forest Service, "Transcript of Board of Review of Mann Gulch Fire," 194.

221   Lois Jansson included a copy of the Board of Review's final report in Lois Jansson, *Have You Ever Stopped to Wonder?* (n.p., 1965), 52–53.

221   Lois Jansson recorded the sense among some Forest Service employees that the Board of Review's report was a whitewash in *Have You Ever Stopped to Wonder?* 54.

221–222   The unsuccessful attempt of Henry Thol Sr. and other families to press their cases in court is documented in *Have You Ever Stopped to Wonder?* 54.

222   The Forest Service's acceptance of Henry Thol's main point that "the value of lives of men should be given first consideration" is documented in U.S. Forest Service, "Transcript of Board of Review of Mann Gulch Fire," 193.

222–223   Earl Cooley documented the post–Mann Gulch innovations in training and equipment for U.S. Forest Service firefighters in *Trimotor and Trail,* 129.

223   For more information about the LCES training program, see Mark Matthews, "LCES," *Wildland Firefighter* 4, no. 8 (August 12,

2000): 44–48. The quotes from Paul Chamberlin in this chapter are from this article.

CHAPTER THIRTY-ONE

227   "I really think that fire we saw when we flew over there was a typical smokejumper fire. . . . If they had, they'd have all been safe, the ones that had the chance to get in there": Bob Sallee's video interview with Stevan Smith for *Fire Fighters from the Sky: The History of Smoke Jumping* (Missoula, Mont: Smoke Jumpers Association, 2000), 12:27:50.

228   "Some people have said that they thought Wag's fire burned the people who got past where he lit his fire. . . . So there's no way, in my mind, that Wag's fire burned anybody": *Fire Fighters from the Sky*, 13:01:30.

228   "I went thirty-five or forty years without talking to anybody. . . . But I finally decided there wasn't any answer to that question and just went on with my life"; video interview for *Fire Fighters from the Sky*, 12:11:35.

229   "I came at it one way and Rumsey came at it another and we were fifty feet apart and there's no question"; video interview for *Fire Fighters from the Sky*, 13:20:39.

229   "In Rumsey and Sallee's memory . . . only a few pieces appear where they are in reality": Norman Maclean, *Young Men and Fire* (Chicago: University of Chicago Press, 1992), 212.

229   Bob Sallee uttered the words expressing his disagreement with Maclean and Robinson's reconstruction of the events of August 5, 1949, at a press conference at the 50th-anniversary commemoration of Mann Gulch in Helena, Montana.

229–230   Biographical information about Bob Sallee is in X-CEL Productions, *Mann Gulch Remembered* (Helena, Mont.: Helena High School, 1999).

230   Biographical information about Walt Rumsey was provided by his daughter Peggy Bale and published in X-CEL Productions, *Mann Gulch Remembered*.

230   Patsy Dodge recalled Wag Dodge's words that "the Old Boy upstairs has been riding in my hind pocket" for X-CEL Productions, *Mann Gulch Remembered*.

230   Skip Stratton and Fred Brauer told me in an interview that Wag Dodge spoke with all the parents of the fallen smoke jumpers.

230   Fred Brauer told me in an interview that Wag Dodge was unable to jump from a plane after the Mann Gulch fire.

232   Fred Brauer told me during an interview about the distribution of Wag Dodge's ashes in the lake.

232   Bob Sallee's statement that smoke jumping is the best job in the world is in the video interview for *Fire Fighters from the Sky*, 14:13:20.